CAMBRIDGE IBERIAN AND
LATIN AMERICAN STUDIES

GENERAL EDITOR

P. E. RUSSELL, F.B.A.

EMERITUS PROFESSOR OF SPANISH STUDIES

UNIVERSITY OF OXFORD

Poverty and Welfare in
Habsburg Spain

# Poverty and Welfare in Habsburg Spain

## The Example of Toledo

LINDA MARTZ

CAMBRIDGE UNIVERSITY PRESS

CAMBRIDGE

LONDON   NEW YORK   NEW ROCHELLE

MELBOURNE   SYDNEY

Published by the Press Syndicate of the University of Cambridge
The Pitt Building, Trumpington Street, Cambridge CB2 IRP
32 East 57th Street, New York, NY 10022, USA
296 Beaconsfield Parade, Middle Park, Melbourne 3206, Australia

First published 1983

Printed in Great Britain at the University Press, Cambridge

Library of Congress catalogue card number: 82-19725

*British Library cataloguing in publication data*
Martz, Linda
Poverty and welfare in Habsburg Spain.
–(Cambridge Iberian and Latin
American Studies)
1. Toledo (Province) (Spain) – Economic
conditions – History   2. Toledo (Province)
(Spain) – Social conditions – History
I. Title
946.43   HN590.T/
ISBN 0 521 23952 4

To my Mother and
the memory of my Father

# Contents

# Figures

# Tables

# Preface

Poverty and welfare is an enormous topic, but in the sixteenth century its scope is limited somewhat by the documents that are available. For the first part of the book, which deals with crown policy and welfare reforms, much information has been printed, and I have relied heavily upon the British Library's excellent collection of sixteenth-century books and other printed material. As for documents, the state archives of Madrid and Simancas have been consulted, together with other smaller collections, but the Archive of Simancas has provided the most useful information, especially the sections *Patronato Eclesiástico*, which contains much information about charitable institutions, and *Consejo Real* and *Estado*, which yielded facts about the policy of the crown and the city of Toledo. In Toledo, the archives of the city, the cathedral, the diocese, the parishes, the notaries, the Diputación, and the Hospital of Tavera, as well as the Lorenzana Collection in the Toledo Public Library, have been consulted and all have contributed useful material. The minutes of the city council meetings and other documents in the municipal archive have provided the core of information about the city's policy toward the poor. If it appears that the policy of the church has been neglected, or that the discussion of the Toledo prelates is uneven, this is because many important church documents are inaccessible, a great loss in a city where the church played such an important role in poor relief.

To explore all the documents relating to sixteenth-century poor relief would be a life-long task. The state archives are vast and contain no catalogues relating to the subject, so finding information is somewhat hit-or-miss. It is possible that much information remains buried in an unlikely section or an unexplored *legajo*. On the local level there is a surfeit of documents about the finances of charitable institutions but very little about church policy or the people who received relief. If and when all the collections of the cathedral and the diocese are catalogued and made available to the public, it is likely that a more definite evaluation of the role of the church will be feasible. The book attempts to present a broad outline of the major events that occurred in Spain and Toledo relating to the poor, an outline that future research will amplify and possibly modify.

In instances where a document is not paginated and it forms but one small portion in a collection of three hundred papers, it is briefly described when first mentioned. Also, since the great part of the research for this book was carried out between 1970 and 1974, the description should enable any interested party to locate the document in archives that have recently changed the numbers of their cataloguing system, as is the case in the Toledo diocesan archive.

Throughout the book the Benedictine abbot who defended the 1540 Castilian welfare reforms has been called Juan de Robles, even though he originally wrote his treatise under the name Juan de Medina, alias Robles. This course has been adopted to conform with modern Spanish usage and to avoid confusion with another contemporary, also named Juan de Medina, who was a theologian at the University of Alcalá de Henares.

Many people have contributed to the making of this book. I am especially grateful to John Lynch and H. G. Koenigsberger, who read the original manuscript and offered suggestions for improvement; to Brian Pullan, who also read and commented on the original manuscript and has since provided valuable ideas and bibliography; to Richard Kagan and Julian Montemayor, who have contributed bibliographic material; and to John Elliott, who offered guidance and moral support through the formative stages of the research and has since read and given helpful advice on the final product. I have also benefitted from the interest and assistance of Spanish archivists and friends: doña Adela González of the Archive of Simancas, don Clemente Palencia and his successor doña Esperanza Pedraza of the Toledo municipal archive; don Emilio Rodríguez and his successor doña María-Jesús Cruz of the Toledo Diputación archive; don Ignacio Gallego and his ex-assistant don Manuel Gutiérrez of the Toledo diocesan archive; the staff and the patron of the Hospital of Tavera; and Julio Porres, who has generously shared with me his knowledge of Toledo's history. To the other people who offered assistance, whether in the form of a reference, an idea, or general interest in the topic, I would also like to express my thanks and appreciation.

# Abbreviations

ARCHIVES AND LIBRARIES

ACT    Archivo de la Catedral de Toledo
LAC    Libros de Actas Capitulares
OF    Obra y Fábrica
ADT    Archivo Diocesano de Toledo
ADPT    Archivo de la Diputación Provincial de Toledo
SC    Santa Caridad
LC    Libro de Crianza (Hospital de Santa Cruz)
ADPZ    Archivo de la Diputación Provincial de Zamora
AGG    Archivo General Guipúzcoa
AGS    Archivo General de Simancas
CC    Comisaría de Cruzada
CG    Contadurías Generales
CR    Consejo Real
DGT    Dirección General del Tesoro
Est    Estado
EH    Expedientes de Hacienda
MPD    Mapas, Planos y Dibujos
PE    Patronato Eclesiástico
PR    Patronato Real
AHN    Archivo Histórico Nacional (Madrid)
AHPT    Archivo Histórico Provincial de Toledo
AHT    Archivo del Hospital de Tavera
AF    Arca Fuerte
LB    Libro de la Botillería
LD    Libro de Despensa
LO    Libro Ordinario
LR    Libro de Rentas
LRE    Libro de Recepción de los Enfermos
AMT    Archivo Municipal de Toledo

| AP | Autos de los Pobres |
|---|---|
| AS | Archivo Secreto |
| CJ | Cabildo de Jurados |
| LA | Libros de Actas |
| AMZ | Archivo Municipal de Zamora |
| APSA | Archivo Parroquial de Santiago del Arrabal |
| APSJ | Archivo Parroquial de San Justo |
| APSN | Archivo Parroquial de San Nicolás |
| APST | Archivo Parroquial de Santo Tomé |
| AVM | Archivo de la Villa de Madrid |
| BL | British Library |
| Add. | Additional MSS |
| Eg. | Egerton MSS |
| BNM | Biblioteca Nacional, Madrid |
| BRME | Biblioteca del Real Monasterio del Escorial |
| BPT | Biblioteca Pública de Toledo |
| BPUG | Bibliothèque Publique et Universitaire, Geneva |
| FC | Favre Collection |
| RAH | Real Academia de la Historia, Madrid |

## OTHER ABBREVIATIONS

| *AC* | *Actas de las Cortes* |
|---|---|
| caj. | cajón |
| cap. | capítulo |
| carp. | carpeta |
| *DHEE* | *Diccionario de Historia Eclesiástica de España* |
| exp. | expediente |
| leg. | legajo |
| lib. | libro |
| *MHSJ* | *Monumenta Historica Societatis Jesu* |
| mr(s) | maravedí(s) |
| n. | note |
| no. | number |
| *NR* | *Novísima recopilación* |
| pet. | petición |
| secc. | sección |
| t. | tomo |

## NOTE ON CURRENCY

In sixteenth-century Castile the ducat and the *real* were coins of gold and of silver, respectively, while the *maravedí* served as a unit of account. Payments were recorded in all these units. The relationship between them is:

1 *real* = 34 *maravedís*

1 ducat = 375 *maravedís*

Throughout the book, *maravedí(s)* is abbreviated to mr(s).

# Introduction

Recent studies throughout much of Europe have led to what one historian has described as 'a quiet revolution' in the history of poor people and poor relief.[1] Earlier generations developed and debated the distinctions between Catholic and Protestant forms of charity, crediting Protestantism with ushering in a new form of rational, discriminating relief, directed by secular authorities, while relief in Catholic countries was seen as disorganized and haphazard, controlled by an over-indulgent church that sought to preserve a class of paupers so the rich would have ample opportunity to exercise their charitable obligations.[2] Having jettisoned the old belief that almsgiving and other good works could assure salvation to those who performed them, it was argued that Protestantism was able to concern itself with the long-term benefit of the recipients of relief and society in general by encouraging the poor, through education and employment, to be self-reliant and industrious, whereas the practice of indiscriminate charity, thought to characterize relief in Catholic societies, had the opposite effect of encouraging idleness and dependence, thus destroying the will or the need to work and demoralizing the recipients.[3]

Many of these familiar and pervasive distinctions have been displaced. In a recent study of Venice, Brian Pullan has demonstrated that this Catholic city pursued welfare policies that were efficient and highly discriminating, especially against public beggars, and were directed toward long-term social improvement by providing the poor with education and opportunities to work.[4] In two other areas of Europe, the similarities between the Aumône-Général founded in the much-studied Catholic city of Lyons and the General Hospital founded in Protestant Geneva are striking. Both institutions were created to improve welfare services by centralizing and coordinating available resources, both were controlled by secular authorities (though Calvin did absorb the Geneva hospital staff into his clerical establishment), public begging was prohibited in both cities, and relief was limited to deserving natives with transients given but temporary assistance.[5] Nor did Protestant societies possess a monopoly on schemes to confine and employ the poor and the idle: in the sixteenth century beggars' hospitals were founded in many Italian cities, including Rome, and they came into full flower in the seventeenth century when Hôpitaux-Généraux were founded in many French cities.[6] It appears that wandering beggars and vagabonds were viewed with fear and condemnation in both Catholic and Protestant communities.[7] Such similarities have precipitated more objective, sophisticated analyses to establish the distinctions between Catholic and Protestant welfare and charity.[8]

Spain has played little part in this 'quiet revolution'. What has received some attention is Spain's rich sixteenth-century literary tradition, which begins with the influential 1526 treatise of the Spanish exile, Juan Luis Vives, followed by the 1545 debate between Juan de Robles and Domingo de Soto, and ending with the late sixteenth-century schemes of Miguel Giginta and Cristóbal Pérez de Herrera, both of whom supported the foundation of special institutions for beggars.[9] Despite the fact that four of these five men supported reforms designed to eliminate or control public begging, and that the latter two, lesser-known individuals have been the subject of recent studies, the Spaniard whose name seems to have achieved European fame is that of Domingo de Soto, the Dominican theologian who defended the right of all needy persons to beg wherever they chose.

The fame of Domingo de Soto and the lack of knowledge about what actually went on in Spain has led historians to assume that the Iberian peninsula was untouched by the events, reforms and ideas that affected much of western Europe in the late sixteenth century, an assumption that is evident in two recent surveys of European poor relief. J.-P. Gutton, for instance, has concluded that of all the countries in western Europe, only the Iberian peninsula 'perhaps escaped' the development of ideas condemning idleness and countenancing labour;[10] and C. Lis and H. Soly, who attempt to explain poverty in terms of an exploitative economic system, have concluded that because Spain lacked industrial centres of significance the need for a disciplined, controlled labour force (one of the three pre-

requisites the authors posit as causative factors for welfare reforms)
was absent.[11]

The primary purpose of this book is to explore what happened,
both in theory and in practice, in sixteenth-century Spain concerning
the poor and their relief and to determine if Spain did indeed remain
aloof from the reforms and ideas current in other parts of western
Europe. To achieve this goal, the book has been divided into two
parts, the first dealing with what might be best described as national
issues. These include the numerous treatises written about relieving
the poor, the formulation of crown policy, the implementation of the
Tridentine hospital decrees, and the growth of the new hospital
orders. If the crown usually determined policy, it was translated into
action on a local level and Part II is devoted to the city of Toledo. As
the see of the Spanish primate; a commercial, manufacturing, and
intellectual centre; and one of the largest and wealthiest cities of
sixteenth-century Castile, Toledo seems an ideal place to observe
poverty and welfare. This second part begins with a discussion of the
city's population from 1528 to 1625 and an analysis of the distribution
of wealth and poverty in the city parishes in 1561; the remainder deals
with the various methods by which the city attempted to relieve the
poor, the care offered by two of the city's numerous charitable
institutions, a description of recipients of relief, and tentative
conclusions concerning the deteriorating living conditions of the
city's poorer inhabitants.

That the poor of sixteenth-century Castile were numerous is
affirmed by voluminous testimonies of contemporary observers. They
were numerous in terms of the accepted pyramid structure of society,
which ordained that the vast majority at the bottom of the pyramid
laboured long hours for low pay; they became more numerous as a
result of population expansion; and, as a result of migration to the
cities and towns, they became more concentrated and more visible.

For the subsistence economy of sixteenth-century Castile, increasing population meant more mouths to feed and it also meant more
labour that might be productively employed. For much of the
century many areas in Castile responded positively to this challenge.
In some cities, commerce and the cloth industry prospered while in
the countryside more land was brought into cultivation and farm
labourers could supplement their meager income by performing some
operation for the cloth industry.[12] Outbreaks of sickness and famine

were, of course, common occurrences throughout the period but by the early sixteenth century most Castilian cities had attempted to mitigate the ravages of famine by establishing a grain reserve that was sold off at cheap prices when bread was scarce and expensive.

If expansion and prosperity characterized some areas of Castile in the first half of the sixteenth century, by the 1570s this was no longer the case. To explain this change in Segovia the Malthusian dilemma of too many people pressing upon inadequate resources has been suggested.[13] This explanation might also hold true for Toledo, where, in addition to finding grain to feed its own population, the city was confronted by competition for grain by the nearby expanding city of Madrid. In this same decade the city experienced a long depression caused by the crown's suspension of payments, an enormous increase in taxation that struck particularly hard at the cloth industries, and an outbreak of sickness that was one of the worst of the sixteenth century. Signs of trouble are obvious in the 1570s, but it was not until the first two decades of the seventeenth century that the economy of Toledo virtually collapsed.

And how did all these changes affect the inarticulate, long-suffering poor? The poor of early modern Europe were lucky if they managed to get adequate food on a regular basis, not to mention shelter and clothing. For those who laboured in the fields and for the unskilled and semi-skilled workers of the urban areas the struggle to earn enough money to meet expenses was continual and frequently unsuccessful. Even the better-off skilled labourers, retailers and peasants could see their reserves wiped out by one of the unending disasters that struck sixteenth-century society. It could be a work stoppage caused by a lack of raw materials, plague restrictions that prohibited the movement of merchandise and people, or a crown bankruptcy; it could be some natural disaster, whether drought, flood or locusts, that drove up the price of grain to such a high point that the poor could not afford to buy bread; or it could be a more personal problem such as sickness, the birth of another child or death of the breadwinner. These insecurities were constant in the lives of the poor of Toledo as were their crowded and insanitary living conditions, minimal to poor diets, and hard labour for very low pay.

Yet, since migrants continued to pour into Toledo for most of the sixteenth century, one must conclude that life there was better than the life they left behind. A young person might hope to learn a useful skill or to find food, shelter and clothes in domestic service, while an older unskilled person might hope for temporary employment. Toledo also boasted an abundance of charitable institutions and wealthy charitable givers who attempted to help the poor through periods of hardship. While it might have been more difficult for the poor in Toledo to find employment and bread from the 1570s to the end of the century, it was not until the first two decades of the seventeenth century that the inarticulate poor gave physical evidence that the city could no longer support them. After a hundred years of migrating to Toledo, the poor reversed the process and migrated away in search of the employment, cheap bread and charitable assistance that Toledo could no longer give them.

While the relationship between poverty and economic developments might seem obvious to a modern observer, this connection was not usually made by sixteenth-century welfare reformers. They were convinced that the poor should work but this conviction was not based upon any stated observations that a pauper's labour could be utilized by an expanding textile industry or that such labour would bring material well-being to the pauper. The employment of the poor was urged on moral and religious grounds, with occasional references to political expediency, public health and aesthetics. The reformers also shared the conviction that institutional changes – a new hospital, a reform of the old hospitals, a consolidation of charitable funds, or the elimination of public begging – would resolve the problem of the poor and their relief.

As for the great mass of humanity who comprised the poor, they were usually lumped into three groups: the deserving poor, those unable to maintain themselves by labour; the undeserving poor, those who were physically able but preferred not to labour; and, in Catholic countries, the *envergonzantes*, those people in need of relief who did not beg publicly. These first two groups were well-nigh universal in western Europe as was the opinion that the former should be helped and the latter punished. Discords arose, however, in determining the means by which the deserving poor should be relieved, with some cities or countries adopting a system of licensed begging and others prohibiting begging. If and when public begging was outlawed, funds were necessary to support the poor. Frequently the existing charitable resources were consolidated into one central fund or institution, which charitable givers were urged to support, and, in many cases, the wealthier citizens of the community were taxed to support the poor. The usual corollary to such welfare reforms was that under normal circumstances poor relief was limited to natives or long-term residents of a community, though outsiders might receive a donation for their journey when they left a town and a sick person might be taken into a hospital. This brief explanation of the sixteenth-century ideas, terminology and reforms will be amplified by Juan Luis Vives, the first of a long line of Spaniards who wrote about the poor and their relief.

# I

# Castilian legislation, debates and innovations

## JUAN LUIS VIVES AND THE EUROPEAN REFORMS

Within the vast domains of the Emperor Charles V, it was the Netherlandish cities that were among the leaders in providing welfare controversies in the 1520s and 1530s. As a resident of one of these cities, the Spanish humanist, Juan Luis Vives, was able to keep abreast of the latest welfare reforms, hear the debates, and formulate his own ideas. Vives is an important figure in the history of sixteenth-century welfare because in his 1526 treatise, *De subventione pauperum*, he crystallized and articulated what are usually known as the 'new' ideas about the poor and their relief, ideas that were to enjoy, in one form or another, success throughout much of western Europe.

Though a Spaniard by birth, the Iberian affiliations of Vives should not be overemphasized since he left his native Valencia in 1509 and never again set foot on Spanish soil. It is now well known that the humanist suffered the stigma of Jewish blood; his father was arrested by the Inquisition in 1522 and executed three years later,[1] so Vives' life of exile was dictated as much by necessity as by choice. After several years in Paris and then in England at the court of Henry VIII, Vives settled amidst the congenial colony of Spanish merchants who inhabited the city of Bruges where he met and married the daughter of another Jewish refugee from Valencia. His treatise about poor relief was dedicated to the magistrates of Bruges but the book gained a European audience. It was reprinted several times in Latin and translated into Italian and German though apparently not Castilian.[2] In 1527 it achieved the dubious notoriety of being declared heretical by the Franciscan vicar of the bishop of Tournai, much to the disgruntlement of Vives who considered the treatise extremely moderate.[3]

It is easy enough to understand why a Franciscan would consider

7

the treatise as objectionable if not heretical. Though Vives makes no
direct reference to the Mendicant Orders, he is clearly outraged by
poverty, especially the most visible aspects of it: 'It is certainly a
shameful and disgraceful thing for Christians . . . to find so many
needy persons and beggars in our streets' ('Del socorro de los pobres',
p. 280). The Valencian argued that in a truly Christian city the poor
should be relieved so that they were not reduced to the humiliating
and degrading spectacle of stretching out their hands to those more
favourably blessed in the distribution of wealth. Poverty was a
condition into which one might fall, but it was by no means an
estimable condition, nor should the fallen linger there any longer
than necessary. As Vives explained it, 'these our councils do not
remove the poor, but help them; they do not preclude that someone
should be poor, but that he should not be poor for much time' (p.
287). Melioration of poverty was not only the moral obligation of a
Christian community, it was also an expedient measure for those who
governed the city since poverty fostered uncivil and asocial behaviour. It sowed the seeds of discord that led to sedition and
rebellion, and it led men, women and children into wicked and
immoral activities by depraving their morality. Vives shared the
contemporary belief that contagious diseases were transmitted
through the infected breath of the poor, so poverty was also
considered a threat to the physical health of a city. Finally, the
humanist found beggars offensive to the eyes, ears and nose.

Poverty was then a multifarious evil calling for action on the part of
all Christians, but where should action begin given the 'multitude of
poor'? Vives began by dividing the poor into several groups. Beggars
were placed in one of three categories: the impotent, the able bodied,
and the foreigners, that is those not born in Bruges. Persons who fell
into the latter category were to be banished from Bruges to their place
of origin though they would receive a small travel allowance 'because
it would be an inhuman thing to send away a needy person without
provision for his journey' (p. 282). The exclusion of foreign beggars
from relief did not apply during periods of famine or warfare when the
residents of nearby afflicted villages could be taken into Bruges and
treated as natives. Native-born beggars who did not have a domicile
would be housed in the city hospitals or specially designated houses,
while those who had a place of residence would be relieved there.
Public begging was prohibited except for brief periods when a person
had not yet been placed in a house or with a master. Beggars were not

the only persons in need of relief for there were many needy citizens who were too proud to take to the streets as public beggars. These individuals, known as the *envergonzantes* or shamefaced poor, would be noted and relieved secretly by parish deputies.

With the exception of the *envergonzantes*, all persons who sought or needed relief were to be inspected by the city council or its deputies. Those who had a domicile would be visited there by two parish deputies and a scribe who would record their needs, the number of children, and their manner of living; they would be provided for according to their 'quality, estate and condition'. People in the city hospitals were also subject to inspection. Beggars were to be convened in a public square, 'so that such rabble does not enter a house or a room of the government' (p. 284), where they would be registered and interrogated as to why they begged. Anyone who claimed infirmity as a cause for begging was to be inspected by a doctor, and anyone who resisted these proceedings was to be put in jail.

After the inspection process was completed and the list drawn up, Vives was confronted by the troublesome issue of supporting all these people, a problem he never adequately resolved. The only concrete proposal he offered was a reform of the city hospitals which were to be taken over and administered by the city magistrates. Vives seems to have believed sincerely that the hospitals were extremely wealthy: 'It is said in each place that the wealth of the hospitals is so great that if it were administered and dispensed properly it would be enough to relieve all the needs of the citizens' (p. 282). In addition to their great wealth, Vives also believed that the hospitals were crowded with malingerers, 'drones maintained by the sweat of others' (p. 282), who would be ousted and their places filled by homeless beggars. But if the hospitals of Bruges were filled with beggars, there is the question of where the sick were to find relief, a question Vives never addressed.

Aside from the hospital reform, the humanist made vague suggestions about money contributed by prelates, collected in poor boxes, given by testators, or earned by the labour of the poor; temporary loans from the rich; and money that the city could donate if it would eliminate its expenditure on such frivolous items as festivals and receptions for dignitaries. Vives' final resort was Divine Mercy which had recently helped the city's school for poor children to increase its enrollment from eighteen to a hundred.

The lack of adequate financing may be explained by the author's fear of making any suggestions that might be considered heretical. On the other hand, Vives had, at least in theory, eliminated most of the conspicuous welfare candidates. Foreign beggars were sent home and the natives were put to work. Vives was convinced that labour was the cure for poverty and few of the city's poorer residents were omitted from the humanist's suggestions for employment. Native-born beggars of an appropriate age and disposition would be taught a trade; those who did not meet the age and disposition qualifications could dig ditches, draw water, or carry things in baskets or wheelbarrows. Then, too, there were the numerous public works projects of the city such as repairing walls, buildings and statues. Even the blind would be employed in cultivating their musical talents, while the lame would take up basket weaving. If the ideal city of Vives bears a great resemblance to a giant anthill, all the activity was not justified in terms of the expanding economy of Bruges[4] or the amount of money a hard-working person could earn for his labour. In fact Vives suggested that some of the unemployed should be sent to a nearby town that had a booming woollen industry, and the silk weavers of the city, who needed young boys to assist them, could find no candidates because the parents of the boys said their children made more by begging than they did by working.

But if Bruges had no need of workers and parents found it more profitable to send their children out begging than to work, why should Bruges eliminate public begging and initiate a complicated reform that entailed an expensive public works programme? This was to be done in the interests of the poor themselves who would be spared the vice of idleness and be led to a more civil, purer, and wiser life. As Vives explained, when the unemployed were 'occupied and working, the evil thoughts and inclinations born to them by being idle will cease' (p. 280). They would be taught habits that would make them useful rather than pernicious to themselves and others, and in the end, when the poor had been transformed, they would say, 'The senate of Bruges saved us even against our own will' (p. 288). Of course it was not just the poor who benefited from this reformation but also the city of Bruges: 'The city will have an incomparable benefit and imponderable gain with so many citizens made more modest, more civil, well bred and more social . . . the poor will not think of changes, seditions and tumults' (p. 290).

It need hardly be said then any charitable relief dispensed by the city was to encourage virtue in the recipients. If Vives is silent on such technical points as who should distribute the relief and whether it consisted of money or food, he is adamant that any recipient who spent his stipend 'on games, prostitutes, concubinage, extravagance or gluttony' (p. 282) should be punished. The offender would be given the hardest work and have his food rations cut 'so that he will repent of his previous life and will not easily fall into the same vices' (p. 282). The punishments were not to be severe enough to kill the offender, merely enough to 'soften him and debilitate his passions' (p. 282). Supervision of the comportment of the poor fell under the all-encompassing scrutiny of two officials, appropriately entitled censors, who also supervised the activities of the youth of the city, including the children of the rich. In the interests of cultivating desirable habits at the earliest possible moment, the city magistrates were also to provide for the care and education of foundling children. They would be sent to a public school where they would be taught reading, writing, Christian piety, a trade, to live moderately and content themselves with little.

In the entire treatise, Vives hardly mentions the clergy except in the desultory remarks that prelates should contribute to poor relief and priests should not be permitted to use the funds given to the poor; presumably the clergy were to play a negligible role in relieving the poor.

There is, of course, much more to Vives' treatise than what is presented in this brief discussion, but it is fair to say that the humanist has presented a limited view of sixteenth-century poverty. For example, those people who needed assistance through no fault of their own but because circumstances – another child, sickness, death of the breadwinner – compelled them to supplement their meagre income are given only cursory attention by Vives. What remain in the reader's mind after reading the treatise are the clouds of rhetoric used to describe the vicious lives of an inadequately defined 'poor'. On the other hand, Vives' dislike of the squalor, ignorance and sin that he found in the lives of many of the poor and his desire to bring about a moral reformation of these people were to become sound principles of Counter-Reformation mercy and charity.[5]

Vives should not be credited with prompting the welfare reforms of Bruges since his treatise was published after the city had taken this step, and the magistrates may have been influenced by the reforms already carried out in Mons, Ypres, Strassburg and Nuremberg.[6] In the first half of the sixteenth century the publication of social legislation seemed to be common throughout Europe.[7] These early reforms usually adopted a programme similar to that outlined by Vives, though charitable resources were frequently consolidated into one central fund or into a large institution such as a hospital.

One explanation for the rash of laws and reforms having to do with the poor and their relief is the increasing population of Europe,[8] which meant that there were more people in need of relief. Cities and large urban areas were particularly sensitive to the pressure of an expanding population because many people migrated to the cities in search of work or charitable assistance. If migration to cities was a long-term trend over the century, it was also a short-term trend during periods of famine, war, or epidemics when villagers sought relief in cities where food reserves and charitable institutions were more abundant. It was during periods of such short-term dislocation that many cities promulgated poor laws, as the increased demand for assistance forced a more discriminatory policy in the dispensation of relief and better utilization of the available resources.

However, it was not just increasing population that forced cities and states to promulgate legislation against idleness and ablebodied beggars; decreasing population could have the same effect. From the mid-fourteenth century to the mid-fifteenth century, when Europe was suffering from depopulation as a result of the Black Death, many cities and states issued laws that attempted to prohibit the ablebodied from begging, to force them to work, and in some instances, to prohibit them from migrating.[9] In Castile the city of Toledo in 1400 issued a savage law that threatened vagrants with exile, removal of their ears and, on the third offence, death.[10] Thus punishments for vagrancy were not unique to the sixteenth century and cannot be explained entirely by increasing population.

The sixteenth century witnessed the development of certain ideas which, if not exactly new, were stated with greater vigour and more frequently than heretofore. These ideas, expressed by Vives and his fellow humanists, by Luther and other Protestant reformers, and by Loyola and other good Catholics, viewed public beggars as distasteful and as candidates for moral improvement. In addition to their questionable morality, beggars were also viewed as carriers of disease and thus a threat to the physical health of a community; it was the attempt to preserve good health that frequently prompted public officials to regulate or proscribe the movement of beggars. Such ideas about beggars were in obvious conflict with the old belief that the poor were representatives of Christ on earth, and the conflict of these opposing ideas was echoed throughout the century.

One example of such a conflict occurred in the Netherlandish town of Ypres.[11] As early as 1525 Ypres had banned public begging, formed a Common Fund and instructed the Mendicant Orders of the city to make monthly alms collections to sustain themselves. This arrangement lasted until 1530 when the Mendicants formally presented a list of grievances to the city council, arguing that the prohibition of begging and forcing foreign beggars to leave the city was against the divine law and that laymen had no right to administer and distribute charitable revenues. The friars further contended that since they had been deprived of their principal source of revenue by the abolition of begging, they should be maintained by the Common Fund. The Ypres case was referred to the theologians of the Sorbonne who, in January 1531, handed down their frequently quoted decision pronouncing the reform as 'pious and salutory'. The approbation was tempered by qualifications, however: begging could not be prohibited if the Common Fund lacked revenues to support the poor; the Mendicant Orders could not be deprived of their right to beg; ecclesiastical revenues should not be tampered with; and no one could be restrained from making private alms donations.

The Sorbonne decision met with a mixed reaction. The cardinal of Lorraine and the papal legate, Cardinal Campeggi, granted indulgences to those who contributed to the Ypres Common Fund, while Charles V was persuaded to support and encourage welfare reforms in the Netherlands. In October 1531 an edict was promulgated which prohibited begging to all but religious, prisoners, lepers and any deserving pauper who could not be maintained by the Common Fund.[12] The edict also recommended that all charitable revenues should be consolidated to form a Common Fund. Despite the royal decree, the friars continued to publicize their grievances. One Franciscan of Bruges, Jean Royart, published a pamphlet protesting against the reform, though, under the threat of being charged with the crime of *lèse-majesté*, he publicly retracted his criticism. The superior of the Franciscans in Bruges was reprimanded by the Council of Flanders in 1531 for preaching against the new institution, while the scribe and Latin poet, Chretien Cellerius, condemned all attempts to restrict public begging.[13] Clearly, Catholic opinion concerning the poor and their relief was very much divided in the third decade of the sixteenth century.

## THE CASTILIAN REACTION

While the Netherlandish cities initiated welfare reforms that were supported by Charles V and the theologians of the Sorbonne, there is evidence that the cities of Castile were moving in a similar direction. The *procuradores* of the Castilian Cortes who, as representatives of the rapidly growing cities and towns of Castile, were most sensitive to the problems of the poor and their relief, registered continual complaints about the poor in the numerous Cortes sessions convened from 1518 to 1539.

The earliest petitions of 1518 and 1523 complained of wandering poor persons whose peregrinations spread disease and incited vagabondage.[14] The *procuradores* recommended, and the crown concurred, that the poor should remain in their birthplace where they would be given a licence to beg or, if they were afflicted with some contagious disease, they should be confined to a hospital. This early legislation had some effect because in 1521 the city of Córdoba ordered that foreign beggars be expelled, 'seeing that other cities do not permit foreign beggars and order them to return to their birthplace'.[15] However, in 1525 and 1528 the *procuradores* again requested stronger enforcement, and in 1534 it was suggested that the municipal authorities should appoint a special deputy to handle the licensing of poor persons since the justices 'do not want to carry out the laws'.[16] The petition of 1534 brought a lengthy response from the crown. The justices were ordered to appoint 'two good persons' who would see that the poor and sick were cared for in the bishopric of their birth, preferably in hospitals, that vagabonds were punished and that children were not taken to beg. Idlers in the court (presumably those in Valladolid where the royal family resided) were to be punished, while no pilgrim could remain in the court for more than one day. The suggestion made in 1534 that the poor and sick should be cared for in hospitals is the first hint that the Castilian crown favoured a policy of eliminating public begging. Aside from a tepid petition from the *procuradores* in 1537,[17] the next pronouncement concerning the poor came with the promulgation of a poor law in 1540 which, in turn, led to the famous debate between Juan de Robles and Domingo de Soto.

Another supporter of welfare reform was Ignatius Loyola, who in 1535 persuaded the city council of his native town, Azpeitia, to adopt a plan to eliminate public begging.[18] In Loyola's reform the city council was to appoint two deputies, one a cleric and the other a layman, who would collect alms for the poor on Sundays and holy days. The city council was also to compile a list that included the name and ailment of each pauper, and the two deputies, known as the *mayordomos de pobres*, would see that the people on this list received alms 'with respect to the need and quality of each poor person'. Public begging was prohibited to everyone, including the professional alms collectors (*demandores*) of 'hospitals, houses, or churches within or outside of this jurisdiction'. Any foreign beggars unable to work would report to the *mayordomos* who would provide them with relief for one night. Even hospital administrators were forbidden to take in any poor person capable of labour or any *demandores*. The punishments for anyone who broke the no-begging rule varied: on the first offence beggars received three or six days in jail; on the second offence foreign beggars were subject to a hundred lashes while natives were imprisoned for six days. Any hospital administrator who took in an ablebodied beggar received a three-day jail sentence and a fine of 100 mrs, and any citizen of Azpeitia who gave alms directly to a beggar instead of the *mayordomos* was fined 2 *reales*; all fines were used to relieve the poor.

The prohibition of begging was but one reform accomplished during Loyola's stay in Azpeitia. The entire programme included:

The ringing of the church bells for those who found themselves in mortal sin; that there should be no beggars but all the poor should be relieved; that there should be no card games or sellers or buyers of cards; and that the wearing of head ornaments by women, a bad habit and offensive to God, should be extirpated.[19]

Elimination of public begging and provision for those in need was then a matter of moral reform for Loyola as it was for Vives. Beggars joined those who lived in mortal sin, the card players, and improperly dressed females, as people in need of improvement and correction, while other members of the community were urged to confess and communicate at least once a month.

Whether the reforms in a Basque town would have much resonance in Castile, or whether Loyola's ideas about beggars would have any greater influence than the theologians of the Sorbonne, is open to question. But Loyola or his followers might have circulated copies of the Azpeitia statutes. In his defence of the Zamora poor laws, Juan de Robles mentioned that in the poorest provinces of Spain – Galicia,

Viscaya, and Asturias – 'there is not (according to what they say) one poor person who begs publicly . . . . and this is observed most rigorously in the poorest province of all which is Viscaya'.[20]

Instrumental in the formulation and promulgation of the new Castilian poor laws was the cardinal–archbishop of Toledo, Juan Tavera, described by one Spanish historian as 'one of the most eminent men of Spain, comparable to Francisco Jiménez de Cisneros'.[21] Cardinal Tavera was also a staunch supporter of the Jesuits. One contemporary cited him as the best friend the Company had in Castile, and one of Tavera's closest associates, Bartolomé de Bustamante, joined the Company of Jesus in 1552 at fifty-one years of age.[22]

One of a long line of unusually long-lived individuals to occupy the see of Toledo in the sixteenth century, Cardinal Tavera, who was sixty-eight years of age when he signed the 1540 poor law, had behind him a life of service to the Castilian crown and church. Born in Toro in 1472, the second son of an *hidalgo* family, he was educated in Salamanca and became a *licenciado* in canon law in 1500 (Salazar de Mendoza, *Tavera*). Tavera was the nephew of the reforming Dominican theologian, Diego de Deza (1443–1523), a fervent exponent of Thomism and a *catedrático* at the University of Salamanca until he was called upon by the crown to act as tutor and chaplain for the heir apparent of the Castilian throne, Prince Don Juan.[23] In 1497 Diego de Deza returned to Salamanca as bishop of the diocese and conferred upon his nephew his first prebendary, the first of a long series of preferments. The Dominican was translated to the archdiocese of Seville in 1504 and three years later Tavera became his vicar-general. Deza had been inquisitor-general of Castile and Aragon since 1499 and his nephew was elected to the Council of the Inquisition in 1506. In 1513 Ferdinand the Catholic appointed Tavera to reform the chancery court of Valladolid and the following year rewarded him with the diocese of Ciudad Rodrigo. Rapidly translated to the bishoprics of León, Osma and, in 1524, to Santiago de Compostela, Tavera became a cardinal in 1531 and three years later was awarded the plum of Castilian ecclesiastical preferments when Charles gave him the archdiocese of Toledo. The one position which still eluded him, inquisitor-general of Castile, he received in 1539.

Though Cardinal Tavera seemed to prefer administration and diplomacy to theological disputation, he inherited his uncle's preoccupation with church reform. He was concerned with the education and comportment of the clergy,[24] and in 1536 he convoked a diocesan synod in Toledo, the first held since that of Cardinal Cisneros in 1498. Another synod was scheduled for 1546, but it was never convened because of the cardinal's death in 1545.[25] While concerned with church reform, Tavera was a diplomat; the tactful reprimand he sent to the wealthy and quarrelsome cathedral chapter of Toledo in 1536 gives some idea of his concerns and his discretion.

They have said here that on the Day of the Innocents certain games or representations were performed in the cathedral which important persons did not find edifying; afterwards, they whispered in the court about you and me. I know full well that things did not go as far as they say, but still it is most unfortunate that in the principal church of Spain and in the head, which should provide an example for all the others, that occasion should be given for such whisperings. . . . What I desire and you ought to desire, as I believe you do, is that there is such good order, silence and propriety in the cathedral in celebrating the Divine Cult that all those from Spain and outside Spain can take it as an inspiration and example of honesty and seriousness as, thanks be to God, up until now has been done.[26]

As Tavera continued his ascent up the ladder of ecclesiastical preferment, he became more active in affairs of state. He presided over numerous Castilian Cortes held between 1528 and 1539 and was president of the Royal Council from 1528 until 1539 when the Emperor appointed him regent during his absence, an appointment that lasted until 1541. Clearly the archbishop was a close and trusted servant of Charles I, as Charles V was known in Castile. Tavera was certainly successful in prising subsidies for the emperor from the Castilian Cortes, and he seems to have been successful in maintaining peace in a quarrelsome court while the emperor was absent. For example, in 1543, when all the court was gathered in Valladolid to celebrate the first marriage of Prince Philip, a quarrel over matters of precedence broke out between Tavera and the Duke of Alba. The court immediately broke into factions with 'many great lords declaring themselves on the cardinal's side' (Salazar de Mendoza, *Tavera*, pp. 323–5). The verbal battle was not transformed into a physical one because Tavera wisely withdrew to his quarters where he contented himself with writing a complaint to Charles.

As archbishop of Toledo and a trusted servant of the crown, Tavera was not only one of the most influential personages of the realm, he was also one of the wealthiest. His followers and retainers numbered 400, a quantity that Salazar de Mendoza, writing in 1603, judged to be the largest anyone in Castile had ever supported, before or after the cardinal's death. The cost of feeding this entourage was considerable; Tavera's accounts from February to December 1539 reveal that more than 4 million mrs were spent on food.[27] These same accounts also reveal that the archbishop appreciated the finer things of life. As pontifical rings he had a diamond, a ruby, and an emerald set in gold; a gold cross, adorned with six diamonds and a pearl pendant, was made; two large silver candlesticks that had a combined weight of 56 pounds were made for the altar. Aside from the food bill, Tavera's greatest expense for the year was the 25,000 ducats he loaned the emperor when he left for Flanders in November. Despite this large and unusual expense, his account books showed 3,500,000 mrs remaining at the end of the year. The cardinal did not live beyond his means, but his means, an income of 27,681,996 mrs for the eleven-month period, were ample.

In this same period the cardinal gave some 500,000 mrs in alms, not an impressive figure compared with the 675,000 mrs spent for the gold cross. However, in 1540 Tavera gave 45,000 ducats for poor relief (see chapter 3 below), and he left much of his wealth to pay for the construction and maintenance of the large hospital he founded in Toledo in 1541. It had become a custom in Castile to divide up the estate left by the Toledo prelates into three equal parts: one for the pope, one for the crown, and the remainder to pay for the works stipulated in the prelate's will. According to a 1550 report of the papal nuncio, the crown had received 200,000 ducats from Tavera's estate, which means, if the nuncio's estimate was accurate, that the prelate left an estate of 600,000 ducats.[28]

After his service as regent was terminated in 1541, Tavera was anxious to abandon affairs of state and devote himself completely to his pastoral duties. His later letters are full of pleas to leave the court: 'I beg Your Majesty for a licence to return to my diocese where we prelates are obligated to reside; because of my past absences, my age, and the indispositions I feel, I have even more need to retire.'[29] However, in fulfilment of one of his favourite sayings, 'the ministers of Caesar must die on their feet', Cardinal Tavera died in Valladolid still serving the emperor.

Neither the petitions of the Castilian Cortes nor the predisposition of Cardinal Tavera were the direct cause of the Castilian poor law, but rather the drought of 1539 which led to a disastrous harvest throughout Castile. In March 1540 Tavera wrote to the emperor, 'In all the land there is little bread and in some provinces none at all.'[30]

By April Andalucía had been relieved by grain brought in from abroad, but in the rest of the kingdom the scarcity was such that bread riots were feared. On 26 June Tavera reported that Madrid contained so many poor persons and their need was so great that public begging had been prohibited and all the destitute and needy were being cared for in hospitals and specially designated houses.[31] Two months later, on 24 August 1540, a poor law for all Castile was promulgated.

Was the 1540 poor law a measure foisted upon Castile by an overzealous emperor, infected by questionable foreign influences?[32] As explained above, Charles was absent from Castile when the new poor law was issued, and, though he certainly approved of the new measure, he did not force his opinions upon Castile. It was not until September that Cardinal Tavera received a letter from the emperor, who congratulated him on the passage of the new law and went on to say, 'As you recall, although I suggested [such a law] in consultations, it was never decreed because difficulties were always raised.'[33] The emperor urged Tavera to try and make the new measures permanent, and in December 1540 the cardinal reported that letters had been sent out to all the cities of the realm and the reform was continuing with much benefit to all concerned.[34]

The 1540 Castilian poor law was not a clarion call to drastic innovations.[35] It began with a long introduction, signed by Cardinal Tavera and Francisco de los Cobos, which included a review of the earlier legislation devoted to the poor and their close associates, the vagabonds. The poor laws of John I, promulgated in 1387, were reiterated. Complaining of the lack of labourers in the kingdom, this fourteenth-century edict ordered that any ablebodied beggar or vagabond could be forcibly employed for one month to serve as a soldier, to guard livestock or to fulfil other reasonable tasks, though the captives had to be given food and water; if the labour of the offender could not be utilized, he was to be banished from his place of residence after receiving sixty lashes. From the laws of John I there was a sudden leap to the more recent sixteenth-century legislation, none of which, the law sadly concluded, was being observed or executed. Instead, there was 'a multitude of poor persons who come to the principal towns to beg', many of whom were able to work but preferred not to do so. In addition to setting an evil moral example for the rest of the community and discouraging Christian charity, these persons took the alms that should have been given to the natives of the cities. These injustices and the lack of effective enforcement had forced the Royal Council to issue new, more detailed instructions concerning the poor and their relief.

The lengthy instructions were largely devoted to spelling out the administrative details of a licensed begging system. Persons in need could beg only in the cities, towns and villages where they were natives or residents and, of course, only the deserving poor, that is those unable to provide for themselves through labour, were permitted to beg. These persons would be issued a licence by their parish priest, though the licence was also to be scrutinized by the justices. Anyone found begging without a licence sixty days after the publication of the new law would be subject to punishment: the first offence brought four days' imprisonment, the second offence eight days' imprisonment and two months' exile, and on the third offence the culprit would be considered a vagabond and subject to the punishments prescribed by John I. Mendicant friars also needed a begging licence from their superiors and students one from their rectors. Under normal circumstances, a licence entitled the bearer to beg within six leagues of his place of birth or residence except in times of famine when the six-league limitation was invalid. Only the blind and the pilgrims on their way to Santiago were permitted to beg without a licence, though the latter were warned not to stray further than four leagues' distance from the 'straight' road to Santiago. No one could be licensed unless they had confessed and received the Sacrament, and children over five could not accompany their parents to beg but were to be put in service or taught a trade.

It is only in the concluding paragraph of the instructions, after two pages dealing with the details of a licensed begging system, that it was tentatively suggested that begging might not be the best way to provide for the poor. This brief paragraph instructed the prelates, justices and hospital administrators to ensure that the rents designated for charitable purposes were spent to relieve the poor, 'as it would be of great service to God if the poor could be succoured without begging in the streets'. This brief final paragraph, most notable for its suggestiveness and hesitancy, represents the one statement in the 1540 poor law that public begging might not be the best way of providing for the poor. Begging was not actually prohibited, it was merely suggested that the poor might be provided for by other means. Nor were the other means spelled out in any detail: it was merely suggested that charitable revenues should be spent for the purposes for which they had been given and that alms for the needy might be begged by good persons.

The confusing way in which this law presents directions for two contradictory policies, and the vagueness of the final paragraph, intimate that the crown was hoping to avoid criticism by stating its policy of welfare reform mildly, almost as an afterthought tacked on to the main body of the law. More evidence to support the circumspection of the crown is the fact that the law was not actually printed until 1544, four years after it had been promulgated. Finally, since public begging was not actually prohibited and a consolidation of charitable resources was not mentioned, it is obvious that Charles did not force upon Castile the policies he had adopted in the Netherlands; rather he let the Castilians work out their own means of solving the problem.

The 1540 poor law has been described as a police measure,[36] a judgment that relies more on the opinion of Domingo de Soto than on an objective reading of the law. Compared with the legislation of other European cities and states, which punished ablebodied beggars with enslavement or galley service,[37] or even with the earlier Castilian legislation of John I, which promised vagrants one month's forced labour or sixty lashes and exile on the first offence, the punishments of the 1540 poor law seem relatively mild. The first and second offence brought brief imprisonment, combined with a two-month exile on the second transgression, and only on the third offence were the punishments of John I applicable. Nor were any new officials established to enforce the punishments. Of course the letter of the law says little about the actual enforcement, but judging from the experience of Toledo in 1546 when a poor law was enforced, the needy, including beggars, were treated with great charity and kindness rather than severity. Considering the persons who supported the 1540 poor law – the cardinal–archbishop of Toledo, Juan Tavera; the prior of San Juan, Diego de Toledo, whose kindness to the poor was praised by Domingo de Soto; the bishop of Zamora, don Pedro Manuel; and the Benedictine abbot, Juan de Robles – it is difficult to imagine that a policy of oppression or excessive force would prevail.

The reforms of Zamora, which are probably representative of the type of poor law initiated in other cities such as Valladolid, Madrid, Salamanca and Toledo, are also moderate. The Zamora poor law is famous because it was approved by the theologians of Salamanca and was publicly defended by Juan de Robles in his treatise, *De la orden que en algunos pueblos de España se ha puesto en la limosna.* The law included a prohibition of public begging and set up a type of public almonry dedicated to supporting the disenfranchised deserving beggars and to housing and feeding poor travellers for a period of three days (pp. 154–226). Outsiders were welcomed to the city as long as they agreed to abide by the new regulations. The reform was directed by a committee of eight administrators chosen from the ranks of the cathedral chapter, the *regidores* of the city council, the *hidalgos* (the lesser nobility), and 'the people' (*el pueblo*), each group contributing two members to the committee. This committee was responsible for the examination of the poor and the distribution and collection of charitable funds. They were assisted by a receiver whose financial accounts were checked monthly by the *corregidor* and the bishop, and two *alguaciles* who enforced the prohibition of begging and took poor travellers to the point where they would receive their three days' sustenance. Once a week the poor of Zamora received enough money to provide 12 mrs a day for the men, 10 mrs for the women, and 6 mrs for children.

The Zamora reform involved no consolidation of charitable revenues. In this respect it is similar to the scheme proposed by Vives and it exhibited the same weakness, namely a lack of funds. Money was collected from parishioners on a weekly subscription basis and from poor boxes placed in all the city churches. The candid Juan de Robles was extremely disappointed in the small number of citizens who subscribed to the weekly alms collections; only a third to a half of the citizens had agreed to support the new plan, a lack of support the Benedictine attributed to the opposition raised by some theologians. If financial support was not all that might be hoped for, Robles reported that the poor were pleased with the new arrangement. Under questioning, all the disenfranchised beggars preferred the new method of distributing alms; all but two little women (*mujercillas*), who promptly withdrew their objections when told they would receive no more public assistance if they returned to begging (Robles, *De la orden*, pp. 257, 285–6).

Despite the positive testimony of the paupers and the comparative moderation of the Castilian poor laws, they provoked a reaction. It was the Dominican theologian, Domingo de Soto, *catedrático de vísperas* at Salamanca, who offered the most devastating criticism in his little book, *Deliberación en la causa de los pobres*, published five years after the Castilian poor law had been promulgated. Soto's position on the issue of poor relief between 1540 and 1545 is somewhat inconsistent. He was one of the Salamanca theologians who had signed and approved the Zamora poor laws, and in 1544, when the city of Salamanca initiated welfare reforms, the Dominican was chosen as a representative of the university to accompany the city *regidores* as they visited the poor in their homes, so he had been personally involved in the Salamanca reforms. Yet in the academic year of 1539–40 and again in 1542–3, Soto had lectured on almsgiving and poor relief, the latter lectures serving as the basis of his *Deliberación*,[38] so in principle he opposed the reforms as early as 1539. Why then did he sign the Zamora poor laws? Soto claimed that he signed the Zamora statutes without reading them, trusting the advice of a colleague that they contained nothing objectionable (Soto, *Deliberación*, p. 20). Yet given the theologian's concern with the issue and the brevity of the Zamora statutes, it is difficult to believe that he did not know what they contained, or that he would not take the time to read them personally. Perhaps what provoked the theologian's public criticism was the fact that the 1540 poor law was finally printed in Alcalá and Medina del Campo in 1544.

Whatever sparked the Dominican's open resistance and the publication of his book, for those who favoured reform it was unfortunate that Soto, whose fame was such that it was said 'Qui soit Sotum soit totum',[39] should be an opponent. The *Deliberación* was not limited to criticism of the poor laws of Zamora or even to those of Castile, and Soto did not content himself with a humourless and pedantic correction of biblical criticisms as did a Dominican of Lyons who criticized the sermon of one of the welfare reformers of that city.[40] In a letter sent to Prince Philip to explain his 1545 treatise, Soto observed that 'although this question [of the poor] has been debated, the legitimate principles by which it must be judged have never been deduced by anyone'.[41] Though the letter went on to deny the author's ability to determine these principles, these are exactly what Soto sought. In the process, he challenged the precepts and goals underlying all the early-sixteenth-century welfare reforms and any authority – the theologians of the Sorbonne, the decisions of past church councils and even the pope – to sanction the permanent prohibition of begging in a Catholic state.

Juan de Robles, the Benedictine abbot of San Vicente in Salamanca, published his book in March 1545, just two months after his opponent's had appeared. Robles shared many of the ideas advanced by Vives, but his treatise is far more compassionate and moderate. This is largely because the Benedictine carefully distinguished between the deserving poor and the vagabonds, a distinction not always observed by Vives. Robles wisely reserved his vilification for the vagabonds and emphasized that by eliminating these miscreants the deserving poor would receive more assistance, thereby adding a positive incentive for the reform. 'Those who have need to beg are relieved without so much effort on their own part, and they have the security of daily maintenance instead of having it one day and not on another' (p. 301). Though he did stress the virtue of work, mentioning with some pride that in Zamora sixty-five persons thought to be suffering from incurable diseases had been cured and were employed, Robles did not conjure up visions of anthills by prescribing the activities to be performed by those persons on the public relief roles. Nonetheless, despite the moderation and the more circumscribed goals of the Benedictine, he does not conceal his dislike of begging, 'no more than a public proclamation given by the poor of the little compassion and mercy of the rich' (p. 155), and his hope that Christian charity might move forward to eliminate the causes which forced individuals to beg.

Soto was in full agreement that vagabonds were a disreputable lot deserving of punishment, but he questioned the necessity of mounting such a complicated operation as the new poor laws just to extirpate these delinquents. Would it not be simpler for the *regidores* of a city to convoke weekly gatherings of the poor and execute the laws against them at these times? It seemed to Soto that all the examination of the needs, customs and ailments of the poor was born 'not so much out of love and mercy for the deserving poor as of hate and loathing for the whole miserable estate' (*Deliberación*, p. 72). The Dominican pointed out that in all estates of society – prelates and grandees, friars and public officials – one could find sin, weakness and wickedness but 'they do not mount such an artillery against them'. Nor was it necessary to eliminate beggars to succour the deserving poor, who could be relieved by means of confraternities and special perpetual contributions which would be distributed by the parish priest and charitable parishioners. Finally, Soto questioned whether the new poor laws did, in fact, serve to eliminate vagabondage or if they merely shifted the problem from one place to another. Expelling vagabonds from a city was not a very effective solution for they rarely went home; instead they moved on to other places, frequently the smaller towns and villages, where they did far more damage. A policy of what Soto termed 'rigour' against the poor, whether a vagabond, sinner or saint, did more damage than it did good. It forced vagabonds into robbery and it hardened the hearts of the poor to the Christian message: 'To bring virtue to the poor it would be better to give them alms than deny them, because by treating them with kindness you can soften their hearts; in their desperate condition, seeing themselves excluded from assistance, their hearts are hardened against God' (p. 100).

Much of the debate pivoted round the theological niceties of almsgiving.[42] Both churchmen agreed that giving alms was an act of mercy, but Soto argued that mercy had nothing to do with judgments concerning the merits of the recipient. Mercy was distinct from justice, two virtues joined only in God; justice, which involved a distinction between good and evil, pertained to the ministers of justice, that is the secular authorities; mercy, a higher virtue, involved no such judgments but was merely 'to succour everyone' (*Deliberación*, p. 91). Robles is equally adamant that alms must be given with discrimination and he cited numerous scriptural and canonical references to prove his point, concluding that 'he who gives work or charity without examination of the recipient behaves badly and sins gravely' (*De la orden*, p. 194). The Benedictine's attempts to prove his position logically are rather weak. He argued that since mercy was a work of charity and charity was a virtue that possessed order, then mercy too should possess order; and, if mercy did possess order (a still unproven assumption), it was to prefer a good person to a bad one. But this is not the weakest part of the Benedictine's defence, for tucked away in the latter part of his book is the statement: 'Although as private individuals we should not turn our heads from any poor persons nor concern ourselves with knowing who they are, those who govern the republic must take great care that no one begs who does not have a just cause or who will make evil use of what they receive' (p. 296). Apparently what Robles meant was that public alms were to be given with discrimination while private individuals were to give indiscriminately, or that the justices were to eliminate all undeserving poor so that private individuals would not be forced to discriminate. Whatever he meant, his arguments on this point are not consistent or entirely convincing.

The adversaries agreed that almsgiving bestowed upon the giver a special form of grace. For Soto, the external act of giving was not so efficacious as the inner feeling of compassion aroused in the soul of the giver when he was confronted with the sufferings of the poor; to evoke this feeling of compassion, the poor had to be visible and conspicuous, not enclosed in hospitals or special houses. Also, almsgiving involved a direct spiritual union between the giver and the receiver which could not be relegated to an intermediary. Robles did not deny that one should feel compassion for the poor, but stressed that compassion should arouse a desire to help the poor by improving their condition or curing their ailment. In and of itself, compassion was a very negative virtue: prisoners would not be freed and the sick would not be cured because they aroused our compassion and it was meritorious to give them alms. An individual should strive to remedy misery and poverty as a republic should strive to increase the wealth of its citizens 'so there are many rich and powerful citizens and few or no poor ones' (*De la orden*, p. 263).

But Soto's most devastating argument, reiterated throughout his treatise, was based upon the accepted dictum of the Catholic church that alms should be given voluntarily to be meritorious. Soto mentions some exceptions to this rule, instances when almsgiving became obligatory rather than voluntary, the most important of which was any case of extreme need, when a person was close to death from a lack of food (*Deliberación*, pp. 36, 46-7). But aside from this exception no one could be compelled to give alms. The Dominican then referred to the 1531 Sorbonne decision which stated that the poor could not be deprived of their right to beg unless they were assured of an alternative means of subsistence. How, Soto asked, could the crown assure the poor of an alternative subsistence when it had no power to tax or force its citizens to contribute to poor relief? And since the crown could not guarantee an alternative subsistence, it had no right to deprive the poor of their right to beg or to determine that the poor should be relieved in their birthplace, since it had no means of assuring that their place of birth could or would support them. 'No law can forbid the poor from leaving their birthplace to beg, if at the same time the law does not oblige and compel the people of the birthplace to maintain adequately all their poor and needy' (pp. 27, 35-7, 107-10).

Soto objected to the new poor laws not only because they excluded foreigners from permanent relief, but because a person could be punished merely for begging in a foreign city. He argued that if one was truly in need, begging anywhere was not a crime; thus the new poor laws, which prescribed expulsion for those who continued to break the law, were unjust. The Dominican went through the list of precedents for the new laws – past church councils, the Sorbonne decision, and the Scriptures – and concluded that none of them justified the exclusion of foreign beggars from charitable assistance. To those who brought up the old maxim that charity begins at home, Soto pointed out that beginning at home was a far cry from excluding outsiders. The only time he felt a city might exclude foreigners from relief was during periods of famine when a city was unable to maintain its own poor (pp. 47, 129–31), a conclusion that was just the opposite of what Vives recommended when he suggested that at such times foreigners should be admitted.

What Soto envisioned was a Christian commonwealth in which the poor enjoyed a complete liberty of movement. Extrapolating from the personal obligations of the rich to the poor, Soto argued that the richer provinces and cities of Spain had an obligation to help the poorer ones. This obligation was not to be fulfilled by shipments of grain from one area to another or through taxation but by the poor themselves, who 'like ants have to search for the richest part of the plant'. Depriving the poor of their liberty of movement was not only morally untenable, it was also against the divine law, at least as Soto interpreted it. 'How does Your Highness think that a land of mountains should maintain so many poor as the kingdom of Toledo, or Valladolid, or the Court of Your Majesty' (p. 38).

When Soto wrote his treatise many European cities had enacted poor laws that excluded foreign beggars from permanent relief and some cities did levy at least a temporary poor tax. The Dominican was aware of the reforms in Flanders, Italy and Germany, but, thumping the drum of patriotism, he rejected them all: 'That which is done in other lands cannot be used as a good example for us. . . . They can take an example from us as we have from them . . . . neither the people of Ypres nor any German can be an adequate example for us' (pp. 43, 120, 137).

Was Soto correct in implying that the exclusion of outsiders from relief was unknown in Spain? As early as 1321 the city of Barcelona ordered that all beggars, 'foreign or of another language', leave the city, and in 1521 the Castilian cities apparently adopted a similar expedient.[43] Whether this latter example was based on earlier Castilian precedents or foreign influences is unknown, but Soto's identification of the exclusion of outsiders from relief as a foreign solution should not be accepted as the final word until further research clarifies this question.

To those of us who know the end of the story – state taxation and implementation of welfare – Domingo de Soto appears to be arguing for an outdated system. However, the Dominican raised some issues that continue to be of interest for later generations. Freedom of movement for the poor is what Adam Smith recommended some two hundred years later when he sought to improve the condition of the poor and the wealth of nations.[44] And, if freedom of movement within the confines of national borders is now a generally accepted premise in most of the developed countries of the world, the immigration policies of these same countries are devoted to limiting outsiders, especially those who are poor or unskilled. Nor have the obligations of the rich developed countries to the poorer undeveloped ones received any accepted or comprehensive definition. Thus the problems brought up by Domingo de Soto in the sixteenth century linger on, though jurisdictional boundaries have been enlarged from cities and provinces to nations.

It does not appear that Soto had much to say that would encourage any sixteenth-century welfare reformer. However, if one reads his book closely, as all future Castilian reformers and policy makers were to do, there was a ray of hope. Soto did not approve of the poor being shut up in buildings and kept out of public view, but when eulogizing the great charity of the early Christian church he mentioned that in those golden days there had been hospitals for all needs, even to house beggars. At another point, when discussing the voluntary nature of almsgiving, he stated that in the case of hospital endowments people could be forced to give alms, a remark that is never clearly explained in the treatise and could be interpreted in a variety of ways (pp. 136, 108). But for any Catholic welfare reformer searching for a way out of Soto's dilemma, these two remarks might provide the basis for a new approach: give the beggars a hospital of their own.

On one point the protagonists agreed completely: poor relief should be administered and implemented by ecclesiastics. In the case of Soto, who carefully distinguished between mercy and justice and limited the role of the secular authorities to one of meting out punishment to vagabonds, this is a consistent conclusion. In the case of Robles, who argued that justice and mercy must be exercised jointly and that morally corrupt or idle persons should be excluded from assistance by 'those who govern' in the best interests of the republic, it seems a bit incongruous. It may have been personal experience that convinced the Benedictine of the need to keep poor relief in the hands of the clergy. When the poor laws were first introduced in Zamora, the nobles behaved in a very tactless manner by entering the houses of the poor in the company of all their servants and retainers and then publicizing the confidential information they gathered about the persons in need of relief. Robles admitted that the nobility had been overzealous in its mission and he hastened to add that the visits were now being carried out in a more discreet fashion.

Both theologians dedicated their books to Prince Philip. If one might dispute how to administer and implement poor relief, no one doubted who would finally decide the issue. As Soto put it, 'We will all follow where Your Highness leads and we will favour, defend, preach and counsel what Your Highness decides' (*Deliberación*, p. 140). Despite Robles' pleas that he come to a quick decision on the matter, Prince Philip, prudent at an early age, made no public pronouncement about relief of the poor until 1565 when new poor laws were promulgated.

After the 1545 debate Juan de Robles was appointed by the Inquisition to serve as a censor of the writings of the unfortunate archbishop of Toledo, Bartolomé de Carranza. The Benedictine died in 1572 in the monastery of Montserrat with his greatest work, a translation of the New Testament, unpublished, possibly because he feared the adverse judgment of the Inquisition. His opponent, Domingo de Soto, moved on to even greater acclaim. Soto was sent to the Council of Trent in 1545 where he contributed to the formulation of the council's legislation on justification. The emperor's urbane ambassador to the first session of the council, Diego Hurtado de Mendoza, found the Dominican 'excessive and frenetic' though he admitted that he was one of the best and 'most secure' theologians in attendance.[45] Presumably it was the ambassador's latter judgment which persuaded Charles V to appoint Soto as his personal confessor in 1549. The fact that Soto's commission as imperial confessor lasted little more than a year has given rise to much speculation, though it seems likely that the emperor felt the need of a more accommodating spiritual advisor and Soto preferred books and theology to the courtly life. In 1552 the Dominican resumed his teaching duties at Salamanca as *catedrático de prima*, a position he held until his death in 1560. Soto did not lose contact with the crown however, for he corresponded with the royal family, acted as a consultant in difficult theological matters and was frequently suggested as a candidate to fill vacant episcopal sees, including the archbishopric of Toledo in 1557.[46]

One might think that the Soto–Robles debate would inspire discussion and commentary in Castile since both treatises were published in the vernacular, but this does not seem to be the case. From 1545 until the termination of the Council of Trent in 1564, little was said by the crown, the Cortes, theologians or concerned citizens. However, one historian has recently traced echoes of the 1545 debate in the famous novel, *Lazarillo de Tormes*, whose author and date of composition are still unknown.[47] If this theory is correct then the 1545 debate did inspire at least one Castilian to reflect openly upon the causes and effects of poverty.

While the crown said nothing specific about the poor until 1565, it made some attempt to deal with the unruly and idle of the kingdom in a new pragmatic of 1552.[48] As Soto had pointed out, expulsion of vagabonds was not a very effective solution since they preferred travelling about and merely created more of a nuisance somewhere else. The 1552 pragmatic ordered that these miscreants should be subjected to galley service, a solution favoured by most sixteenth-century governments that had need of oarsmen. Anyone found begging without a licence was considered a vagabond and, as such, was subject to four years' galley service on the first offence, eight years' on the second, and a lifetime on the third offence.

The representatives of the Castilian Cortes, unusually reticent about the poor since the promulgation of the 1540 poor law, returned to the subject in 1555 when they again complained about unlicensed begging and the ineffective enforcement by the justices. The *procuradores* proposed the appointment of a new official, euphemistically entitled the Father of the Poor, who would act as a type of employment officer for those persons 'not inclined to labour'. This official would see that the idle were given daily employment; if anyone refused to accept the proffered task, they would be thrown out of the city or town where they resided 'as a work of mercy, Christianity and good government'.[49] Either the crown's 1552 pragmatic had not received much diffusion, the overworked justices had no time to enforce it, or the *procuradores* felt that galley service was too severe a punishment for ablebodied idlers, for exile continued to be the suggested remedy to deal with them.

The crown gave a non-committal response to this proposal, but two years later it was forced to some definite, if temporary, statement about poor relief. In 1556–7 a period of famine and plague struck two of the largest cities of the realm. As a chronicler described the situation in Seville: 'it was a very sterile year and a multitude of beggars from the neighbouring district came to Seville. More than 500 had died in the streets, so the beggars were confined in order that their illness would not endanger the rest of the city' (Órtiz de Zuñiga, *Annales de Sevilla*, pp. 279–80). Similar conditions prevailed in Toledo and in November 1557, the city council wrote to the crown requesting permission to begin an organized plan of relief 'because the high price of bread and other foods means that the poor and needy cannot maintain themselves and many have become sick and died'.[50]

The response from the Royal Cámara, whose membership included the influential Dominican theologian Melchor Cano, was a qualified assent. Permission was granted on grounds of the many people in need of relief, especially the shamefaced poor and other honorable persons who, because they did not beg, were not receiving adequate assistance. The city authorities were cautioned to meet with the regular clergy and other persons 'zealous in serving God and the public good', not to force anyone to give to the alms collection against their will, and to pay particular attention to the relief of the non-begging poor. However, this permission was not to be considered as a policy that was permanent or that applied to the whole of Castile: 'This organization [of poor relief] cannot be given generally for all the provinces and places of the realm since each of them is different and distinct, and it can be better accomplished on an individual basis according to what seems most suitable and the possibilities and conditions of each area.' In other words, in 1557 any relief effort that involved an organized collection and distribution of alms, a prohibition of public begging, and confinement of beggars had to be approved by the crown, and approval was contingent upon 'conditions, suitability and possibilities'. Presumably famine and sickness were conditions that justified at least a temporary approval.

Judging from the 1557 letter to the city of Toledo, the crown no longer supported the tentative welfare reforms of the 1540 poor laws as a permanent policy. Another indication that the crown had modified its position on poor relief came in the Netherlands, where an edict of Philip II allowed the needy of Bruges to beg publicly.[51] Forced to modify its earlier reforms, the senate of Bruges attempted to control begging by taking over all the charitable institutions of the city, a decision defended by Gil Wyts, pensionary of the city, in a book entitled, *De continendis et alendis domi pauperibus*. Two years later a Spanish Augustinian, Lorenzo de Villavicencio, appointed to Bruges as a preacher and also as a secret agent of Philip II, published *De oeconomia sacra circa pauperum curam*, which criticized Wyts, Vives and any secular authority that attempted to take over charitable institutions or to forbid public begging to the poor. The issue was submitted to Louvain for arbitration but in the meantime tempers ran high as Wyts tried to have the Augustinian's book burned by the public executioner and Villavicencio tried to have Wyts' ideas declared heretical by the theologians of Salamanca and Alcalá.[52]

Compared to the events in Bruges, matters proceeded quietly in Castile as the crown published a new poor law in 1565.[53] Philip's law, like that of his father, began with complaints about the increasing number of vagabonds who, because of their crimes and evil lives and because they took the alms that belonged to those truly in need, should be punished. The law went on to elaborate the procedures for a licensed begging system, but there were no hidden surprises tacked on to the end of the law. Rather the justices were ordered to ignore all previous welfare legislation, and the 1540 poor law was directly rescinded.

The administration and implementation of poor relief was placed in the hands of two deputies to be delegated by the justices in every parish of the kingdom. The deputies were to examine all beggars and give licences to those unable to sustain themselves through labour; they were to see that children of five years or older did not accompany their parents to beg, but specific directions as to what should be done with these children were not given; they were to draw up a list of the *envergonzantes* in their parish and to see that persons with contagious diseases were confined; finally they were responsible for collecting and distributing alms to the latter two categories of non-begging poor. The deputies received some assistance from the parish priests who signed all begging licences and helped to determine the *envergonzantes*. The justices played a more passive role by approving the begging licences and ensuring that a hospital or house was available for those persons with contagious diseases. The licence a beggar received was usually valid for one year but short-term licences for 'temporary impediments' were also mentioned. A licence allowed begging within the jurisdictional area of the justice, no one could receive a licence unless they had confessed and received the

Sacrament, and begging was prohibited in any church while the Divine Offices or 'sung or spoken masses' were being celebrated.

The punishment of vagabonds and other minor delinquents was the subject of a new pragmatic issued one year after the new poor laws.[54] The continual complaints of the Cortes about the lack of effective enforcement against idlers and vagabonds suggests that the justices were either overworked or negligent in their duties. Thus a new official, the *alguacil de vagabundos*, was created, whose function was to see that beggars, bigamists, ruffians, robbers and the like were brought to justice. The 1566 pragmatic also clarified the legal and administrative process by which these minor delinquents were to be condemned and transported to their respective ports of embarcation for the galleys. With the appointment of the *alguacil de vagabundos* in 1566, the crown legislation and officialdom relating to the poor was complete, and it remained largely unchanged until the eighteenth century when the poor and their relief again became a subject of import.

The poor law of 1565 was a traditional solution which attempted to regulate public begging, limited the role of the secular authorities to distant supervision and left the actual administration and implementation of poor relief to parish officials. A comparison of the 1565 poor law with that of 1540 indicates some changes in crown policy. With the exception of persons suffering from contagious disease, nothing was said in 1565 about placing the poor in hospitals and the poor were not ordered to return to their birthplace. If the validity of a beggar's licence was limited to the jurisdictional area of the justice who approved it, this did not mean that the licensee could not migrate to another parish in another city and receive a licence there. As Domingo de Soto recommended, the crown did not attempt to prohibit public begging and it did not suggest that the place where a pauper was born was responsible for maintaining him.

However, the stipulation that poor persons must have evidence of having confessed and communicated before they could receive a begging licence was one point that Domingo de Soto lost. Twenty years earlier the Dominican had objected to this requirement by arguing, among other things, that if there were many poor people who had not confessed in ten or twenty years, there were as many rich people in exactly the same condition 'and they do not take away their life or their food' (p. 95). The perceived need for more frequent confession and communication among all estates of society was one expression of Counter-Reformation spirituality that surmounted the objections of Soto.[55]

The publication of a new poor law and the creation of a new official to enforce the law did not end the crown's concern for the poor and their relief. Nor did the law end the circulation of new ideas designed to eliminate or control begging, but after 1565 reforms and ideas centred upon the hospitals.

### HOSPITALS AND THE GROWTH OF A NEW ORDER

The reform of hospitals had been a topic of discussion in Castile since the late fifteenth century when a movement to improve hospital efficiency swept through much of southern Europe. The fifteenth-century reform involved a fusion of the services and revenues of the numerous small hospitals into one large hospital, usually known as a consolidated or a general hospital. The medieval concept of 'hospitality', the services to be rendered by hospitals, was extremely ample.[56] It included the duty of housing pilgrims or travellers, whether rich or poor, a form of hospitality today relegated to hotels, hostelries or hospices; the provision of permanent living quarters for the old, the infirm, the poor or those afflicted with contagious diseases such as leprosy; and medical or surgical care for the sick and injured. The usual medieval response to the multifarious purposes of hospitals had been to found an abundance of small institutions, each with its own administrator or hospitaller, its own endowments and dedicated to treating a certain type of ailment or need. The fifteenth-century hospital consolidations centralized the services and sometimes the rents of the small hospitals within one large hospital. Centralization eliminated some of the prevalent abuses in the use of hospital rents, which were frequently spent to support an absentee administrator who viewed this income as an additional increment to subsidize his personal expenses; or a resident administrator, who, together with the hospital staff, managed to consume all the available income themselves leaving no revenues for relief of the needy. A fusion of all hospital rents, properties and endowments into one central fund meant that investments could be made on a larger scale under the supervision of one central committee; also checking accounts was simplified since it was far easier to check one central fund than it was forty little ones. The larger hospitals also offered benefits to patients. Since the new hospitals maintained a full-time staff, many of whom lived in the hospital, a patient could receive the benefit of spiritual or physical consolation at any hour of the day or night. Nor would a sick patient need to wander from one hospital to another in search of one which had space and treated his particular ailment.

The hospital consolidation movement appears to have begun in Italy where, by the third quarter of the fifteenth century, several towns had formed large consolidated hospitals.[57] Castilians might also have been inspired by the formation of such hospitals in the Iberian peninsula. In 1479 Prince Dom João of Portugal received papal permission to consolidate all the hospitals in Lisbon, and by 1502 forty-three small institutions had been fused into the new Hospital of All Saints.[58] By the second decade of the sixteenth century, consolidated hospitals were a standard practice in all Portuguese cities. Similar reforms were initiated in the crown of Aragon where consolidated hospitals emerged in Zaragoza, Lérida, Tarragona, Valencia and Barcelona and in the Basque provinces.[59]

Though hospital reforms proceeded apace in many parts of the peninsula, the results in Castile were negligible despite the support of many influential persons. The Mendoza family, who dominated the Castilian ecclesiastical hierarchy in the last decade of the fifteenth century, strongly pressed for hospital consolidation. Diego Hurtado de Mendoza, cardinal–archbishop of Seville from 1486 to 1502, had attempted to consolidate the hospitals of Seville, but was forced to abandon the reform, owing to what one chronicler describes as, 'the strife of terrible controversies' (Órtiz de Zuñiga, *Annales de Sevilla*, p. 566). Pedro González de Mendoza, uncle of the Sevillan prelate and cardinal–archbishop of Toledo from 1483 until his death in 1495, pressed for a similar reform in Toledo and finally included the hospital consolidation as one of the clauses of his will. The Toledo prelate left a sizeable portion of his worldly wealth for the foundation of a hospital in Toledo, to be known as the Hospital of Santa Cruz. Mendoza's will specified that the rents and services of all the small, badly administered hospitals of the city and two of the hospitals administered by the cathedral chapter, one for the insane and another for foundling children, were to be fused into his new hospital.[60] However, despite the fact that the cardinal had received papal permission for the consolidation,[61] when the Hospital of Santa Cruz was officially opened in 1514 it included only the rents dedicated to supporting foundling children.

If Castilian prelates favoured reform, the innovative and imaginative measures of the Catholic kings indicates that they too were concerned with improving the charitable institutions of their realm. In Santiago de Compostela in 1499 they founded a general hospital, one of the largest and most beautiful in Spain, which was dedicated to housing pilgrims, the sick and the infirm as well as caring for foundling children.[62] Another foundation of the Catholic kings, the Royal Hospital of Granada, was devoted to treating syphilis, the new disease of the late fifteenth and early sixteenth centuries.[63] In 1500 the Toledo hospital of the military order of Santiago de los Caballeros was instructed by the crown to treat the same illness. They were also concerned for the well-being of soldiers who had served the crown. An old, almost inactive royal hospital in Seville, Nuestra Señora del Pilar, was converted into a retirement hospital for poor or injured soldiers,[64] while one of the earliest military field hospitals was constructed in Granada during the campaign to reconquer that kingdom.[65] It is probable that the Hospital de la Corte, a mobile hospital that accompanied the Castilian court in its peregrinations, was founded by the Catholic kings (Quintana, *Madrid*, p. 445). In view of all these crown reforms, it is difficult to explain why hospital consolidations were not effected in Castile, especially since Ferdinand actively supported consolidation in the crown of Aragon.

Of course hospital consolidation was not popular with all parties, especially with those persons, corporations or pious congregations destined to lose their hospital building and rents, undoubtedly those who created the 'terrible controversies' in Seville. An example of how one individual felt about the reform is provided by the testament of Juan Múñoz, a *vecino* of Granada who in 1501 founded a small pilgrim hospital in his native city:

> Because it is my determined will that this my hospital should remain forever dedicated to the advocation of the Mother of Christ, I order that neither the house nor the rents or properties may be removed, transported or converted into any other pious work in any manner by a king, queen or prelate, on pain of falling under the damnation of the Mother of Christ.[66]

Disposing of wealth for charitable purposes was, after all, a very personal matter and the donor had every right to stipulate how his money should be spent and to hope that his foundation might last into perpetuity. No matter how rational or practical consolidation might appear to prelates, monarchs or city authorities, it did not arouse enthusiasm amongst the persons who were destined to lose their foundation in the interests of establishing a large, amorphous consolidated hospital.

Furthermore the opponents of reform could raise some valid objections. Was it morally just to tamper with the last will and testament of a charitable giver, or to alter the purposes he had stipulated and to convert his bequest to a new cause? And, if so, who should undertake such conversions, the crown, the prelates or the pope? The legislation of the Council of Trent answered some of these questions, but in the meantime they confused the issue of hospital reform and offered a certain amount of protection to those who chose to resist such changes. Vives, who recommended a sweeping hospital reform in Bruges, had no doubts about the legality of converting pious funds or who should do the converting.

Those who govern the city must know that [hospitals] pertain to their care. No subject is permitted to excuse or exempt himself, alleging that the laws of the founder remain inviolable forever. These laws are not to be heeded to the letter, but according to justice . . . the rents or property left [by testators] should be distributed in the best uses and spent in the most worthy manner without so much concern as to who does it or in what manner it should be done ('Del socorro de los pobres', p. 281).

No matter how adamant Vives might have been in his conviction that pious funds might be converted to new uses, the fact that he mentioned it at all indicates that there were doubts and controversies. It would appear that in Castile those who objected were powerful and well armed, for Charles V, who had sanctioned a consolidation of charitable revenues in the Netherlands in 1531, did not attempt a similar reform in Castile even though there was support for it.

The Castilian Cortes, for instance, openly advocated hospital consolidation. From 1518 to 1559 the *procuradores* had offered numerous petitions suggesting that the small, inefficient hospitals of the realm should be consolidated into one or two larger hospitals.[67] They recommended that the larger cities should have two hospitals, one for contagious diseases and the other for non-contagious ailments, while the smaller populations should have only one general hospital. The *procuradores* added that the large wealthy hospitals were not to be included in the consolidation since they provided a useful and necessary service.

Another supporter of hospital consolidation was Cardinal Tavera who, like his predecessor Cardinal Mendoza, founded another large hospital in Toledo. When the cardinal wrote to the emperor explaining his intentions, he also suggested that the poor, small hospitals of Toledo should be consolidated into his new hospital. Though enthusiastic about the new foundation, the emperor postponed the question of consolidation until his return to Castile when the proposal could be discussed at length and any 'disorders' might be avoided.[68] As was the case with Cardinal Mendoza's consolidation reform, the proposal of Cardinal Tavera was never effected.

Whatever the causes inhibiting consolidation, in retrospect, the era of the Catholic kings and that of Charles I was one of increasing hospital foundations. Castile's increasing prosperity and the growing preoccupation with religious reform encouraged charitable giving, the foundation of pious works, and active involvement and concern for the poor and their relief. If Cardinal Cisneros stimulated the religious revival in Castile,[69] in later years many of his reforms were actively propagated by the evangelical movement fostered by Master John of Ávila, also known as the Apostle of Andalucía.[70] One of the many followers of the Apostle was John of God, whose hospital in Granada was to serve as a centre for a new type of religious order devoted to hospital service and the care of the poor and the sick. By an ironic twist of history the convert became more famous than his master, but that was a post-Tridentine development unforeseen by a contemporary in the mid-sixteenth century.

The only son of a well-to-do *converso* family of Almodóvar del Campo, a village in the Mancha region of New Castile, John of Ávila (1499–1569) attended the University of Alcalá from 1520 to 1523 where he studied under Domingo de Soto, recently returned from his studies in Paris, and formed an enduring friendship with the future archbishop of Granada, Pedro Guerrero. After leaving Alcalá, the young man journeyed to Seville where he met a former protégé of Cardinal Cisneros, Francisco de Contreras.[71] A fervent exponent of church reform, Contreras devoted his life to evangelism and education; many of his educational goals were expounded in his book, *Doctrina Cristiana*, and he founded two schools dedicated to spreading the Christian doctrine, one in Torrijos (province of Toledo) and the other in Seville. The school in Seville included twenty-four children, some of the poorer ones supported by Contreras, who were taught singing, grammar, art, and theology as well as the weaving of esparto grass.[72] Inspired by the reforms and the Seville school of Contreras, John of Ávila spent the rest of his life preaching and founding schools throughout Andalucía. By 1555, he had founded a total of fifteen schools; eleven served to instruct children in the rudiments of reading, writing and the Christian doctrine, while three were dedicated to the higher studies of arts and theology. The most famous of these foundations was the University of Baeza which served as the intellectual centre of John of Ávila's coterie and as a training centre for future priests, instructed in the art of preaching instead of speculation. In the 1550s the printing presses of the University of Baeza were enormously active, turning out a plethora of spiritual guides, prayer books and devotional tracts. 'Books of contemplation for carpenters' wives', as Inquisitor Fernando Valdés called them when many of the Baeza publications were placed on the Index promulgated by Valdés in 1559.[73]

The unfavourable judgment of the Inquisition was one of the factors contributing to the decline of the Baeza school and the movement founded by John of Ávila. The Master had one experience with the tribunal in 1531 when he was denounced and arrested for suspicious practices and preaching, though after a two-year imprisonment he was freed and completely exonerated of all the charges brought against him. The other factor contributing to the decline of his movement was a purely Castilian phenomenon relating to the Jewish background of the Master and many of his followers. When the Jesuits first arrived in Castile in the 1540s, many of them viewed John of Ávila as a precursor of their own movement and there was much talk of absorbing the apostle, his disciples and all his educational foundations into the Company of Jesus.[74] However, if Ignatius Loyola always favoured admitting John of Ávila, other Jesuits were not so favourably disposed. Nor was the Company of Jesus in an advantageous position in Castile. The primate of Spain from 1546 to 1558, Cardinal Silíceo, disliked the Jesuits almost as much as he did *conversos* (those of Jewish descent), so the Company, struggling for recognition and acceptance in Castile, could hardly afford to fill its ranks with New Christians. Though some of John of Ávila's followers did become Jesuits, the Master himself did not.

Probably because of his *converso* origins and his fear of the Inquisition, John of Ávila never wrote any systematic treatise, but his letters and sermons indicate that he was concerned with the poor and their relief. In 1547 he wrote to his friend, Pedro Guerrero, newly appointed to the archdiocese of Granada, 'it is necessary to appoint a discreet and loyal person to examine the needs of the poor in their homes and provide for their needs'.[75] The prior of San Juan, Diego de Toledo, contacted the Master about the new poor laws initiated in one of the Castilian towns in the 1540s, requesting that the Master send one of his followers to assist in the reform. Though John of Ávila declined to send his disciple, he consoled the prior concerning the reforms: 'Strengthen yourself in the justice of the cause you are dealing with . . . it is nothing other than the perfect remedy for succouring the poor and miserable.'[76] The Master was also active in founding hospitals, some for syphilitics, and he and his followers had briefly served in one of these foundations. Of course the most famous hospital came to be that of John of God in Granada, inspired by a sermon of the Master in 1537. Though John of Ávila always considered himself the spiritual advisor of John of God whom he constantly counselled, and though he supported the Granada foundation in every possible way, John of God's hospital was one of many achievements of the Andalucian apostle.

The conversion of John of God was dramatic, noisy and public. Certainly the early life of Juan Ciudad or Cidade gave no indication of future sainthood (Castro, *Juan de Dios*). It is impossible to say where he was born. The traditional story, much embroidered by his followers, was that he was born in Portugal and transported to Castile by a priest, but recent studies support the theory that he was born in Casarrubios del Monte, a village in the province of Toledo, of *converso* parents.[77] He spent his early life as a shepherd, served with little distinction in the army, and journeyed to Africa where he was employed in building fortifications, a task that sounds suspiciously like forced labour rather than profitable employment. When he returned to Spain, he settled in Gibraltar, peddling religious books and images in the city and nearby villages; finally he bought a small shop in Granada where he followed the same trade. After John of Ávila's sermon, the sudden spectacle of the bookseller giving away all his books, screaming, walking through the streets half naked and beating himself convinced the local citizenry he had taken leave of his senses. He was committed to the Royal Hospital of Granada where the insane were treated by means of floggings, thought to be necessary to drive out evil spirits. Fortunately, with the assistance of John of Ávila, he was released from the hospital and together they developed a more productive plan for channelling the religious fervour of the bookseller by setting up a hospital.

John of God's first hospital was a rented house in the most humble neighbourhood of Granada and it admitted any person who requested admission, no matter what his ailment. The hospital housed beggars, pilgrims, travellers, prostitutes, lepers, syphilitics, the aged, the insane, the blind, cripples as well as anyone in need of temporary medical treatment. John of God was always concerned with the prostitutes of the city, an activity which caused much displeasure to Master Ávila who warned him to, 'guard against dealing too much with females because you know they are a trap sent by the devil so that the servants of God should fall'.[78] Apparently the city authorities also sent undesirable persons to the hospital. Francisco de Castro, the biographer of the saint and a later administrator of the Granada hospital, reports that some persons were brought to the hospital by force, 'so that the public squares were cleansed of these lost persons' (Castro, *Juan de Dios*, p. 49). Castro also mentions that the hospital inmates were encouraged to work and that John of God visited the merchants of the city asking for silk, wool and flax to be spun and woven in his hospital. This policy might have been adopted in an attempt to earn money, for the hospital was always short of funds despite generous contributions from the duque de Sesa, the conde de Tendilla, doña María de Cobos y Mendoza and John of Ávila. It was in search of financial support that John of God visited the court in Valladolid in the 1540s where he reportedly met Prince Philip and gained many contributions, most of which were spent before he had returned to Granada.

The hospital of John of God met with mixed reactions. Some called it 'the tippling house of vagabonds and the graveyard of the poor',[79] while others supported it morally and financially. The hospital was moved to a vacant nunnery in the 1540s, probably in the interests of space, for it sometimes housed as many as two hundred patients. The quality of the care given to such a multitude of people with such a mixture of ailments is certainly questionable. Castro reports that one of the factors contributing to the founder's death were the injuries he sustained when he was pushed down a flight of steps by one of the patients, 'who did not see who it was' (p. 62); apparently there was nothing extraordinary about pushing people down steps, though exceptions were made for the provider of the hospital. When Pedro Guerrero was appointed to the Granada archdiocese in 1546, he visited the hospital having heard that it housed many idle, dissolute and wicked persons. The outcome of this visit was the appointment of a cleric, Father Portillo, who was to act as the administrator and supervisor of the institution. John of God was unhappy about the new arrangement and complained to Master Ávila, but the master was unsympathetic to his pupil's complaints, pointing out that 'God did not call you to govern, but to be governed; therefore you do not serve Him if you do not obey.'[80]

Part of the conflict between John of God and Father Portillo centred around the admission policies of the hospital, for John of God had always accepted any person who requested admittance. Master Ávila argued that this practice was unacceptable:

Although to you it seems a lack of charity to throw anyone out, you are deceived, because there are times when by not offending someone, everyone loses ... thus brother, sometimes it is necessary to refuse something asked of us and to remove that which is not good, for the benefit of the hospital and other things which you do not understand.[81]

Discrimination in charitable assistance clearly pertained to hospitals as well as almsgiving. John of God shared the ideas of Domingo de Soto, that mercy was to succour everyone, while his master argued for the necessity of discrimination. The question of who was to receive the benefits of hospitality and who was to be excluded was never clearly resolved in sixteenth-century Castile, though John of God's experiment in Granada provided a precedent for those who argued that beggars too should be included within the hospital system.

When John of God died in 1550, he left behind him a hospital in great debt and five very poor followers. It was Archbishop Guerrero who salvaged the movement by paying off the hospital's debts, taking the brothers under his protection, providing them with an institute or rule, and helping them to found, construct and pay for another new hospital (Castro, *Juan de Dios*, pp. 74, 80–3). The land for the new hospital was donated by the city council and an Hieronymite monastery, and the brothers and their hospital were placed under the supervision of the Hieronymite superior, an arrangement which eventually led to great discords. In 1552, Antón Martín, considered as head brother after the death of John of God, was called to Madrid to found a hospital in that city, the first of the brothers' foundations outside Granada.

Shortly after the Madrid foundation, the brothers established hospitals in Montilla, Lucena, Seville and Jerez de la Frontera, but their greatest success was in Córdoba, where Philip II gave them an old, royal San Lázaro to convert to their own purposes.[82] Success and royal favour gave the brothers new confidence. Also the movement had attracted more educated persons like Rodrigo de Sigüenza, an Aragonese noble, Pedro Soriana and Sebastián Arias, who found the brothers' subservience to the Hieronymite superior in Granada intolerable and sought to forge a more independent and cohesive movement. In 1571 Sebastián Arias persuaded Pius V to acknowledge the brothers as a religious congregation which was placed under the rule of Saint Augustine, though the brothers added service to the poor to the traditional three monastic vows (Castro, *Juan de Dios*, p. 103). Appeals to Rome by any of the Castilian ecclesiastical establishment were not encouraged by Philip II, yet the brothers managed to achieve still higher recognition from the papacy. In 1584 they took over what had originally been an old leper house on the Tiber Island in Rome, renaming the institution the Ospedale di San Giovanni Calibita, and Italians began joining the movement. Impressed by the determination and the achievements of the brothers, Sixtus V declared them a religious order in 1586, an elevation that exempted them from episcopal supervision, and allowed them to elect their own superior and to expand into a truly international movement.[83] Vexed by the papal preferment, in 1592 Philip prevailed upon Clement VIII to demote the Brothers Hospitallers to their former status of a religious congregation.[84] The demotion was but a temporary interlude however, for in 1611 the brothers were again elevated to the status of a religious order, despite the violent objections of the prelates of Granada, and Valladolid; in 1630 John of God was beatified, and sixty years later he was canonized. In the seventeenth century the Brothers Hospitallers continued their expansion not only in Castile, but throughout the Catholic world, founding hospitals in France, Austria, Poland and in the New World.

Philip's attempt to maintain the brothers' status as a congregation was based largely upon the fact that if they attained the rank of a religious order, they would be exempt from the supervision of the Castilian prelates. Since 1564, when the Tridentine decrees were promulgated in Castile, the Castilian prelates and the king had been struggling to reform the religious orders and all pious and ecclesiastical foundations in Castile. In a country obsessed with reform and supervision, the papacy's decision to create yet another exemption from episcopal visitation was destined to elicit resentment. In addition, as the papal brief demoting the brothers to a congregation explained, they were largely persons of humble origins who had little education, facts which made episcopal supervision even more imperative. In 1586 the vicar-general of the Granada diocese was openly derisive of the congregation. He accused them of spending pious money illicitly to subsidize their appeals to Rome and described the brothers as: 'imposters, who take money from the faithful for their own ends. This is not surprising since they are all the dross of society who do not want to work, so they take this habit to enrich themselves quickly . . . and afterwards leave and marry.'[85]

Yet if the humble origins of the brothers left them open to the abuse of the more nobly born, it also accounted for a great deal of their success. No matter what the Granada vicar-general might think of the brothers, his report clearly indicated that the hospital of John of God was the wealthiest in Granada and the only one not in debt. More than half its total income of 2,237,750 mrs had been collected by the brothers through begging alms. Not only did the brothers beg alms, but, being humble men, they were accustomed to labour and they offered the fruits of their labour to the poor and the sick without remuneration. In Córdoba, for instance, they converted the old San Lázaro to a hospital suitable for housing fifty patients, they cultivated many of the lands the hospital possessed and they cared for the patients.[86] The only salaried officials in the Córdoba hospital were the doctor, the surgeon, and the barber, none of whom were members of the congregation. The money saved by not paying salaries to a professional staff could be invested in treating the poor or, as the vicar-general would have it, in appealing to Rome. Since hospital service was a career open to any person, no matter what his background, the movement provided a productive means of absorbing the energy of the common man who chose to dedicate his life to active good works and service to the poor. As Francisco de Castro explained, to be a follower of John of God, 'letters and studies are not necessary; rather, a great deal of contempt for the world and oneself, and much charity and love of God' (p. 84). Nor did hospital service involve any novel theological interpretations to disturb the Inquisition or the religious orders of Castile. Since the brothers limited their attentions to service of the poor and were willing to care for the most humble of persons and the most unattractive of diseases, frequently not welcomed in other hospitals, they were guaranteed success in an era when there were continual complaints about the multitude of poor and sick.

# The reform of charitable institutions

## THE TRIDENTINE REFORMS

Throughout the last third of the sixteenth century, the hospitals of Castile were subjected to a continual barrage of reforms. Incentive for one reform movement was fostered by the hospital decrees of the Tridentine legislation which urged episcopal supervision of the services, expenditures and administrators of charitable institutions. Before the Council of Trent the jurisdictional status of hospitals, like that of most institutions pertaining to poor relief, was vague and uncertain.[1] On the one hand hospitals were frequently founded, administered and paid for by laymen, either as individuals or as members of a confraternity or a municipality, facts which lent support to those who maintained that hospitals were secular institutions subject to the control of secular authorities. On the other hand, even the smallest hospice possessed an altar and the larger hospitals usually boasted a full-scale church, facts which placed the institutions in the jurisdiction of ecclesiastical authorities.[2]

Consider, for example, the hospital at the Escorial, founded by Philip II in the early 1570s to treat the workmen who laboured to erect the eighth wonder of Christendom, as well as any poor persons in need of hospital care. The lengthy constitutions for this thirty-bed hospital were studied and amended by the most eminent men of Castile, including the king, so they might be taken as the last word in the goals of Castilian hospital service.[3] Though many of the ninety-one articles of the constitution were devoted to the minutiae of bed making, food rations and the virtues of keeping a flock of chickens, the first priority for every new patient was that he confess and receive the Sacrament 'so that having cured his soul, Jesus Christ will give His grace, which, with the intercession of His glorious mother and Saint Lawrence, will soon cure his body'. It was also recommended that the

Hieronymite monks of the Escorial monastery might occasionally visit the hospital to give 'small sermons and exhortations to the patients'. If spiritual attention was of primary importance in the treatment of any hospital patient, the hospital also provided medical services for the poor and it had been founded and was subsidized by Philip II, so surely he had some right to supervise and direct his own hospital.

Castilian legislation prior to the Council of Trent provides little clarification of the jurisdictional ambiguities of hospitals. The only institutions that gained special attention from the crown were the ubiquitous leper houses, usually found outside the city walls of the larger Castilian towns. In 1477 the Catholic kings created two new crown officials, the *protomédico* and the *alcalde examinador mayor*, who were responsible for supervising persons involved in trades or professions relating to public health.[4] Aside from examining and licensing physicians, bone-setters, apothecaries, and spice and herb sellers, these officials were to ensure that all persons suffering from leprosy were confined to a leper house. The rectors of the San Lázaros were ordered to admit all the lepers sent to them by the crown officials or suffer a fine or loss of office. In 1528 Charles I enlarged the crown's concern in the leper houses by decreeing that they should be visited by officials appointed by the Royal Council and their accounts audited every six months by the *corregidor* or the justice (*NR*, lib. 7, tit. 38, ley 1). The emperor did not claim all the San Lázaros as royal hospitals however, since a special provision was made for leper hospitals not of the royal patrimony; these institutions were to be visited jointly by the prelates and the justices. Thus, in the interest of safeguarding public health the crown had, long before the Council of Trent, asserted its right to supervise the leper houses of Castile.

Nor does the question of crown taxation offer much illumination concerning the status of hospitals. Since the era of the Catholic kings, if not before, the Castilian church had been subjected to paying the crown a periodic tax known as the *subsidio*.[5] Sanctioned by the papacy, the *subsidio* was levied upon clerical rents and incomes, though the exact amount to be collected was determined by the crown, the papacy and the degree of resistance offered by the Castilian church. Until 1540 hospitals were included as contributors to the *subsidio*, but, by means of a complicated rebate system, some hospitals received a donation from the *subsidio* proceeds. In 1530 Cardinal Tavera suggested to the emperor that the reformed religious orders, the hospitals and other pious works should receive a rebate from the *subsidio* 'as the Catholic kings and Your Majesty have done in the past'; the cardinal added that only those hospitals which exercised 'continual care of the poor' should be granted this favour.[6] The list of hospitals which received a donation in 1534 included only forty-four institutions, a very small number in view of the hundreds of hospitals in Castile.[7] Nor is there much logic to the selection of favoured hospitals since many royal hospitals were excluded yet other very wealthy private ones, like Cardinal Mendoza's Hospital of Santa Cruz in Toledo, were included.

Perhaps the complicated method of collecting the *subsidio* and then repaying some of the proceeds to certain religious orders and hospitals was devised as a means of avoiding the insidious custom of exemptions, for all rebates had to be personally approved by the emperor.[8] Whatever the explanation, a papal brief of 1540 provided a simpler system by exempting from the *subsidio* all hospitals that 'exercised effective hospitality'.[9] However, it does not appear that the exemption recommended by the papal brief was in effect very long, since in 1548 a Cortes petition urged that hospitals be exempted from the *subsidio*.[10] If the early-sixteenth-century hospitals taxation policy seems uncertain, it could be argued that by having imposed the *subsidio* on hospitals the crown considered them as part of the ecclesiastical establishment of Castile.

Hospitals were but one institution that the Tridentine legislation classified as 'pious works', subject to episcopal supervision. Also included were the confraternities, the ubiquitous brotherhoods that proliferated in Castile. Confraternities are difficult to describe briefly since they served a multitude of purposes. They usually provided some sort of charitable assistance, in some instances limited to members and their immediate family, in other instances, particularly if it was a wealthy confraternity, relief was given to outsiders. The brotherhoods were also concerned with religious and spiritual matters. They were organized around devotion to a certain saint, cult, or penitential practice, and many of them saw that the spiritual obligations – masses, anniversaries, vigils – of their deceased brothers were celebrated. Confraternities also served an important social function for the brothers by providing a convenient opportunity to eat, drink and socialize; to march in processions; and, on occasion, a chance to exercise their competitive spirit by verbally or physically assaulting rival confraternities.

The crown viewed some confraternities with suspicion. In 1473 Enrique IV prohibited all confraternities founded since 1462 except those created purely for spiritual and pious purposes, and even these brotherhoods had to have a licence from the crown and authority from the prelate. The king was particularly anxious to prohibit those confraternities that 'sheltering under the name and advocation of a saint . . . and pretending to be honest and well intentioned . . . spend money pursuing evil desires that result in great scandal, disturbances and other mischief' (*NR*, lib. 12, tit. 12, ley 12). This law was repeated by Charles I in 1534, and in 1552 the emperor prohibited all confraternities composed of skilled labourers (*oficiales*).[11]

The confraternities were a constant thorn in the side of the ecclesiastical authorities who, before and after the Council of Trent, sought to control their growth and eliminate some of their secular activities. In 1536 the Toledo diocesan legislation, complaining of the confraternities 'which have increased and increase in such number that harm could result', established a licensing system for the brotherhoods.[12] All confraternities were to present their constitutions to the diocesan authorities for inspection, and any who did not comply would be fined or have their constitutions annulled.

The question of the jurisdictional status of hospitals and confraternities was partially resolved by the Tridentine legislation, which was accepted promptly in Spain. Pius IV confirmed the conciliar decrees on 26 January 1564, and the official bull of confirmation was published on 30 June 1564. On 12 July, less than two weeks after the decrees were officially confirmed, Philip II signed the royal *cédula* of acceptance for Castile.[13] It is possible that the king of Spain was the first monarch of Christendom to accept the decrees; his acceptance antedated that of the cardinal–infante of Portugal (7–12 September), Sigismund of Poland (7 August), not to mention the Emperor Ferdinand who expressed serious reservations about the decrees, or the French crown, which never did officially accept the Tridentine legislation.[14] It is also possible that the Castilian clergy were the most rapidly informed of the contents of the reform. In April 1564 Philip authorized the printing of the decrees, and in that same year nine editions of the legislation were printed throughout Spain. In 1565–6 provincial councils were convened in Toledo, Granada, Valencia, Santiago-Salamanca, and Zaragoza, though for some reason no council was held in the archdiocese of Seville despite the king's letter to the archbishop, Fernando Valdés.[15]

The Tridentine legislation dealing with hospitals consisted of four decrees, the first of which classified hospitals as 'pious places', subject to the visitation and correction of the ordinary. The fathers of Trent had precedents for their decision in the 1311 'Quia Contingit' formulated at the Council of Vienne.[16] This early decree recommended that the ordinaries should correct hospital rectors who did not spend hospital rents in their determined purpose of relieving the poor and needy, and stipulated that a hospital rectorship should not be given to the secular clergy as a benefice. The earliest hospital decree of the Tridentine council was no more than a reiteration of the fourteenth-century decision (*Concilio de Trento*, sess. 7, cap. 15) and it was not until the last years of the council that any original policies for hospitals were formulated. Two of the later decrees proclaimed the bishops as executors of all pious dispositions and subjected to episcopal visitation all places of charity, including hospitals and confraternities, except those under royal protection. All administrators of pious works were ordered to render their accounts to the ordinary, though some concessions were made to privilege and custom in this matter: in instances where a hospital's foundation documents prohibited episcopal intervention or, if by custom or privilege accounts were rendered to another party, the ordinaries were limited to attending a joint account rendering session in the company of the traditional auditors (sess. 22, caps. 5, 8, 9).

The last and most innovative of the Tridentine hospital decrees gave the bishops authority to correct all hospital administrators except those of the regular orders who were subject to the correction of their respective superiors, a mandate that included the right to deprive a negligent administrator of his post, and it was suggested that hospital administrators should be appointed for only three years. Also the conversion of pious funds to other purposes was approved 'if the purpose of a hospital was to care for a certain type of pilgrim, sick or other person who can no longer be found' and if such a conversion was not prohibited by the foundation statutes of the institution (sess. 25, cap. 8). All conversions of pious funds were to be effected by the bishops with the advice of two well-informed members of the cathedral chapter.

Philip sent a crown legate to all the 1565–6 provincial councils, and each legate received a detailed list of the crown's opinions and recommendations for the execution of the Tridentine legislation. The instructions sent to don Francisco de Toledo, crown legate at the provincial council in Toledo, noted the ample mandate given to the prelates in the visitation of the hospitals and urged the legate to be aware of the exemptions to this commission.[17] All the royal hospitals, including those of San Lázaro and San Antón, those of the military orders and 'other hospitals which His Majesty or his ministers customarily visit', were exempt from episcopal visitation. The hospitals of the universities and those of the regular orders were also exempt as they fell under the supervision of their respective superiors.

In disagreement with the Tridentine decrees, the Castilian prelates were not to visit any hospital where the foundation statutes expressly prohibited episcopal visitation, though surprisingly the crown instructions said nothing about the joint account rendering sessions that the prelates were supposed to attend in such instances. Since conversion of pious funds 'could be dangerous and prejudicial', such conversions had to be done with the 'wisdom and consultation of His Majesty'. In the question of episcopal visitation of lay confraternities, the king decided that the prelates could concern themselves with matters relating to the fulfilment of masses and pious works, 'but in matters of property, accounts and other things this would be prejudicial to royal jurisdiction'; thus the bishops were limited to inspecting only the books relating to pious dispositions.

This latter decision brought a response from the clergy convened at Toledo who pointed out that 'in this kingdom there are many confraternities who spend their money badly, in meals and other profane things, which is not corrected because they are never visited, the secular justice always impeding it by saying that they are laymen and of royal jurisdiction'.[18] There is no record of any crown response to this complaint, but it is doubtful that Philip changed his mind on this issue.

If the Tridentine legislation enjoined activity on the part of the prelates, it also prodded the Castilian crown into a detailed investigation dedicated to locating, cataloguing and in many instances reclaiming what came to be known as the royal ecclesiastical patrimony. The delicate question of lay presentation to ecclesiastical benefices had been touched upon in one of the Tridentine decrees which instructed the bishops to review the rights and privileges entitling laymen or lay communities to make such presentations. Though the presentation rights of emperors, kings and 'other sublime and supreme princes who possess the right of sovereignty in their dominions' (sess. 25, cap. 9) were exempt from episcopal scrutiny, the sovereign obviously had to know exactly what presentation rights he possessed. The Castilian ecclesiastical patrimony included a vast array of pious foundations such as monasteries, chapels, hospitals and colleges, the right of presentation to many ecclesiastical benefices and other special concessions granted by the Holy See.[19] Certain portions of this patrimony had been more jealously guarded than others: no Castilian monarch was likely to forget his right to present bishops, but the presentation of an obscure abbot or hospital administrator was another matter. Thus, royal agents were dispatched throughout the kingdom to read foundation documents, bulls and privileges, to decipher old inscriptions and to interview venerable citizens. The reports sent back by these agents were very gloomy, especially concerning the royal patrimony of Oviedo and Granada, much of which had been usurped.[20]

Part of this neglect stemmed from a lack of adequate machinery to supervise the affairs of the crown's ecclesiastical patrimony, considered as one of the many duties discharged by the Royal Council of Castile and its offspring, the small cabinet council known as the Cámara de Castilla. In the 1560s, as the Tridentine reforms were being discussed and disseminated in Castile, affairs of the church were dominated by the powerful Diego de Espinosa, cardinal of Sigüenza, inquisitor-general of Castile, and president of the Royal Council. However, soon after the cardinal's death in 1572, Martín de Gaztelu emerged as the Cámara secretary for the ecclesiastical patrimony, a position he retained until his death in 1580.[21] It was not until 1588 that the king officially regularized administrative aspects of the Cámara. The president of the Royal Council was to preside over the Cámara, and three secretariats were created: one for the church, one for justice and another for the Cámara. According to Philip's *cédula*, the Cámara was to deal with 'all the affairs relating to my royal patrimony of the church in these my kingdoms of Castile, Navarre and the Canary Islands, of whatever nature they may be, whether of justice or grace' (*NR*, lib. 1, tit. 17, ley 11). In 1588 the secretary of the church was Francisco González de Heredia, who retained his position at least until 1614.

Hospitals comprised only a small portion of the royal patrimony, but they were included in the crown's attempt to locate, reform and provide closer supervision of its pious foundations. Of the numerous hospitals included within the royal patrimony, those of the military orders were visited with a regularity that would have delighted the most ardent hospital reformer. For example, the Hospital of Santiago de los Caballeros in Toledo was visited seventeen times from 1480 to 1637; thirteen of the visits occurred in the sixteenth century, which means the hospital was inspected on an average of every eight years.[22] Possibly the regularity of the visits in this hospital is explained by the superior administrative machinery of the military orders.

Other royal hospitals, even those of fairly recent foundation, were not subjected to such strict surveillance. The Royal Hospital of Granada, founded by the Catholic kings to treat syphilis, was a constant scene of mismanagement. Charles V had ordered a visitation of the hospital sometime between 1518 and 1519 and the results of this inspection underlined the need for reforms. The hospital had no constitutions and was also badly in debt, largely because the episcopal Hospital of Santa Ana had appropriated a portion of the tithe which should have gone to the Royal Hospital. Though Charles ordered that constitutions be written and sent to special *cédula* to the cathedral chapter and the archbishop of Granada inquiring by what right they took the tithe for their hospital,[23] it appears that none of these royal decrees had any effect. In 1589 Philip ordered the bishop of Gaudix, Juan Alfonso Moscoso, to visit the Royal Hospital. The prelate, one of the rare Castilian bishops who managed to combine a glimmer of humour with his reforming zeal, was appalled by the condition of the hospital. He began his report with the disheartening observation that 'the Royal Hospital had very good and firm walls and nothing else'.[24] The foundation statutes, bulls and title deeds had completely disappeared or were destroyed by neglect, while the deeds for the hospital's lands and properties were scattered about the archive or had vanished. The bishop calculated that the institution was 2,500,000 mrs in debt, and the episcopal hospital still received that portion of the tithe which should have gone to the Royal Hospital. Worst of all was the condition of the insane, housed in the hospital since 1541,[25] who were treated like brutes; they were deprived of beds, clothes, shoes and medical attention and their food rations were eaten by the staff. The syphilitics received such poor treatment that many left sicker than when they entered. As for the administration, there were more staff members than patients, theft of clothes, grain and meat was a common practice, and no constitutions had ever been written to govern the institution.

The Royal Hospital of Granada was reformed.[26] In 1593 a new administrator was appointed and constitutions were written which included procedures for collecting and spending income, treatment of patients, and closer supervision of the institution by crown visitors. Nonetheless, according to the 1628 report made by the president of the Granada chancery, one of the crown visitors, things were still not quite as they should be, though his criticisms were moderate compared with those of 1589.[27]

Since the Royal Hospital of Granada was a fairly recent foundation, no one had any doubts as to who should appoint the administrator or govern the institution. It was an established portion of the royal patrimony, even if its condition indicated that it suffered from neglect and mismanagement. Many of the royal hospitals were older and smaller foundations which, in the absence of any crown activity, had been occupied by confraternities whose members treated the sick, administered the hospital's rents and governed the hospital. Once the confraternities were installed, it was not easy for the crown to establish its rights to appoint an administrator to govern the institution.

In 1611 a dispute arose in Toledo when the crown appointed an administrator to an institution that had always been known as the Hospital del Rey. Aside from the obvious implications of its name, the hospital also had royal arms over the doorway and royal arms were displayed on the tunics of those persons who solicited alms for the hospital. According to the testimony of the crown-appointed administrator, Luis Moreno, a chaplain of the Toledo cathedral, soon after he was appointed the royal arms so prominently displayed mysteriously disappeared, the name of the hospital was changed to El Refugio de los Pobres Incurables, and the hospital archive was robbed of all its foundation statutes and other important papers.[28]

Luis Moreno notified the crown of these activities, and the crown ordered the *corregidor* of Toledo to investigate the matter. A lengthy hearing was held, but it was obvious that none of the witnesses who appeared was willing to testify against the wealthy and prestigious brotherhood that operated the hospital, Nuestra Señora de la Paz y Corpus Cristi. Not even the historian, cathedral canon and hospital administrator, Pedro Salazar de Mendoza, was willing to say anything about the missing royal arms and foundation documents, though he did conclude that, based on the history and past experience of the hospital, 'one could presume it was a foundation of the king'. Other witnesses explained that the royal arms had been removed from the building during recent renovations and the hospital's name had been changed in order to collect more alms.

The *corregidor*, also an obvious partisan of the confraternity, took the same line in his final opinion. He noted too that none of the important papers had been missing from the archive when he visited the hospital in 1612, and, based on documents he found there, he argued that the hospital belonged to the confraternity, not the king. In conclusion, the *corregidor* noted that the confraternity was composed of 'virtuous, rich, Christian and honoured persons' who served the hospital without salary, investing a great deal of time and money in its maintenance. If the crown took over the administration, all local support would cease, and 'if Your Majesty wants to enter into the administration, it will be necessary to assign a large rent for the conservation of this work'. It was probably this last remark that saved the brotherhood and its hospital for the crown was not in a position to subsidize a hospital that housed 150 to 200 patients and was supported by the alms and energy of the local citizenry.

One of the crown's most successful and tenacious battles was fought over the San Lázaros of the kingdom. In the instructions sent to the crown legates who attended the 1565–6 provincial councils, Philip had claimed the San Lázaros of the realm as royal hospitals, exempt from episcopal visitation. This claim was based upon the crown decree of 1528 which was, in fact, a very vague piece of legislation. This decree stated that those San Lázaros known to be of the royal patrimony should be visited by the *corregidores* and justices, while those outside the royal patrimony should be visited by the *corregidores* and the prelates. What was not stated was how the jurisdictional status of these hospitals should be determined or who should determine it. In an age devoted to litigation, such ambiguities were guaranteed to cause confusion and afford contemporaries a cause for argument.

The city of Toledo had a San Lázaro that was built in the fifteenth century. In 1561 the city council had given the Confraternity de las Angustias permission to use the building on condition that the brothers exercised some type of hospitality for the poor and sick;[29] twenty years later, the San Lázaro had become an active centre for treating all manner of ailments, especially young boys with contagious skin diseases. In 1580 the visitor-general of the Toledo diocese, Doctor Juan López, had visited the San Lázaro, much to the disgruntlement of the confraternity, which claimed it was a royal hospital and therefore exempt from episcopal visitation.[30] Though feathers were ruffled in 1580, it was not until 1591, when Doctor López attempted a second visitation, that an open breach occurred.

This time the confraternity refused to admit the visitor, who in turn excommunicated some of the brothers. Incensed by their mistreatment, the brothers appealed to the crown for justice in May 1591.[31]

Shortly after the confraternity's appeal reached Madrid, the crown began collecting facts and opinions from all parties concerned in the dispute, a process which included a lengthy hearing attended by much of the episcopal hierarchy of the Toledo diocese. The cardinal–archbishop of Toledo, Gaspar de Quiroga, was at the hearing, and the vicar and the visitor-general each presented a lengthy testimony. The Toledo San Lázaro possessed no foundation statutes. The only written record that could be located was an inscription in the church which read: 'This church of San Lázaro, built by Juan Sánchez de Trevino, steward of Fernán Pérez de Guzmán, was completed in 1418.'[32] The vicar presented this inscription as evidence that the institution was not a royal foundation. Nor, the vicar continued, were the royal arms displayed on any part of the building, the hospital had never received a royal endowment and 'no house of the royal patrimony had ever been so neglected and poverty stricken'. Since the crown had no obvious claims to the institution, the vicar argued that it should be visited by the ordinary according to session 22, chapters 8 and 9 of the Tridentine decrees as well as the laws of the land. Doctor López testified that as he had no knowledge that the San Lázaro was a royal hospital and the laws of Castile stated that all San Lázaros not included in the royal patrimony should be visited by the ordinary, he had included it in his visitation as a matter of course. When Doctor López had completed his testimony, Cardinal Quiroga stated that it was his right to visit the San Lázaro, requested a transcript of the proceedings so he could reply, and left the hearing. Unfortunately the cardinal's reply is not included among the documents, but whatever he said was of little avail. The crown prosecutor, Rui Gómez de Ribera, concluded that in accordance with the laws of the land and also by precedents established through past visits of the San Lázaro carried out by Toledo *corregidores*, the hospital enjoyed the protection of the king; therefore His Majesty would appoint persons to administer and visit the institution.

The jurisdictional status of other leper houses in the kingdom must have been less dubious because by the 1590s the crown had a collection of San Lázaros scattered throughout Castile in the cities of Burgos, Granada, Córdoba, Arévalo, Seville, Gijón (Oviedo),

Zamora, Segovia, and Toledo.[33] The condition and size of these hospitals varied from the one in Toledo, recently enlarged and housing up to 500 persons, to that of Zamora, which was in danger of collapsing and housed one poor woman. Philip II showed great concern for even the smallest of these hospitals. Capable and wealthy administrators were appointed for a period of only three years and periodic visitations were sanctioned. Some of the San Lázaros were converted to new uses. Though it had been acknowledged in some areas of Castile that leprosy had died out by the end of the sixteenth century, in 1594 three specially appointed crown physicians determined that it still existed in Seville,[34] so the San Lázaro of that city continued to house lepers. Philip gave the San Lázaro of Córdoba to the followers of John of God who enlarged the hospital and offered to treat any type of infirmity, especially long-term or incurable diseases. In 1594 the Discalced Franciscans were given the San Lázaro of Arévalo to use as a monastery, though the monks were ordered to place the royal arms on the building.[35]

Thus the crown did attempt to locate, supervise and improve the hospitals of the royal patrimony. Conflicts over rights of appointment and visitation, and the provision of adequate bureaucratic machinery to handle the royal patrimony verify the crown's concern. There is every reason to believe that the Castilian prelates emulated, if they did not exceed, the activity of the crown. The dispute over the Toledo San Lázaro is one example of episcopal zeal, for the Toledo visitor-general had no right to visit the hospital. In his testimony to the crown the Toledo vicar admitted that the *corregidores* of Toledo had previously visited and taken the hospital's accounts, while the laws of the land, to which the vicar and the visitor referred, clearly stated that in instances of non-royal jurisdiction, the prelate was to be accompanied in his visitation by the *corregidor*, a qualification the diocesan witnesses did not mention. Also Philip had claimed the San Lázaros as exempt from episcopal visitation in his 1565 comments to the Toledo provincial council. Given the perspicacity and legal acumen of the diocesan witnesses, it is difficult to imagine they were ignorant of the crown's position. Yet had the Confraternity de las Angustias not appealed to Madrid episcopal visitation would have continued, and the crown, having no knowledge of events in Toledo, presumably would have done nothing. As it was, the case over the Toledo San Lázaro stirred the king into more concerted action; on the day the decision of the Toledo hospital was handed down, the crown sent out a letter to all the *corregidores* urging them to visit the San Lázaros in their jurisdiction and report on their condition. Though this was a case where the overzealousness of the diocesan officials misfired, it appears that the church asserted its visitation mandate wherever possible and only a concerted defence on the part of the crown, a city council or a confraternity could frustrate this offensive.

Not only were the Castilian prelates pervasive in establishing their newly defined authority, they also interpreted the process of visitation in the broadest sense, considering that it unavoidably included an inspection of a hospital's financial accounts. In 1568 the bishop of Pamplona, Diego Ramírez Sedeño de Fuenleal, a doctor of civil and canon law who had attended the third session of the Council of Trent, was engaged in a visitation in his diocese. It happened that the town of Estella (Navarre) had a general hospital which, according to the city council, had been founded in 1524 'without approval from any prelate or ecclesiastical judge, but merely with the approval of the Royal Council'.[36] When the bishop arrived in Estella, he insisted not only upon visiting the general hospital, but also auditing the account books. The city magistrates and the two *mayordomos* they had appointed to administer the institution refused to accede to the bishop's latter demand, whereupon Diego Ramírez excommunicated the recalcitrant *mayordomos*, and the city of Estella appealed to the Royal Council of Navarre for assistance. In search of a compromise, the Royal Council recommended various solutions and finally suggested that the bishop send a representative to Estella when the hospital officials presented their accounts to the municipality. Such a joint account-rendering session was what the Tridentine decrees advised, but the bishop, arguing that the administration of his diocese would be ruined if diocesan officials were called hither and yon at the discretion of hospital administrators or municipalities, rejected the compromise and refused to absolve the excommunicated *mayordomos*. Through with temporizing, the crown dispatched an *alcalde de corte* to Pamplona and on 26 June 1568 the bishop's temporal goods were sequestered and his rents placed under an embargo. Diego Ramírez was outraged of course, but the two *mayordomos* were finally absolved and the city of Estella considered it had won a major victory. It was a short-lived victory however, for two years later the bishop initiated legal proceedings against the *mayordomos* of the hospital who were found guilty of negligence and improper expenditure of pious funds.

The bishop of Pamplona might be judged as uncompromising, but he could not be accused of neglecting his duty. If his interpretation of episcopal visitation was broader than that recommended by the Tridentine decrees or even the crown, judging by the diocesan legislation published after 1565, he represented the majority opinion of the Castilian prelates. The Toledo diocesan legislation of 1566 exhorted and ordered the visitors of the archbishopric to inspect confraternities and hospitals, to take their accounts, and to see that their wealth was well spent.[37] The 1583 diocesan legislation of Salamanca was even stronger, ordering the *mayordomos* of hospitals, hermitages, confraternities or other pious works to render their accounts to the visitors 'on pain of excommunication'.[38] What is notable in both these decrees is that no exceptions were made for royal hospitals, for confraternities of laymen, or for hospitals that excluded episcopal visitation in their foundation statutes. Thus none of the exceptions noted by the king or included in the Tridentine decrees were mentioned in the diocesan legislation.

This is not to say that the Castilian prelates were always successful in executing such a broad mandate: the skirmishes between church and crown in Estella and Toledo are evidence that they were not. However, the policy of the prelates seems to have been to visit all pious foundations, leaving the administrator with the burden of knowing the exceptions and protesting to the proper authorities. The prelates did not usually attempt to visit hospitals that were obvious and known portions of the royal patrimony. For instance, the bishop of Oviedo notified the crown of the existence of two royal hospitals in his diocese,[39] and it was a chaplain of the royal chapel in Granada who informed the crown of the need to visit the hospital in that city.[40] However, these cases underline the fact that it was the church which took the initiative and the crown that reacted.

Aside from the inspiration given the prelates by the Tridentine decrees, the church had long been dispatching visitors to inspect ecclesiastical institutions in the administrative units of the diocese. Thus it already had adequate administrative machinery to implement visitations. However, the office of visitor took on more importance after 1565. The archdiocese of Seville had four visitors, one for the city of Seville and three for each administrative unit of the diocese. In the 1580s these officials were paid the sizable salary of 80,000 mrs and 90 *fanegas* of grain 'because these are offices of importance and require persons of knowledge and conscience'.[41] In 1583 the city council of Toledo, in a list of recommendations compiled for the provincial church council held by Cardinal Quiroga, stressed the importance of the office of visitor and urged that 'serious men of good conscience' be appointed.[42]

As the office of visitor took on more importance, the duties assigned to the visitors were enlarged and codified. The 1583 diocesan legislation of Salamanca included a special section of instructions to visitors, who were to inspect all pious places, even if exempt, to take the accounts and to correct 'whatever seems necessary to correct'.[43] They were to inform themselves of the poor in each place they visited, especially the young women, poor orphans, children of poor parents, and to know the need, quality and customs of each person and how they might best be succoured. They were to be sure that in years of high grain prices the parish priest and two rich, honorable parishioners would beg alms for the poor of their parish every feast day.

Even more detailed were the instructions given to the visitors of the archdiocese of Toledo in 1622. Aside from checking the account books of all hospitals, confraternities and other pious places, they were to track down and record all endowments left for charitable purposes or pious works and find out how the money was spent. They were to inform themselves of the *envergonzantes* in each place they visited and to keep a record of these people and to see that healthy poor travellers stayed only one day in the same hospital and that all hospital patients had confessed and received the Holy Sacrament. The tariff of fees that the visitor and his scribes could charge in each place they inspected was established, and the visitor was to be prepared to appear personally before the archbishop's council to give an account of his visit.[44]

The visitation books for the vast archdiocese of Toledo indicate that the visitors were successful in fulfilling the first part of the diocesan mandate.[45] Records of the financial condition of churches, chapels, confraternities, hospitals, hermitages and other pious works are comprehensive, as are the notes about the physical condition of the buildings and the comportment of ecclesiastics. However, if the visitors did compile a list of *envergonzantes* in the places they visited, it is not recorded in the visitation books.

In fact, the information relating directly to the poor and their relief is meagre. There is the occasional pious work that was founded to provide alms to the poor or to marry poor orphan girls, and these accounts were checked along with the rest, but the visitor did not include any information about the recipients. As for the confraternities, except for the brotherhoods that operated a hospital, their welfare activities, if they performed any, are not mentioned. Their expenditures are limited to the money spent for processions, fiestas, vespers, masses and wax. Possibly some paupers of a community were included in the confraternity's fiesta celebrations, but this is not mentioned by the visitor. Hospitals were also inspected and their accounts taken. In instances where a building was 'badly treated', which are numerous, the visitor ordered repairs either at the expense of the hospital or, in one case, by transferring money from another pious work. In terms of directly helping the poor, possibly the most constructive guidance given by the visitor was related to *pósitos* or *montes de piedad*, foundations providing a reserve of grain that was loaned to peasants for a modest sum $-\frac{1}{2}$ *real* or 1 *celemin* per *fanega* – at planting time. These grain reserves insured that even the most impoverished persons would at least be able to plant their fields, though the harvest obviously depended upon other factors. The visitor checked the accounts and actual grain reserves of the *pósitos*, and in cases where the *pósito* was no longer functioning, ordered that the patrons re-establish them.[46]

The seventeenth-century visitation books of the archdiocese of Toledo indicate that the church was well informed about the people, institutions, pious foundations, and wealth that fell within its dominion. Equally apparent is the prestige and intelligence of the visitors, who kept track of a bevy of chapels, *pósitos* and other pious foundations and ordered their patrons to repair or refinance these works if the visitor deemed it possible to salvage them; who reassigned money from one pious work to another; and who imposed fines or more serious penalties on those who did not fulfil their obligations, such as a sacristan who paid a 100 mr fine because the altar had dust 'two fingers thick', or a priest who paid 6 ducats because he neglected to keep a book of masses he celebrated, or another priest who was imprisoned for 'evil customs'. This is not to say that the church's means of enforcing its rules – fines, legal action, imprisonment or excommunication – were always successful. In Escalona, for example, the diocesan authorities had proceeded 'with all rigour' against the church of that town, but the lawsuit and excommunication had never achieved anything 'but disturbances, causing great scandal to the people who saw so many lawsuits among ecclesiastics'. Alonso de Palomino, the would-be visitor of Escalona, sadly reported that the town had not been visited for twenty years and accounts of pious foundations had not been checked for thirty years. The result was that 'the customs are depraved and everything is suspended; they enjoy their exemption and the rest of the people are suffering, awaiting a decision of Your Eminence'.[47] However, since Escalona was but one town of the seventy-seven visited by Alonso de Palomino, it is really the exception to the rule. By the third decade of the seventeenth century, it appears that the archdiocese of Toledo had established control over the wealth and property left for charitable purposes that fell within the jurisdiction of the church.

### HOSPITAL CONSOLIDATIONS AND BEGGARS' HOSPITALS

While hospital visitations proceeded, the crown embarked upon its most energetic reform directed towards the amelioration of Castilian poor relief, the consolidation of the numerous small, poor hospitals into larger, multi-purpose institutions. The idea of hospital consolidation had been circulating in Castile for some time, but it does not appear that any actual consolidations were effected until the last third of the sixteenth century. The Tridentine legislation said nothing specific about hospital consolidations, although a broad interpretation of the chapter authorizing the conversion of pious funds to new uses might have justified the reform. Contemporary Castilian opinion did not seem to accept such a broad interpretation however. In the list of instructions Philip sent to the crown legates who attended the 1565–6 provincial councils, hospital consolidation was treated as a separate issue which the prelates were urged to discuss and support, and, following the advice of his prelates, Philip appealed to Rome for a special papal brief to sanction the reform. The brief granted in 1566 placed the hospital consolidation under the supervision of three prelates: the bishop of Cuenca, Bernardo de Fresnado, the bishop of Palencia, Cristóbal Fernández de Valtodaño, and the bishop of Segovia, Diego Covarrubias y Leiva. These three prelates, together with the bishop in whose diocese the reform was to be effected, were to coordinate and supervise all the details of the consolidations. This arrangement proved to be difficult and costly so the king requested a new brief, granted by Pius V in April 1567, which placed the reform directly in the hands of the prelates of each diocese. Not all hospitals were included in the consolidation. The brief mentioned those hospitals which 'have such tenuous annual revenues that they scarcely serve to sustain the officials and administrators . . . that offer little or no hospitality and are unable to fulfill the duties and foundation statutes of the founders'.[48]

Even with the arrival of the new brief authorizing each prelate to effect the reform in his own diocese, there was not a great flurry of activity. Instead there was, as Philip later described it, 'a great deal of procrastination and confusion'. However, the powerful Diego de Espinosa, president of the Royal Council until his death in 1572, was obviously a supporter of the reform. Cardinal Espinosa was born in Martín Múñoz de las Posadas, a village in the diocese of Ávila which boasted a population of five to six hundred *vecinos* in 1569. It was customary for Castilian men of wealth to shower gifts upon their place of birth and for this reason, under the auspices of the cardinal, Martín Múñoz received a new chapel and the benefits of a consolidated hospital. In October 1569, the Royal Council sent out letters to the *alcaldes* of Martín Múñoz and the bishop of Ávila, Álvaro de Mendoza, informing them of the proposed consolidation and ordering them to attend a meeting in Martín Múñoz to discuss the reform.[49] The examiner-general of the Ávila diocese, Master Gaspar Daza, arrived in the village on 24 October, and, in the company of two *alcaldes* and two *regidores*, made an inspection of all the five hospitals of the village.

During their tour of inspection the committee compiled a report which gives some idea why hospital consolidation was considered a necessary reform. The total endowments of all the hospitals amounted to seventy-five *aranzadas* (approximately 447 deciares) of vineyards that rented for a total of 38,000 mrs a year, forty-five *fanegas* of wheat land, one perpetual *censo* paying 450 mrs a year, two small houses given rent-free to two paupers, and a bull of pardons. Five confraternities administered the rents of the hospitals and were responsible for fulfilment of any spiritual obligations stipulated by the founder of each institution. However, since none of the hospitals had a patron, and the founder of only one hospital was known and he had not specified any spiritual obligations, the masses, vigils and anniversaries celebrated by the confraternities had nothing to do with the last testament of the founders of the hospitals. As for hospitality, each hospital had two beds for travellers or pilgrims. Though the five hospitals could have housed a total of ten patients between them, according to the committee's report none of the hospitals admitted any patients. Only one hospital employed a hospitaller, a man so poor that he had to work to sustain himself, so he went to work leaving the hospital doors closed for the better part of the day. What was worse, the hospitals were unable to treat any sickness so these patients were forced to wander to the next village in great danger of losing their life. All the committee members recommended that the hospitals should be fused into one of the old ones which could then be enlarged to treat the sick and to house poor travellers and would have adequate rents to offer decent hospitality.

The Royal Council was, of course, in complete agreement with the committee's recommendation and in November 1569 sent out instructions to effect the consolidation. Because of delays in passing down the chain of command among the diocesan officials, it was not until April 1570 that the parish priest of Martín Múñoz, Jerónimo Bravo, received a commission from the diocese of Ávila to act as representative for the bishop in the impending consolidation. The Royal Council had decided that the Hospital of Santa Ana should be retained and receive all the revenues, rents, landed and movable properties of the other four hospitals. Any property that Santa Ana did not need was to be sold off in public auction, as were the four old hospital buildings. The proceeds from the auction were to be spent in enlarging and improving Santa Ana or invested in useful and secure rents, preferably wheat land or perpetual *juros*. When the auction was finally completed in September 1570, the profits amounted to nearly 100,000 mrs,[50] a tidy sum that should have permitted the hospital to make improvements and useful investments and to offer effective hospitality.

Before the auction was completed the *regidores* and the *alcaldes* of Martín Múñoz drew up a list of regulations for the government of the new hospitals which was forwarded to Cardinal Espinosa. Probably the only persons in Martín Múñoz who could have objected to the reform were the brothers of the five confraternities who lost their meeting place, the rents they had administered and the opportunity to offer charitable assistance to the poor. The new regulations excluded the confraternities from any administrative or charitable obligations in the new hospital, though they were each permitted to celebrate a yearly reunion, a mass and a vigil in a special room of the hospital. Cardinal Espinosa, who scrutinized and amended the city's regulations, ordered that the new room for the confraternities was to be built immediately and terminated within six months. The Hospital of Santa Ana should have taken over any spiritual obligations specified in the testaments of the founders of the extinguished hospitals, but since there were none, the regulations merely suggested that three masses should be celebrated every week for the consolation of the patients and the souls of all the founders. For fairly obvious reasons, the *regidores* and the *alcaldes* who drew up the new regulations recommended that they should be the patrons of the new hospital, a recommendation vetoed by Cardinal Espinosa, who appointed the *alcaldes* and the parish priest as patrons, establishing a more favourable balance between ecclesiastical and secular authorities. The patrons were to appoint a *mayordomo* to administer the hospital rents, a hospitaller and a chaplain, and they were responsible for making a yearly visitation and taking the hospital's accounts. The city's suggestion that a 'moderate' banquet should be consumed on visitation day at the expense of the hospital was also vetoed by the cardinal, who specified that all banqueters should pay 3 *reales* for their food and drink.

When the consolidation was completed, the Hospital of Santa Ana should have been a better administered, wealthier hospital, capable of offering many more services to the poor and sick. Two infirmaries were to be added, one for men and another for women (segregation of the sexes was an important prerequisite in sixteenth-century hospital reforms), while travellers and pilgrims were to have their own dormitory. There was as well a chapel so the patients could easily receive spiritual consolation. The regulations never actually established exactly what type of patients should be admitted or how long they might stay in the hospital, but they definitely excluded all 'healthy, rich men and outsiders who live evil lives'.[51] The only persons inconvenienced by the reform, the brothers of the five confraternities, apparently made no protests, or if they did they were not recorded in the documents. Probably the confraternities of Martín Múñoz were not rich or powerful enough to resist the combined forces of royal and diocesan officials.

The Martín Múñoz hospital consolidation exhibits all the earmarks common to most sixteenth-century Castilian poor relief reforms. It was sponsored, supported and executed by the combined forces of church and crown. If the city *regidores* made an attempt to upset this balance by trying to take over the patronage of the hospital, they were thwarted by the provision of Cardinal Espinosa. There is no doubt that the motivating force behind the reforms of Martín Múñoz was Diego de Espinosa. One might wonder if the president of the Royal Council, who signed all the conciliar letters fostering the reform as the bishop of Sigüenza, considered himself as a servant of God or of Philip II, but the *vecinos* of Martín Múñoz were quite clear about who had sponsored the consolidation. All public proclamations for the auction of the old hospital buildings and property included the mitigating provision that the property was being sold 'by order of a royal provision of His Majesty'.

Though the enlarged Hospital of Santa Ana promised better services to more people, it was not intended to serve as a permanent home for any paupers of the community. The sick were given medical and spiritual attention while poor travellers were provided with sleeping accommodation, but these services were offered on a limited, short-term basis. The hospital did not offer to feed and house the needy of the village on a permanent basis. Those people unable to earn a living because of some physical handicap, or temporarily in need of assistance because of too many children, high bread prices or no work would be forced to seek assistance from their family, friends, confraternity or parish priest, or to join the ranks of public beggars. There was nothing unusual about a hospital limiting its services to treating the sick and housing travellers on a short-term basis. One of the reasons why the Granada hospital founded by John of God created such a stir was that it did offer temporary or permanent assistance to anyone in need. But as John of God had learned, the maintenance of such a hospital was expensive, and there were also theological and moral objections.

Despite these objections, the idea of providing beggars with their own hospital met with some success in Castile. A brief discussion of the advantages of beggars' hospitals is contained in an anonymous manuscript written as early as July 1560. However, the title of the manuscript, 'That general hospitals are a good means to remedy the poor if the entire republic is responsible for maintaining them',[52] is deceptive. The term 'general hospital' denoted two distinct types of sixteenth-century institutions. The traditional meaning referred to a hospital that treated all types of ailments. As Sebastián de Covarrubias explained it, 'in those hospitals that are called general or are well-endowed, they treat fevers, wounds, syphilis, the insane and foundling children' (*Tesoro*: 'hospital'). However, what the anonymous author of the 1560 manuscript had in mind was an institution that housed nothing but beggars. To avoid confusion and ambiguity in the use of this term, an institution devoted to housing beggars has been described as a beggars' hospital, while the term 'general hospital' has been reserved for the type of establishment described by Covarrubias.

Though the 1560 document is no more than a brief outline which left many questions unanswered, the author was insistent that beggars' hospitals had to be founded throughout Castile. He accepted the fact that the poor must retain their liberty of movement, meaning that they could leave and enter the hospitals as they chose. It was precisely this liberty of movement which necessitated nation-wide action because

if there are hospitals in some parts and not in others, aside from the inequality which arises out of burdening one part with all the poor, if the undeserving poor have lands or free outlets where they can loiter and continue their lives of ill-gotten gain, they will flee from the hospitals as from a prison and will never be brought to a better life.[53]

The author was also adamant that these hospitals must have adequate income because 'to enclose the poor without giving them food, clothes, habitation and medicine would be like a prison and a confinement'. Adequate income would be raised by voluntary donations, taking out loans on a city's rents or properties, and through a hospital consolidation that would give to the new hospitals the rents and properties of some extinguished hospitals. A *hermandad*, composed of people from the various regions of the country, would provide some centralized direction by redistributing alms and paupers according to the needs and resources of each area.

While the 1560 manuscript never clearly explained how it was to be achieved, the author promised that his hospitals would eliminate the undeserving poor, thereby leaving more relief for those who truly needed it. Thus the 1560 reform promised a result similar to that propounded by Juan de Robles in 1545; what had changed was the means of achieving this goal. Instead of a common fund or a central committee that collected and distributed alms to the poor, all that was needed was a hospital, an old familiar institution. Even Domingo de Soto had claimed that in the golden days of the early Christian church there had been hospitals for beggars. Nor was there any mention of limiting relief to the native-born poor and sending outsiders back to their birthplace to find assistance. In theory, the beggars' hospitals would remain open to all the deserving poor provided that each large urban centre founded such a hospital.

The 1560 manuscript was probably read by a very small circle of people, and it was not until the late 1570s that the subject gained wider support and a more vocal audience in Castile, thanks to the tireless activity of Miguel Giginta, a canon of the cathedral of Elna (Rosellon) in the diocese of Tarragona. Born in Perpignan in 1534, Miguel's father, don Francisco Giginta, was comfortably placed as regent of the Council of Aragon and later as chancellor of the University of Perpignan. One of the younger of at least four children, Miguel was destined for the church, and he received a bachelor's degree from the University of Perpignan before being awarded the canonry of Elna. He did not stay in Elna long however. From 1576 to 1588 he wandered about the Iberian peninsula attempting to persuade prelates, monarchs and city authorities of the utility of his hospitals.[54]

According to his own description, Giginta was in Madrid in 1576 when he presented to the king a brief outline explaining his reform, 'Representación para que se remedien los pobres'. Though his ideas found no immediate success with the king, the *procuradores* of the Cortes were impressed. To study the reform in more detail, they appointed four commissaries who 'took twenty written opinions from the gravest persons in letters and experience, all of whom approved it'.[55] Convinced of the wisdom of the canon's plan, in 1576 the *procuradores* sent a petition to the king, asking that the reform be effected in all the cities of the kingdom (*AC*, vol. v¹, pp. 80–1). However, after the initial flurry of enthusiasm, impetus for the reform was lost when the president of the Royal Council, Diego de Covarrubias, died in late 1577. Assessing the situation, Giginta decided to abandon Madrid and try his luck in Portugal. His sojourn in Portugal lasted until 1580 during which time he visited Lisbon, Oporto and Coimbra, but the death of King Sebastian in 1578 and the consequent disputes over the royal succession frustrated plans to enact the canon's reforms in that kingdom. However, while he was in Coimbra Giginta published his *Tratado de remedio de los pobres* (1579), a treatise that provided a fuller exposition of his ideas, written in the form of a dialogue. With the publication of this book, Giginta's ideas about relieving the poor are essentially complete.

Sixteenth-century beggars' hospitals combined elements of punishment and salvation in varying degrees, depending largely upon the disposition of the proponent, but the idealistic Giginta inclined towards the more positive side of salvation. It was his hope that if the poor were provided with adequate living quarters, food, edifying leadership and employment, they would become happy, well-behaved and contented citizens of the Christian commonwealth. The persons lodged in Giginta's hospital would have histories read to them as a form of recreation; they would receive continual instruction in the Christian doctrine and frequently attend mass, rosaries in hand, to be brought ever closer to salvation. All the inmates would be employed in useful productive tasks such as spinning and weaving; young girls would be taught to sew and knit while the boys would be trained in a profession or a trade, depending upon their ability. All the work of the hospital – the cooking, sewing, washing and cleaning – would be done by the residents who, Giginta believed, would be animated by communal spirit and good will when their necessities had been provided for. The poor of Giginta's hospital resembled nothing so much as a species of religious community. If, however, there should be some particularly difficult and unruly inmate, the canon recommended a mild form of physical persuasion suggested by Vives, namely a cut in food rations. Giginta placed great store by this method arguing that no matter how incorrigible the individuals, 'in five or six hours . . . even if there are five or six thousand . . . they will be brought [to government and order] . . . without any need of *alguaciles*, whips or cudgels' (Giginta, *Tratado*, fol. 16v).

Up to this point Giginta's debt to Juan Luis Vives is fairly obvious, but no theorist writing about the poor of Castile could ignore Domingo de Soto. Giginta devoted one chapter to reconciling his ideas with those of 'that great theologian' and allusions to Soto appear throughout the treatise. One concession made to Soto was the issue of public begging. Despite Giginta's objections to mendicity which are scattered throughout his book, the inmates of his hospital went out begging, though they did so in a very orderly fashion. The most unsightly residents, chosen because they would inspire the most charity, were dispatched to certain appointed places every day; they went out in pairs and wore a distinctive insignia to mark them as worthy poor. The attempt to organize and discipline begging is very much in the style of Giginta, but the fact that he permitted it at all was probably a concession to Soto's objection that by confining the poor, Christians would be deprived of a direct confrontation with the poor and the opportunity to discharge their charitable obligations on a personal, individual level. Giginta made sure that his pairs of beggars covered every important place in a city at all hours of the day so that no citizen would lack the opportunity to exercise his charitable obligations.

Secondly there was the question of liberty of movement of the poor prescribed by Soto. Possibly because he attempted to meet this charitable prerequisite, or possibly because he was not a very systematic thinker, Giginta's solution for dealing with vagabonds or healthy beggars is unclear. He argued that all the persons in his hospitals were free to come and go as they pleased and that no examination was necessary for admittance. But if the inmates could come and go freely, why would anyone choose to enter or remain in an institution that promised enforced fasting for five or six hours? If the project to lead the poor to a happier, more productive existence included punishment, then surely some compulsion was necessary to make them stay. A degree of compulsion was exerted by the fact that individuals who left the hospital lost, at least in theory, their right to beg: they had refused the offer of an alternative means of subsistence plus the opportunity for spiritual salvation. Any resident who left the hospital was to find some way of earning a living other than begging, and the local citizenry were to cooperate in enforcing this ban by giving alms only to the specially designated beggars from the hospital.

Giginta also mentioned that vagabonds would not want to enter his hospitals because of the work requirements and the 'sobriety' of the institution, yet at another point he argued that they would all be productively employed, though he never explained how this was to be achieved (fols. 26–7, 30–1, 37). In answer to Soto's criticism that the wilfully idle would merely flee to a place where they could continue their non-productive existence, Giginta insisted that all the cities and larger towns of Castile should institute a hospital so there was no escape, while the villages should remit any sturdy beggar to the nearest city. But since he never explained exactly what the cities should do with them, this is hardly a constructive suggestion. While one may admire Giginta for emphasizing the more positive aspects of his hospitals – vocational training and spiritual salvation – his omission of a practical solution of dealing with vagabonds leaves his scheme incomplete.

The Catalan was equally unsuccessful in resolving the other difficulty which relentlessly pursued all the poor relief reformers, the question of finances. All his money-raising schemes were entirely unoriginal: donations from private individuals, the profits gained through the work projects and the begging forays of the inmates, and the proceeds resulting from a consolidation of the small, poor hospitals in each city. Giginta was never too concerned about finding more income for his hospitals because he believed that the work projects of the residents would be profitable enough not only to pay for the operational expenses of the hospital, but also to accumulate a surplus that would be divided between those who did the work, poor people in prison, and other needy hospitals. So convinced was the canon of the profitability of his scheme that he was eager to take in any person who sought admittance and was willing to work for his or her food: people who were temporarily unemployed, as well as poor travellers and pilgrims who got two days' free food before they had to start working.

If Giginta was optimistic about finances and vague about administrative details, he was wise in his choice of potential supporters. His treatise of 1579 was dedicated to Antonio Mauriño de Pazos y Figueroa, bishop of Ávila, successor to Diego de Covarrubias as president of the Royal Council and a close friend of the cardinal–archbishop of Toledo, Gaspar de Quiroga, to whom Giginta dedicated another book, *Cadena de oro* (Perpignan, 1584). Giginta dedicated books to these prelates because they were his staunchest supporters in Castile. Cardinal Quiroga, usually considered as a model Counter-Reformation prelate, was a strong supporter of the Jesuits who were usually in evidence when a beggars' hospital was founded.[56] Both these prelates had spent many years in Italy, Pazos as a student at San Clemente in Bologna and then as bishop of Patti (Sicily) before he returned to Castile as bishop of Ávila (c. 1578–81) and bishop of Córdoba (1581–d. 1586); Quiroga was auditor of the Roman Rota and visitor of Naples and Sicily before he returned to Castile as president of the Council of Italy (1567–94), bishop of Cuenca (1571–77), inquisitor-general (1573–94) and finally archbishop of Toledo (1577–d. 1594). The Italian experience of both men is worth emphasizing because Italy was in the vanguard in founding beggars' hospitals. As early as 1563 the city of Bologna had founded a beggars' hospital, apparently with papal approval. In 1565 Cardinal Carlo Borromeo urged that such hospitals be founded in his diocese, a suggestion that was implemented in 1577 by the city of Brescia. Similar hospitals were founded in Turino (1583), Modena (1592) and Venice (1594), and in 1587 Sixtus V, in the bull *Quamvis infirma*, ordered the foundation of a beggars' hospital in Rome, continuing a project begun by Gregory XIII.[57]

Giginta dedicated his books to prelates, but this does not mean that laymen were excluded from the administration of his hospital. To the contrary, the confraternity that was to govern the hospital would be composed of 'a *señor*, six merchants and four *caballeros*' and the city *regidores* and the Council of State were also urged to support the reform. Well aware that it was the decision of the king that would determine the issue, Giginta devoted one chapter of his treatise to elucidating the obligations of a monarch, who as 'Protector of the Poor', should foster the reform.

Aside from his duties as president of the Royal Council, Antonio Pazos was at the same time president of another special committee known as the *Junta de Reformación*, clearly a predecessor of the more famous junta of the same name established in the second decade of the seventeenth century and apparently one of many juntas convened in this period.[58] As fate would have it, there is no mention of Giginta's reform among the surviving documents of the junta, but the committee did discuss all manner of related topics. They deliberated upon relieving the poor of Madrid, the role of the ecclesiastical and the secular authorities in reforming certain monasteries, granting licences to hospitals to perform 'representations', the need to improve public morality, the usefulness of the *alguacil de pícaros*, and whether the bull *In Coeno Domini* issued by Gregory XIII in 1579 did, in fact, derogate the bull granting the *Cruzada*.[59] It is possible that the committee never had time to get to Giginta's reform. In March 1579, President Pazos reported that the junta was so overwhelmed by memorials that it would have to meet an extra day every week; the delay was exacerbated by the sullen attitude of the Royal Council which refused to dispatch any decisions of the junta. The members of this junta fluctuated, but aside from President Pazos those most regular in attendance were the ubiquitous secretary, Juan Vázquez de Salazar; Philip's grand almoner, Luis Manrique; the Dominican theologian, commissary-general of the *Cruzada* and Philip's confessor, Diego de Chaves; and the Augustinian friar who had objected so violently to the welfare reforms of the city of Bruges, Lorenzo Villavicencio. Surprisingly, Giginta reported that Villavicencio had approved the 1576 memorial supporting his reform, though the Augustinian may have been persuaded to give his approval by the pressure of his peers.[60]

The interminable discussions about Giginta's reform finally gave way to action soon after the canon returned to Castile when the city of Toledo publicly proclaimed the foundation of a beggars' hospital in January 1581.[61] All the beggars of the city were ordered to report to the hospital, which consisted of two converted houses in the parish of San Nicolás, where they would be provided with the necessities of life, or, if they were sick, they would be sent to another hospital to be treated. On 1 March, when the hospital was officially opened, all public begging in the city or its environs was prohibited. At the top of the broadside announcing the opening of the hospital appeared the names of the Toledo *corregidor*, the illustrious don Fadrique Portocarrero y Manrique; the equally illustrious cardinal–archbishop of Toledo, Gaspar de Quiroga; the Toledo cathedral chapter; and the city council. Conspicuous by its absence is the name of the king. At the time Philip was in Portugal consolidating his sovereignty in the newest embellishment to the vast Spanish empire and his temporary absence may have given courage to the persons who supported the Toledo foundation. Also, Toledo had just emerged from one of the severest subsistence crises of the century, a fact which may have emboldened the city to take the audacious step of founding a beggars' hospital without a licence from the crown.

The founders of the Toledo hospital were well aware of the connection between the 1540 poor law and the 1581 beggars' hospital, as the introduction of the proclamation sheet for the new hospital makes clear:

This city, desiring to implement the laws and orders of the Emperor, of glorious memory, and of Your Majesty, which speak of the confinement of poor beggars, consulted with the cardinal–archbishop of Toledo and the Toledo cathedral chapter, and, with their agreement and good opinion, instituted and founded a general hospital where all the poor who beg are confined.[62]

Since the poor law published by Philip never mentioned confining any beggars except those with contagious diseases, the founders of the Toledo institution were forced to justify their reform on the basis of the 1540 poor law, which, as they must have known, was no longer in effect.

Toledo's move inspired other Castilian cities. The city council of Zamora invited Giginta to come to their city and assist them in founding a hospital. Because he was busy in Toledo, Giginta declined the invitation, but he cautioned the councillors that if they did found a hospital it should not be 'a school or a prison, but an ordered house of innocent artisans and good Christians'.[63] In July the *procuradores* of the Cortes again discussed the reform and voted to petition the king a second time to ask that 'the universal confinement of the poor be effected throughout the kingdom'. The president of the Royal Council discouraged this second petition on grounds that it was a 'novelty and His Majesty has ordered that no more papers be sent to him because he is so busy' (*AC*, vol. VI, pp. 655–74). Despite the preoccupations of the king, the persistence of the *procuradores* was at least partially rewarded when in January 1582 the city of Madrid proclaimed the opening of a beggars' hospital to which all the beggars of Madrid were to report.[64] Public begging was prohibited after 1 February when the hospital officially opened. The Madrid proclamation bore a great resemblance to the earlier one published in Toledo except that the former institution boasted a licence from the king and an order from the Royal Council.

At what seems the pinnacle of success for Giginta's reform (the canon reported that a hospital had also been opened in Granada),[65] he rushed off to the crown of Aragon. It is probable that his return was prompted by the threat of the cathedral chapter of Elna to cut off his emoluments on grounds of his absence from the diocese. In 1583 Giginta returned to Elna to plead his case, apparently with little success because in 1584 the city council of Barcelona wrote to the Holy See to support the canon's cause.[66] Aside from worrying about his finances, Giginta visited many cities – Perpignan, Barcelona, Zaragoza, Monzón and Tarragona – in an effort to found more beggars' hospitals. The canon reported success in Perpignan, but it was in Barcelona that his reform received the warmest reception, thanks to the efforts of Doctor Diego Pérez de Valdivia, a follower of John of Ávila, who had been preaching in favour of such a foundation since 1581. The arrival of Giginta gave the scheme the necessary impetus, and in 1583, with the support of the bishop of Barcelona, Joan Dionas Loris, the city council and the Jesuits, the Hospital de la Misericordia dels Mendicants was founded.[67]

The name of the Barcelona hospital brings up the subject of the name of Giginta's other foundations, which modern historians invariably call Casas de Misericordia. This is a misnomer for the foundations in Toledo and Madrid, both of which were called General Hospitals of Beggars or simply General Hospitals, not Casas de Misericordia. The correct name of the Castilian foundations is important since it may serve as a link between the Castilian hospitals and the better-known *hôpital général* that flourished in seventeenth-century France (see below, p. 237, n. 6).

In 1586 Giginta was again in Madrid where he personally appeared in the Cortes to drum up support for his reform. At this time a hospital consolidation was being implemented in many Castilian cities, including Madrid, and it seemed to Giginta a convenient moment to found beggars' hospitals, which could receive the rents of the small hospitals that had previously housed pilgrims and paupers. Impressed by this idea, the *procuradores* decided to send to all the cities who voted in the Cortes a copy of Giginta's book and a paper they had compiled on the subject and to ask the cities for their opinion as to the feasibility of founding a beggars' hospital.[68] More support for the reform appeared in 1587 with the publication of a papal bull recommending the foundation of a beggars' hospital in Rome. Giginta brought a copy of the bull to the Cortes, and the *procuradores* ordered that the bull be translated into Castilian and eighteen copies be made and sent out to the cities of the realm.[69] Despite papal approval, the answers sent by the cities were discouraging. Only León expressed interest in the idea, while Salamanca, Córdoba, Granada and Soria were negative, largely for reasons of economy (*AC*, vol. ix, pp. 27, 172, 244, 317, 358).

The Castilian cities were wise, and probably well-informed, to plead penury in their decision not to found a beggars' hospital. The Toledo hospital had proven to be a sinkhole of money, and it was largely the munificence of Cardinal Quiroga, who gave approximately 30,000 ducats to support the foundation, that kept it afloat. The number of people in the Toledo hospital varied: in a year of good harvest there were about 300; in a year of bad harvest there were 500. However, in an era of continual grain shortages and rapidly rising prices, the cost of maintaining 300 persons, even if they were fed the most frugal rations, was expensive. In July 1581, after only five months of operation, the hospital was short of funds; by October the city council estimated that 3,500 ducats had been spent, nearly six times the sanguine estimate of Giginta, who thought the hospitals could be maintained for 600 ducats a year. In November the rector of the hospital, Juan de Figuerado, testified that the beggars lacked all the essentials of life – clothes, wheat, beds, coal, wood and blankets.[70] The original Toledo beggars' hospital, which is discussed in more detail in chapter 3 below, led a very sketchy hand-to-mouth existence until it finally expired in the 1590s.

It appears that the beggars' hospital in Barcelona did not prosper either. In 1584, the first full year of operation for the hospital, Catalonia suffered a bad harvest and the number of people in the institution reached 560, probably the maximum number ever admitted. In July the hospital administrators sought and received a special donation of 2,000 pounds from the city council. In August the city council sent out a petition, which included official approval from the bishop, to the prelates of Tarragona, Lérida, Gerona, Vich, Tortosa, and the cathedral chapters of Urgel and Elna, asking them to contribute to the hospital. The justification for seeking this outside assistance was that the Barcelona hospital was open to all beggars no matter what their place of origin and 'the greater part [of those in the hospital] are from bishoprics outside that of the city'. This letter was sent out again in 1586. A city proclamation made in 1589 to combat plague indicates that either the hospital was not operating at this time or, if it was operating, it did not house many beggars. Nor had public begging been eliminated. The city council ordered all vagabonds to leave the city 'within twenty-four hours on pain of 100 lashes', while other beggars were ordered to the Hospital de la Misericordia. Like the hospital of Toledo, that of Barcelona was financed by a bevy of complicated money-raising schemes, all indirect or voluntary, none of which yielded enough income to maintain the people in the institution.[71]

The language used in the proclamation statute of the Barcelona hospital was far milder than that used in the Toledo proclamation, but that does not mean the beggars were treated mildly. First of all, in violation of Giginta's theories, there was a physical inspection of persons found begging in the streets. Persons appointed by the city council ejected those fit to labour after warning them that they would be severely punished if they returned to beg. Secondly, others were transported to the hospital 'by force', especially young boys and 'others who used their time begging alms instead of studying their lessons with their masters'.[72] Thus the voluntary and idealistic aspects of Giginta's hospitals do not appear prevalent in Barcelona.

Aside from the difficulties of financing the hospitals, other problems emerged. The communal spirit of the hospital residents did not appear to be as strong as Giginta had hoped: 'disorders' broke out in the men's dormitory, unknown people entered or left the hospital at night, and some hospital residents did not choose to do their share of the work. Nor did the people of the city confine their alms to the specially appointed hospital beggars as they were supposed to do. And, instead of limiting the hospital residents to healthy beggars, sick ones had also been admitted, which caused outbreaks of sickness in the institution. What seems to have upset Giginta most of all, however, was the fact that the followers of John of God were trying to take over his hospitals.[73] Possibly Giginta was not a good administrator and the daily routine of operating a hospital did not interest him as much as it did the followers of John of God. On the other hand, had his hospitals functioned as he hoped they would, admitting all those in need of assistance in addition to people temporarily out of a job or merely passing through, it is doubtful that anyone in all Spain would have been capable of managing such an institution. The number of qualified applicants would have been in the thousands rather than hundreds. The primary difficulty of the Spanish beggars' hospitals was the discrepancy between the theory, which promised so much to so many, and actual practice, which frequently was unable to offer more than a small amount of bread to only the most destitute of society.

However, the discrepancy between theory and practice was not what contemporaries saw as the major difficulty with Giginta's hospitals. When the Cortes of 1586–8 attempted to revive Giginta's plan for founding beggars' hospitals throughout the crown of Castile, the final blow to their efforts came in July 1588 when Canon Bobadilla appeared before the assembly to present his objections. What the canon said was basically what Domingo de Soto had said forty years earlier: that the poor should be permitted to beg in the streets and should not be enclosed in a hospital. Giginta appeared seven days later to defend his reform, but this was the last mention by the *procuradores* of the canon of Elna and his beggars' hospitals (*AC*, vol. x, pp. 184–7, 191).

The king's opinion of Giginta's idea remains obscure. In January 1582, just after the Madrid beggars' hospital had been founded, Giginta wrote to don Juan de Zuñiga, viceroy of Naples, that 'His Majesty shows by his letters that he is very satisfied with the reform', but the judgment of the canon is obviously not impartial.[74] However, in the late 1580s the king did support a reform that promised to 'purify' Madrid by removing all the undesirable elements of society, with the ultimate result that 'all Spain will be like a school of virtue'.[75] The purification of society, presumably analogous to the Castilian quest for purity of the blood, and the creation of 'a school of virtue in all Spain' suggest that the king was concerned with achieving a state of reformed morality appropriate to the leading exponent of Catholicism, and that the ideas of Giginta, which promised a moral reformation of at least the poorer members of society, may have exercised some appeal.

It was in 1587 and 1588 that the president of the Royal Council, the conde de Barajas, and Licenciado Gudiel devised a scheme that they promised would reduce the number of robbers, vagabonds, lost women, escaped slaves and 'the many strangers who write and tell of everything that happens in these kingdoms'.[76] To achieve these goals, Madrid initiated a system of supervising non-residents of the city: lists of *vecinos* in each neighbourhood or *cuartel* were compiled, any strangers were to report to an *alcalde*, and all establishments providing beds for travellers were subject to inspection by the *alcaldes*. Any undesirable or unemployed non-resident found wandering about the city or lingering in a tavern was subject to expulsion. The *Junta de Policía* was officially created by a royal *cédula* of 1590, but the system was implemented before then because in 1589 the city of Toledo complained to the crown that their city was being inundated by beggars from Madrid.[77] In self-defence Toledo began its own system of parochial surveillance and reopened its beggars' hospital. A policy of exiling unwanted idlers and excluding them from public relief was confirmed in September 1590 in a crown letter informing the Toledo city council that no one but natives and residents of Toledo should be admitted to the beggars' hospital,[78] a decision that would have disturbed Domingo de Soto, though it should be added that other private hospitals in Toledo remained open to outsiders.

The determination of the crown to eliminate all avenues of escape open to vagabonds and idlers is best indicated by Philip's pragmatic of June 1590, prohibiting any subject of Castile to dress in the habit of a pilgrim or to make a pilgrimage without first obtaining a licence from the justices and the consent of the diocesan officials:[79] foreigners were permitted to wear pilgrim's habits but they also needed a licence. This pragmatic was promulgated on grounds that many ablebodied men used a pilgrim's habit as a disguise to avoid honest labour, to perpetrate crimes or mischief and to escape the scrutiny of the justices. Anyone found disobeying the pragmatic was subject to the punishment of a vagabond.

The most enduring welfare reform of the sixteenth century, the implementation of the long-impending hospital consolidation, was revived again in the 1580s. Since 1568 the crown had assiduously sent out letters to the prelates and the *corregidores*, and in 1578 Philip personally asked President Pazos to find out what progress, if any, had been made with the hospital consolidation in Seville and Córdoba.[80] Until 1586, however, all the royal activity produced little in the way of tangible results. A lengthy report from the provisor of

Granada provides some explanation for the delays in that particular archbishopric. The provisor reported that Archbishop Pedro Guerrero had received a crown letter, written in September 1568, which ordered that a hospital consolidation should be effected in the Granada diocese, but that letter 'seems to have been unanswered perhaps because at that time the *moriscos* rebelled'.[81] Another crown letter was received in 1584 but this one was also unanswered 'perhaps because in this archbishopric there are so few and such poor hospitals that this consolidation seems unnecessary'. The most recent royal letter of October 1586 had at least jogged the provisor into compiling a report about the thirteen hospitals of the city, six of which he felt might be consolidated.

Since a papal bull of 1486 had given the Castilian crown the right of presentation in all the ecclesiastical benefices of the kingdom of Granada, it might be thought that the crown would have little difficulty forcing through a consolidation in that diocese, especially after 1590 when the elderly, steadfast servant of the crown, Pedro de Castro, was appointed archbishop of Granada. Such was not the case however, for Pedro de Castro held out against the reform in the interests of defending the small, continually indebted episcopal Hospital of Santa Ana. The crown was informed of all the disadvantages of the episcopal hospital by the president of the chancery court of Granada, Fernando Niño de Guevara, who also mentioned that the smells, noises and indecencies emanating from the hospital, situated adjacent to the chancery court, disturbed the ministers of justice in the execution of their duties.[82] The president recommended that the episcopal hospital be fused with the royal hospital, more advantageously located outside the city. Pedro de Castro took great exception to the president's opinion and wrote the crown a brief, acerbic letter relating the special virtues of the episcopal hospital and the very poor management of the royal hospital.[83]

As with any reform that threatened to interfere with the privileges, patronage and prerogatives so jealously cherished by sixteenth-century society, hospital consolidation aroused all manner of opposition on the part of those destined to lose their hospital and all its affiliated benefits. Resistance might be passive, such as ignoring the crown letters and hoping that the royal officials would find something more pressing to occupy their time, or more active, such as writing petitions, initiating legal proceedings, fabricating miracles or hiding documents. Only firm, determined and constant crown prodding, supported by an equally determined and aggressive prelate, could overcome all the innate antagonism to the reform and in instances where one of these requisites was absent, as in Córdoba and Toledo,[84] no hospital consolidation was effected. Though the reform was not carried out in every urban centre of Castile, the hospitals of Madrid, Seville, Valladolid, Salamanca, Toro, Jaén, Antequera, Medina del Campo, Plasencia and Segovia were consolidated, and the list of successes would probably be longer were documentation more accessible.[85]

The Seville consolidation, pressed forward by the dauntless cardinal–archbishop Rodrigo de Castro, was certainly the most impressive of the sixteenth-century hospital reforms. An estimate of the 1580s puts the number of Seville hospitals at 112,[86] and the rents, properties and spiritual obligations of seventy-five of these hospitals were fused into the two institutions finally chosen to remain as centres for treating the sick; the Amor de Dios, which admitted patients suffering from non-contagious ailments, and Espíritu Santo, previously Santa Catalina de los Desamparados, where contagious diseases, defined as ulcers and syphilis and their related problems, were treated.[87] At least fourteen hospitals were untouched by the consolidation. These were hospitals of the crown, the cathedral chapter, the city council, or wealthy private institutions that offered adequate hospitality.

The hospital consolidation of Seville followed the pattern of that in Martín Múñoz some twenty years earlier, but Cardinal Rodrigo de Castro had a much harder time executing the reform than did Cardinal Espinosa. Cardinal Castro agreed to implement the consolidation as early as 1584, but it was not until 1589 that the first definite steps toward auctioning off the defunct hospitals were taken. The cardinal attributed the delay to the city council of Seville which, in his judgment, had continually tried to thwart the reform. Equally adamant in their opposition were the confraternities, especially those who governed or administered a hospital or 'offered hospitality', since they were included as part of the vast cataloguing and reshuffling of money and property dedicated to pious works and poor relief. Some confraternities were eliminated, while others were forced to relocate in the churches and monasteries of the city.

By 1596 Bartolomé de Herrera, 'notary of the hospital consolidation of Seville', reported that he had nearly completed the extensive bookkeeping tasks involved in the consolidation process. Each of the two hospitals had a book of their respective properties and houses, a total of more than 3,000 contracts, a book of the tributes that they paid, and a list of the masses, fiestas, remembrances and sermons to be celebrated in the churches and monasteries of the city. Still to be completed were the books of the tributes and *juros* each hospital held, more information as to the spiritual obligations to be performed by the priests of the hospitals, and separate account books for each of the four dowry bequests held by the hospitals. When these latter papers were compiled, Herrera felt that the hospital consolidation of Seville was finished.

A report of 1598 indicates that both hospitals were fully operative and well-endowed. The Amor de Dios had a total income of 4,862,000 mrs, of which 3,211,580 was available to treat the 100 to 150 patients suffering from non-contagious diseases. The Espíritu Santo possessed 4,040,180 mrs with 2,725,725 mrs left to treat the 100 patients hospitalized, in addition to the 60 people who lived at home and came to the hospital in the morning for treatment. However, building repairs in the Amor de Dios continued until the 1620s when the hospital was officially terminated under the auspices of cardinal–archbishop Pedro de Castro, the elderly half-brother of the prelate who began the reform, while repairs in Espíritu Santo continued until the 1670s.

The hospitals throughout the archdiocese of Seville were also to be consolidated, but this reform proceeded more slowly. In 1598 Bartolomé de Herrera reported that the reform was nearly complete in Jerez, while in Arcos, Niebla and Sanlucar la Mayor substantial progress had been made. But in the villages of Puerto de Santa María, Cazalla, Carmona, La Palma and Villaena the consolidation process had hardly begun. Apparently Rodrigo de Castro was unable to complete these consolidations before his death in 1600, because in 1601 Francisco Gallinato, the recently appointed administrator of hospitals, asked the Royal Council for permission to continue the work of Bartolomé de Herrera and reported that much remained to be done in the towns of the archdiocese.[88]

In a recent history of Seville the author reports that Rodrigo de Castro is remembered in the city as 'stubborn, ostentatious, uncharitable and hateful', a description that may owe something to the cardinal's success in forcing upon the city an unpopular hospital reform.[89] However, though the cardinal supported the consolidation and made every effort to have it implemented with dispatch, one of the primary reasons he did so was because 'His Majesty has wanted it so much'.

The Madrid consolidation was probably the most rapidly effected since, as the residence of the court, Madrid was especially susceptible to the dictates of the crown. Nor did the city possess an abundance of wealthy confraternities, a large, powerful cathedral chapter or a recalcitrant bishop; only the vicar of Madrid (presumably appointed by the archbishop of Toledo in whose diocese Madrid fell), who was treated much as a crown servant by the Royal Council. Nor did Madrid have one hundred hospitals in 1586, but a mere fifteen (Quintana, *Historia de Madrid*, pp. 99–100, 445–54). When the consolidation was completed in 1587, the city was left with four hospitals: the Hospital de la Corte, a peripatetic institution that accompanied the Castilian court and cared for courtiers; La Latina, an old, wealthy, private foundation; Antón Martín, the more recent foundation of the followers of John of God who treated contagious diseases; and the new General Hospital, apparently located in the same building as the old beggars' hospital. While the newly consolidated General Hospital occupied these buildings, it is unlikely that its purpose was limited to that of housing beggars. Madrid had no large hospital dedicated to treating non-contagious diseases and it surely needed one. The pattern of the Seville consolidation, where two hospitals were retained, one for contagious and another for non-contagious diseases, suggests that Philip II tried to fulfil the plan presented by the Castilian Cortes as long ago as 1525. This is not to say that a sick beggar would not be admitted to the new hospital, but merely that the institution did not limit its services to providing a home for the destitute.

One historian has denigrated the Madrid consolidation on grounds that the hospitals which treated foreign communities – the Italians, the French, the Aragonese – were not touched,[90] but this is a misinterpretation of the purposes of the consolidation and the foreign hospitals. A licence from the crown was necessary before these hospitals could be founded and in 1578, when the Italians sought such a licence, the president of the Royal Council urged that it be granted:

All the council . . . resolved that Your Majesty should give them the licence since no difficulties can be found; rather it is an advantage to the court and an alleviation to the hospitals of the court. Since this hospital will travel with the court, it does not come under the law that all hospitals should be fused into one (as the Hospital de la Corte does not). The licence should be given to them with the provision that they do not beg alms in the court. . . .[91]

Clearly if the foreign hospitals were sustained by their own funds and alleviated the burden of Madrid's hospitals, it would have been contradictory to the purposes of hospital consolidation, directed towards improving Castilian hospital service, to remove them.

From its inception in 1587, the General Hospital of Madrid was administered by Bernardino de Obregón and staffed by the brothers of a society he had founded in 1567. Since Bernardino de Obregón founded a new hospital order, parallels with John of God spring to mind, but in background, temperament and avocation, Bernardino bears more resemblance to Ignatius Loyola.[92] Born in Burgos in 1540, he was educated in the household of the bishop of Sigüenza, Fernando Niño de Guevara, and in 1552 embarked upon a military career, serving under the duke of Saboya in Italy and Flanders. When he returned to Castile he joined the household of the duke of Sesa, Fernando de Córdoba, as master of the horse and was honoured with a coveted habit of the military order of Santiago de los Caballeros. With all these social advantages, the young man astounded his contemporaries in 1567 when he abandoned the luxuries of the court and devoted himself entirely to serving the poor. He sold all his worldly possessions to found the Hospital of Santa Ana in Madrid and gathered around him a group of followers known as the Siervos de los Pobres. In 1589, two years after Benardino had taken over the task of administering the Madrid General Hospital, his society was confirmed as a religious congregation by the nuncio and Cardinal Quiroga. As with the congregation founded by John of God, the Siervos de los Pobres were given the rule of Saint Augustine, and they added the vow of service to the poor to the usual three vows of poverty, chastity and obedience.

Bernardino de Obregón was a special favourite of Philip II, but unfortunately the king chose to honour his favourite and twelve of his most devoted followers by sending them to Lisbon in 1592 to take over the administration of the Hospital of All Saints, an institution directed by the powerful and wealthy Hermandad de la Misericordia. Shortly after Bernardino left Madrid, difficulties broke out in the Madrid General Hospital and the Hospital de la Sagrada Pasión, which had previously cared exclusively for female patients, left the General Hospital and returned to its old quarters as an independent institution. Meanwhile Bernardino and his followers ran into trouble in Lisbon. Quite understandably the persons who had been ousted from their posts in the Lisbon hospital were not predisposed to view the newcomers with generosity; they launched a systematic attack to undermine the Castilians which ended with Bernardino de Obregón's inglorious appearance before the Portuguese Inquisition. When he finally returned to Castile in 1598, Philip was close to death and Bernardino died two years later, a victim of the plague.

Despite the frequent appeals to Rome by his followers, Bernardino de Obregón was never canonized, nor did the Siervos de los Pobres achieve the widespread fame, following and dispersion of the Brothers Hospitallers. Nonetheless they did found hospitals in Seville and Valencia, and they retained a monopoly in the Madrid General Hospital until the eighteenth century. The head brother of the Siervos de los Pobres served as the administrator of the Madrid General Hospital and also as one of the members of the *Congregación de Caballeros* that governed the hospital. Over and above the congregation was a *Junta de los Hospitales* whose members included the vicar, the *corregidor* and three *regidores* of Madrid, the senior *alcalde* of the court, and three members of the Royal Council.[93] Thus Madrid's hospitals were supervised by crown, church and city officials.

They were subsidized in a variety of ways. As of 1584 they shared in the profits gained through the performances of plays staged in the city, an expedient that was adopted by many Castilian cities and towns.[94] Though moralists like the Jesuit Pedro de Guzmán were scandalized by certain aspects of the plays, the money they brought in was enormously important to the hospitals. Another source of income came from excise taxes or *sisas*; the Madrid hospitals received a portion of the excise taxes levied on coal, oil and meat.[95] They also received a portion of any unapplied merchandise or money confiscated by the judges for legal infractions.[96] The Hospital de la Corte, devoted exclusively to caring for the personnel of the court, received an annual gift from Philip II and enjoyed a special licence to sell livestock.[97] Thus the hospitals profited from an odd assortment of money-raising schemes that contemporaries must have judged as 'voluntary', in addition to any income they might receive from soliciting alms and the last wills of charitable givers.

The Madrid hospital consolidation was not popular with all parties. Even the usually tactful chronicler, Jerónimo de Quintana, flatly stated in his history of Madrid that it was a mistake (pp. 100, 448), and the Castilian Cortes, long supporters of the reform, did an abrupt about face in November 1598 by petitioning Philip III to dismember the General Hospital (*AC*, vol. xv, pp. 729–30; vol. xvi, pp. 651–3). The *procuradores* maintained that the hospital was overcrowded, its rents poorly administered and a great portion of its available income was spent in supporting its large staff. The first of these reproaches was probably true. The population of Madrid had been increasing since Philip II selected it as the residence of the court, and with grain shortages and sickness striking New Castile at ever more frequent intervals in the last third of the sixteenth century, the hospitals were bound to be crowded. Yet the *procuradores*' suggestion of refounding all the old, small, ten-to-thirty-bed hospitals hardly seems an adequate solution for housing more patients, improving the administration of rents or cutting down the expenditure for staff. The *procuradores*' eulogies about the care and attention given by the old hospitals may well have been nothing more than nostalgia for a bygone era when Madrid had been a small, normal Castilian town.

But these objections were only a preface to the true cause of discontent which had to do with the lack of money the General Hospital received from charitable givers. When a hospital was founded, it was customary for a founder to include some type of spiritual obligations for his soul, perhaps prayers to be said by the hospital patients or the celebration of masses, vigils or anniversaries by the rector or the priest of the hospital. As part of the consolidation process, the General Hospital assumed responsibility for fulfilling all the spiritual obligations of each of the defunct hospitals, though the number of masses, prayers and vigils for the souls of the dead was reduced and consolidated. Had this not been done, the priests of the hospital staff would have been fully occupied celebrating masses for the founders, leaving them little time to minister to the needs of the patients. It was just this consolidation and reduction of spiritual obligations which the *procuradores* felt to be a dissuasion to charitable givers:

When there were many hospitals, persons were moved to leave their fortune for something so holy and necessary, seeing that their spiritual obligations were conserved. . . . By fusing all the hospitals into one, the spiritual obligations of the founders are obscured, which is the reason why those persons who ought to leave their worldly possessions to hospitals leave them for other pious works that do conserve these obligations.[98]

The criticism of the Cortes certainly suggests that many Castilian charitable givers were more concerned with the well-being of their own souls than they were with the well-being of the hospitals or the persons in the hospitals. Given the fact that the consolidation was resented by many of the literate, wealthy persons who could afford to found hospitals, it is to Philip's credit that he chose to push through an unpopular reform in the interests of the poor, the beneficiaries of more efficient hospital service.

On the other hand, the crown's policies, or intended policies, may have had a negative effect on Castilian hospitals throughout the century. Castilian charitable givers seem to have been aware of the threat of a hospital consolidation, disliked the prospect, and made efforts to prevent the absorption of their institution into a large general hospital. As early as 1501 Juan Múñoz of Granada had threatened 'the damnation of the Mother of Christ' against anyone who tampered with his hospital, and in 1550 doña Beatriz de Trejo included in the foundation statutes of her hospital in Plasencia that 'neither by bull or any other means may [my hospital] be joined with another, converted to another pious work, sold or exchanged'.[99] The long-impending threat of a hospital consolidation, together with the movement to found large, if not enormous, general hospitals that only the very wealthy could afford, may have discouraged moderately wealthy Castilians from leaving their wealth to hospitals and encouraged them to found chantry chapels,[100] which appeared to be much safer pious foundations in as much as no one discussed consolidating them.

It should be noted that the Cortes appealed to the crown to dismember the Madrid General Hospital and that the administrator of the Seville hospitals wrote to the crown for permission to continue the consolidation in that diocese. The consolidation was very much a crown project and at first glance it appears that Philip II realized the directive of Juan Luis Vives, who had argued that it was the responsibility of the secular authorities to see that hospital revenues were spent to relieve the poor. Certainly the Madrid consolidation established precedents for the eighteenth-century reformers who sought to justify the crown's attempts to take over poor relief.[101] But Philip's actions were tempered by certain conditions and limitations, innate to a ruler of a sixteenth-century Catholic state. First of all he had a papal brief approving the reform. Secondly he accepted the fact that the consolidation had to be implemented by the prelates. Had the king considered himself the final arbiter of poor relief, the consolidation might have been effected throughout Castile rather than in the piecemeal, haphazard fashion resulting from the disposition and enthusiasm of each prelate. The crown might suggest, cajole and urge, but it did not usurp what it clearly reckoned to be the prerogative of the prelates.

Philip III did not dismember the Madrid General Hospital, though it was transferred to a new location, a move which entails some remarks about the last of the sixteenth-century reformers of poor relief, Cristóbal Pérez de Herrera. Born and educated in Salamanca, Herrera became a crown *protomédico* in 1577, served as a doctor in the Spanish galleys for nine years and later treated the servants and staff of the royal household. In the 1590s Herrera settled in Madrid where he formed a friendship with Mateo Alemán, author of the famous picaresque novel *Guzmán de Alfarache* (1599), and in 1595 he embarked on a career as a writer and an *arbitrista*. Until 1618, when he wrote his last and most popular work, *Moral Proverbs and Riddles*, Herrera was unflagging in offering his advice on all manner of subjects, ranging from medicine to improvements for Madrid, the army, and society in general. In addition to his numerous treatises, the doctor also spent a great deal of time petitioning the crown for money or a coveted military habit, the latter of which he never obtained because of his *converso* origins.[102]

So far as his schemes for relieving the poor are concerned, most fully elaborated in the treatise *Amparo de pobres* (1598), Herrera was little more than a popularizer of ideas developed by others. Having had the advantage of seeing what went wrong with Giginta's hospitals, Herrera was able to make a few practical adjustments to the Catalan's scheme. Giginta had been vague about administrative details, so Herrera added a more Castilian note by drawing up an elaborate network of officials, with equally elaborate titles, who were to act as governors for his network of institutions, known as albergues. In the upper echelon of this pyramid of officialdom was the junta-general, which consisted of the protector-general of the poor, a position Herrera hoped would be given to Rodrigo Vázquez de Arce, the president of the Royal Council, and the *procurador-general*, a position Herrera hoped he might fill.

Since one of the major shortcomings of Giginta's foundations was a lack of funds, Herrera suggested that all the albergue inmates should find their own food by begging while the albergue was to provide nothing more than sleeping quarters and occasional sermons on the Christian doctrine; as Herrera put it, the albergues were to serve as parishes and dormitories (*Amparo*, p. 251). Aside from the financial benefits to the albergue's operating expenses, Herrera argued that it was far healthier to send the inmates out begging since they would receive the benefit of exercise and 'the ventilation of the air'. Not everyone was permitted the luxury of being an albergue beggar, recognizable by the distinctive signs and clothing they wore, for the administrators of the albergue were to inspect all candidates to determine that they were deserving paupers. Any undeserving female candidates would be placed in a workhouse, a punishment recommended by Herrera because the unpleasant spectacle of public whippings would be avoided. Herrera seemed especially incensed by female vagabonds and delinquents who contaminated others with syphilis, abandoned their children and caused a general moral laxity in the community. These jezebels would have their hair shorn, be fed the cheapest food, sleep on the poorest beds and be put to work weaving and spinning. Herrera argued that 'with moderate food, threats, punishments, and imprisonment of chains or stocks for those who are incorrigible, all will be amenable and humble, enduring the work with patience, complying with penitence and involving themselves in virtuous works on feast days or Sundays' (p. 124).

The majority of people who would be affected by Herrera's reforms were, of course, healthy male beggars. Their 'reformation' consisted of having them choose between three options: either they went to work, they went to the galleys if they begged or, assuming the plan was enacted on the national level Herrera hoped for, they left Spain. To be sure the male vagabonds were aware of their options, the number of police officials was to be increased. Two fathers, one for adults and another for the young, were to see that healthy beggars found employment. The number of *alguaciles* who were responsible for arresting vagabonds was increased and they were offered a bounty of two *reales* for every vagabond they captured. Perhaps because Herrera was the first layman since Vives to write about poor relief, successful implementation of his plan was largely dependent upon secular police officials (pp. 194, 208–11).

As was true of the other sixteenth-century theorists who wrote about the poor, Herrera seemed to assume that work was available for the beggars if they chose to take it, although at one point he did suggest that healthy beggars might be employed on the 'public works of the albergue' on their first transgression.[103] At least one person did question whether there was work for the beggars. One objection to Herrera's scheme was that 'at present there is nothing in which to occupy these people and thus [execution of the reform] will create robbers, especially on the highways' (p. 168). If this objection is accurate, urban beggars did not have much of a choice: starvation, banditry, the galleys or emigration.

Thus Herrera did not solve the problem of the vagabonds any more than Giginta did, but the doctor was more realistic in suggesting that controlling them depended upon the active involvement of an enlarged police force. Nor did Herrera view work as a means of reforming the older generation of beggars. Except for the cleaning tasks to be done in the albergue, the deserving poor were exempt from work programs: all they had to do was forage for their food. Work was prescribed for female vagabonds and this work was viewed as a punishment, enforced by the even more severe punishments of chains and stocks. All this was a far cry from the idealistic communities of Giginta where the poor were to be revitalized through labour. It was only when he discussed the young that Herrera retained Giginta's optimism about the redeeming values of labour, but the actual training and employment of the young was not the concern of the albergue officials. Instead there was yet another official, the protector of orphans and the poor, who saw that the children of those who lived in the albergue were employed at seven years of age.

By the end of the century, Vives' belief that work was the salvation of the poor and that secular officials should see that all the poor, including the halt, the lame and the blind, were employed in some fashion, had been modified. What the state offered, at least in Herrera's scheme, was a place to sleep and a begging permit for those who could not maintain themselves through labour, a combination penitentiary–workhouse for wayward females, and an enlarged police force to see that the ablebodied did not beg, and, if they did, that they were punished.

As was the case with Giginta's reform, it was the *procuradores* of the Cortes who first championed Herrera's scheme; in 1595 they sent a memorial to the king asking that albergues be established throughout the kingdom.[104] But the Madrid albergue also gained support in high places: from the president of the Royal Council, Rodrigo Vázquez de Arce; the confessor of the king, Diego de Yepes; the tutor of Prince Philip, García de Loaysa; *catedráticos* of the Universities of Salamanca, Valladolid and Alcalá; and one member of each important religious order. Continuing the support they had given to the earlier hospitals of Giginta, the Jesuits provided three signatures of approval (Herrera, *Amparo*, pp. 245–7). In 1597 the crown sent out 'instructions' to the Castilian cities urging that they found an albergue. The king donated 24,000 ducats and allocated certain other funds to the Madrid foundation, and Herrera reported that he visited the albergue while it was being built. The inscription on the foundation stone of the Madrid albergue, dedicated in 1596, read: 'This temple is dedicated . . . by order and with the aid of Philip II and the favour of Prince Philip III, by decree of Rodrigo Vázquez de Arce, president of Castile, and with the agreement of the rest of the Supreme Council' (Quintana, *Historia de Madrid*, p. 449).

But if Prince Philip favoured the Madrid albergue in 1596, he lost interest in 1598 when he became king. With the installation of a new regime Herrera lost most of his supporters at court as the confidants of Philip II died, were dismissed or sent away from court by his son. In 1598 the Cortes agreed to bestow upon Herrera the magniloquent title of protector and *procurador-general* of the albergues, but the reformer's pleas for financial assistance were unanswered. The title was not confirmed by the crown, nor was Herrera successful in persuading the king to grant him any money despite a constant stream of petitions.[105] Only in 1605 did the crown agree to give him 4,800 ducats in rents and saleable offices in the Indies and the kingdom of Naples, suggesting that he get the remainder of the 16,000 ducats he claimed from the city of Madrid.

The Madrid albergue was not much longer-lived than the earlier beggars' hospital. In 1599 it was used as a plague hospital, and in 1603 the Madrid General Hospital was transferred from its old location in the street of San Jerónimo to the albergue, located in the street of Atocha. This change was precipitated by the Cardinal–Archduke Albert who had purchased the property adjacent to the General Hospital. None too pleased to have the sick housed in such close proximity, the Cardinal–Archduke moved them out and gave the building over to the nuns of Saint Catherine, presumably a quieter and healthier sort of pious community.[106] In 1608 Herrera reported that the albergue housed beggars, the General Hospital and a special workhouse for females suitably entitled La Galera, a title popularized by Mother Magdalena de San Jerónimo in her publication, *Razón y forma de la galera real* (Salamanca, 1608).[107]

Herrera died in 1620 and the symbolic end of his albergues occurred in the same year when the remains of Bernardino de Obregón were placed in the recently completed church of what was

known as the General Hospital of Madrid. The only portion of
Herrera's scheme which seems to have enjoyed a degree of lasting
success was the workhouse for wayward females. In 1656 a crown
report relating the financial condition of the Madrid hospitals
mentioned La Galera where more than seventy females were confined
and set upon weaving and spinning clothes to be used in the other
Madrid hospitals.[108]

However, the name of Herrera and his albergues served as an
example to later generations of reformers who hoped to provide a
hospital for the deserving poor and eliminate vagabonds. In the 1660s
and 1670s, during the regency of Queen Mariana of Austria, a
movement to found beggars' hospitals, now known as *hospicios* or
hospices, re-emerged. The various councils and juntas appointed to
study this matter usually began their reports with 'the active and
efficacious dispositions of Philip II' and the treatise of Herrera.[109] In
1666 the Congregation of the Esclavos del Dulcísimo Nombre de
María presented a petition to the queen, asking that a hospice be
founded in Madrid. The fact that the manuscript mentions similar
foundations in 'other well-ordered republics' suggests that Castilians
were aware of the activities of the French crown, which in 1662 issued
an edict ordering that general hospitals be founded in all large urban
centres of France.

However, it took some time for the Madrid hospice to become
operational. In 1666 all beggars in Madrid were examined, and 800
were found who met all the qualifications of deserving beggars, but it
was not until 1668 that the houses donated by the Conde del Puerto
were refurbished and even then only twenty-four paupers were taken
in. From 1668 to 1673 there was much discussion among councils and
juntas, but the hospice was plagued by a shortage of funds. One junta
estimated that 50,000 ducats would be needed for the two buildings to
house male and female beggars, and that each hospice would need
30,000 ducats in rents to maintain all the people. In 1671 the Royal
Council succinctly summed up the problem:

The first, easily recognizable difficulty is that the establishment of an
albergue for all poor beggars seems impossible, or very difficult, in view of the
great number who are in the court and those who enter every day because of
the fatigue and poverty of the provinces; they would increase still more if
they could find a sure meal and shelter.[110]

Somehow money was found by 1673, much of it from private citizens and the guilds of Madrid. The number of paupers in the hospice was increased to 220, and they were moved in a procession to a new location in the street of Fuencarral. The congregation was placed under royal protection and its name changed to the Dulce Nombre de María y San Fernando, Rey de España, or quite simply, the Hermandad del Hospicio; by 1674 the *hermandad* took as many as 800 paupers.

The poor and their relief became a subject of import again in the eighteenth century and in 1724 the Madrid *hospicio* was remodelled by the architect Pedro de Ribera, whose work still stands today in the street of Fuencarral.[111] The eighteenth-century campaign to provide spiritual and vocational education for the poor and to eradicate idleness appears to have met with greater success than that of the sixteenth century, at least in terms of the number of *hospicios* founded throughout Spain.[112] In the long run, however, the later movement foundered on the familiar obstacle of finances. While one might praise the individuals who donated their money and time to help the poor and admire the ingenuity of those who governed in creating yet another indirect tax to support the poor, these fund-raising schemes were never adequate. Even under the best of circumstances the idea that an institution – whether a hospice, a beggars' hospital or a workhouse – would solve the problem of poverty, unemployment and idleness seems somewhat optimistic, but it was a hope that inspired Spanish reformers for three centuries.

# 3

## The city of Toledo

### THE POPULATION, 1528–1625

The sixteenth-century chronicler, Luis Hurtado, acclaimed Toledo as the heart and principal city of Castile, and, even allowing for the partiality of the author, a native of the city, his judgment was correct ('Memorial', p. 523). When Hurtado wrote his history in 1576, Toledo, known also as the Imperial City, was the second largest city in Castile. One need only glance at a map of Spain to see that the city is situated close to the geographic centre of the peninsula, a location that made it a logical spot for the development of trade, commerce and manufacture. During the reign of Charles V the city was frequently host to the itinerant Castilian court and Cortes, but Philip II convened only one Cortes in Toledo (1559–60) and when the king and his court left the Imperial City in May 1561 Madrid became the unofficial capital of Castile. Philip's decision to establish his court in Madrid, only 70 kilometers to the north of Toledo, had disastrous effects for the prosperity and prestige of the Imperial City. Trade routes, commerce and population began to shift northward, leaving Toledo shorn of most of her pretensions to the title of the principal city of Castile.

Toledo possessed one dignity never lost to Madrid, for the city remained the spiritual centre of Castile, the residence of the archbishop of Toledo, primate of the Spanish church. It is true that in the sixteenth century the Toledo prelates were frequently absent from their diocese in fulfilment of their temporal obligations as councillors to the crown, but absence should not be equated with neglect. Five provincial and diocesan synods were celebrated in Toledo between 1536 and 1622, and the ecclesiastical bureaucracy of the city gave no signs of lacking direction. To assist the prelate in governing his vast domains there was the cathedral chapter, which functioned primarily

93

as a consulting body, and the Council of Government, which dealt with legislative and judicial problems.

Aside from its prestige, the church was an important employer in Toledo. In the sixteenth century the cathedral alone boasted 14 dignitaries, 40 canons, 50 prebendaries, 20 'extravagant' canons, 48 choir chaplains, 37 stipendary priests, 40 choir and altar boys, and 275 chaplains for the numerous chapels in the cathedral, a total of 524 persons. This figure does not include the people employed by the cathedral as painters, clock makers, bell ringers, minstrels, bookbinders, dog catchers and the like, whose number probably rivalled those of the ecclesiastics. In addition to the cathedral hierarchy and the 173 judges, visitors and officials of the Council of Government housed in the archbishop's palace, were the numerous private chaplains, the regular religious and the parish priests.[1]

Toledo was governed by a crown-appointed *corregidor* and a city council composed of 24 *regidores* and 42 *jurados* (Alcocer, *Historia*, fols. cxxii–cxxiii). The *regidores* and the *corregidor* were the actual governors of the city since the *jurados* did not vote, though they were expected to offer their opinions on any issue discussed by the city council. The *jurados* were not totally excluded from the governing process however, since they could, and frequently did, complain directly to the crown about any injustices. Originally each parish of the city had elected two *jurados*, who were to oversee the well-being of the poor and ensure that honesty prevailed in the weighing and measuring of food and merchandise, but by 1521 this office had become the perpetual preserve of wealthy families of the city who also controlled the office of *regidor*.[2] When Hurtado wrote his chronicle, the city council had expanded to 36 *regidores* and 52 *jurados* (pp. 495–6), an increase probably reflecting the crown's efforts to bring more money into its depleted coffers. The office of *jurado* was frequently held by merchants, many of whom were *conversos*,[3] while that of *regidor* was usually reserved for the more established members of the community who could afford to live comfortably without indulging in commerce or trade.

One of the most important changes in sixteenth-century Toledo was the growth of population, a development that can be charted with some degree of accuracy thanks to the numerous censuses carried out by the Castilian crown and the baptismal records kept in many of the city's twenty-one parishes. Before plunging into the details of the censuses, a word should be said about the Castilian method of

Table 1. *Sixteenth-century census figures for the city of Toledo*

|  | 1528 | 1561 | 1571 | 1591 | 1597 |
|---|---|---|---|---|---|
| *Vecinos* | 5,898 | 11,254 | 12,412 | 10,933 | 9,000 |
| Inhabitants | 29,490 | 56,270 | 62,060 | 54,665 | 45,000 |

counting inhabitants. All Castilian censuses were reckoned in terms of *vecinos* or heads of households. The question of how many persons comprised a sixteenth-century household has yet to be resolved, with estimates ranging from four to seven, though five is the traditional multiplier and the one used in this book.[4]

The census figures for Toledo, given in table 1, indicate that the city experienced its greatest increase in population in the second third of the century. From one of the numerous Castilian towns that recorded 5,000 *vecinos* in the first third of the century, by 1561 Toledo had become the third largest of the realm, surpassed only by Seville's 100,000 inhabitants and the 11,624 *vecinos* of Granada.[5] Since most of the Castilian censuses were compiled for fiscal purposes, the persons included in these tabulations varied, depending upon what sort of tax the crown hoped to collect. The census of 1528–40 was the first carried out by the Castilian crown and in Toledo it was limited to that unfortunate group of tax-paying citizens, the *pecheros*. The census of 1561 included the *pecheros* and some of the nobility and secular clergy, so it was a more comprehensive census. Despite the fact that the 1528 census excluded some persons who were counted in 1561, the distortions arising out of a comparison of these two censuses should be minimal since those excluded from taxation in 1528, the secular clergy and the nobility, accounted for only 310 persons in 1561.

But 1561 was not the high point of Toledo's population expansion. Nine years later the crown ordered the *corregidores* to take another census for purposes of distributing and resettling the rebellious Granada *moriscos* throughout Castile. According to the 1571 figures of Tomás González, Toledo boasted 62,060 inhabitants, an increase of 4,500 persons since 1561.[6] It is difficult to be certain exactly what groups the 1571 census included, though judging from the large number of inhabitants the secular clergy and the nobility were counted. Nor is it possible to say how many, if any, of the Granada *moriscos* were included. According to records compiled by the *alcalde mayor* of Toledo, Hernán Velázquez, in September 1571 there were

1,879 *moriscos* in the city and 995 in nearby villages.[7] However, either these figures are incomplete or more *moriscos* continued to come to Toledo because a report of 1581 stated that the number of *moriscos* in the city was 3,032. This figure excluded the slaves, which probably accounted for another 750 people, so the city contained some 3,782 *moriscos* in 1581.[8] The *moriscos* who arrived in 1570–1 suffered from typhus and also what one hospital scribe described as 'weakness', and their mortality rate was very high. In April 1571 the *alcalde* reported that of the total 2,508 *moriscos* sent to the city, 635 had been placed in nearby villages but only 350 of these people were still alive, while of the 1,875 who had stayed in Toledo only 1,150 were still living.[9] Based on these figures, the *moriscos* resettled in Toledo suffered a mortality rate of 40 per cent.

Shortly after the *moriscos* arrived in Toledo the overcrowded city was invaded by another group of outsiders, this time from the north of the peninsula. In 1575 the Toledo *corregidor* complained about the influx of northerners who had migrated southward to escape 'the hunger and famine in the mountains and in the kingdom of Galicia'.[10] In July 1578 the president of the Royal Council, Antonio de Pazos, informed the king of the misery and hardship in Galicia caused by another outbreak of plague.[11] The same year Toledo experienced one of the worst subsistence crises in her history. Perhaps the migrating Galicians carried the plague to the south, but after two years of famine conditions, Toledo was ripe for an outbreak of sickness. The *toledanos* spoke of the *catarro*,[12] a type of infectious influenza, rather than the plague, but it is difficult to be precise about the exact nature of sixteenth-century epidemics. Whatever the disease, it deprived Philip II of his fourth wife, Anne of Austria, and dealt a lethal blow to the city of Toledo.

The severity of the 1578–80 crisis is best illustrated by the curve of parish baptismal rates outlined in figure 1. This graph is a compilation of the baptisms in twelve of the twenty-one Toledo parishes; based on the parish population of 1561, it accounts for 58 per cent of the city's population or 6,618 *vecinos*.[13] The graph begins in a period of famine and sickness that lasted from the harvest of 1556 to the harvest of 1559 so the births in the first two years are unusually low. The abrupt upsurge of 1559–61 probably reflects the presence of the court in Toledo as well as a natural recovery. Since the census information already discussed indicates that the city's population increased in the 1560s and 1570s, the low point of 1578–80 is comparable to or more

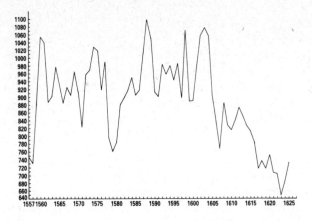

Figure 1. Baptisms in twelve Toledo parishes, 1557–1625

severe than the crisis of the late 1550s. Also, the drop of 1571 indicates that Toledo did not escape the effects of typhus (*febre puncticulari*) spread by the *moriscos* when they were resettled throughout Castile.

The decade of the 1570s brought another misfortune to Toledo when the crown, suffering from the third bankruptcy of the century, trebled the rate of the *alcabalas*, a tax levied on everything sold or exchanged. In 1575 Toledo's share was assessed at 73 million mrs, a sum reduced by 10 million after the city's cries of outrage had been thoroughly aired in the Cortes and the court. After 1575 all the Castilian urban areas suffered heavier taxation, but one expert in sixteenth-century Castilian finances has concluded that Toledo was probably the hardest hit by the 1575 increase, which represented a 50 million mr increase in absolute numbers and tripled the city's tax burden.[14] Since each city's share in the *alcabalas* was determined by its trade, industry and population, in matters of taxation a large population and active trade were dubious assets and the Castilian cities became ever more reticent in providing information to the continually inquisitive and penurious crown.

Many Castilian cities were subjected to a census in 1586 when the crown initiated another investigation concerning the *alcabalas*. A royal commission visited Toledo with instructions to compile a census, but in May 1586 the Toledo *corregidor*, Francisco de Caravajal, wrote to the Council of State suggesting that the census be abandoned, 'taking into consideration the greatness of this city . . . and the novelty and inconvenience caused to the inhabitants by having persons walk through the streets and enter the houses to

record all the *vecinos*'.[15] The recommendation of the *corregidor*
prevailed and Toledo escaped the census of 1586.

The city was equally reluctant to provide census information in
1591 when investigations were underway to determine the city's
share in the most recent crown tax on consumer goods, the *millones*.
Since this tax was to be paid by all citizens, including the usually
exempt clergy and the nobility, the *corregidor* was instructed to list the
exact number of *hidalgos*, the regular and secular clergy as well as the
ordinary *vecinos*. In January 1591 the crown received the estimates
from the Toledo *corregidor*, Perafán de Ribera, which gave the
population of the city as ' 12,000 or 13,000, a few more or less' and
also included the total figures for the clerical establishment. Ribera
ended his report with a note stating that it was impossible to
distinguish between the *hidalgos* and the *pecheros* of the city because
there were no lists that contained this distinction 'since this city is free
of all taxes . . . and all the people are exempt'. Juan Vázquez
continued to press the *corregidor* for more detailed information, and in
March the secretary received another estimate listing 10,933 *vecinos*,
10,000 *hidalgos* (it is impossible to say why 933 *vecinos* were excluded
from *hidalguía*), 739 secular clergy and 1,942 regular clergy. This
estimate contained another note from Ribera who explained that the
only lists of the city's inhabitants were those kept by the parish priests,
which he had used for his latest report, but he had not found any
records for the *hidalgos* and if he pursued the matter to the point of a
public inquiry it would cause 'confusion and notable restlessness' in
the city.[16]

Little has been said about the number of clerics in Toledo. The
1561 census listed only 199 secular clergy while the 1591 census
recorded 739, an increase of 540. However, the 1561 census counted
only those clerics who resided in Toledo and many of the cathedral
canons, prebends and chaplains lived outside the city; the 1591 census
included all the secular clergy, whether they resided in Toledo or
elsewhere. No doubt the number of secular clergy had increased by
1591, but it is difficult to be precise about the increase. But the
number of regular clergy had increased. In 1576 Luis Hurtado
counted 1,494 religious, 1,076 females and 418 males ('Memorial',
pp. 546–52), and by 1591 there were 1,942, an increase of 448, though
the 1,339 females still outnumbered the 603 males.

If the number of regular clergy had increased by 1591, the number
of *vecinos* had not. The 1561 census listed a total of 11,254 *vecinos* that

included 199 secular clerics. If the clergy are subtracted from the total, the 1561 population is 11,055, a figure that should be comparable with the 10,933 *vecinos* of 1591. This means that in the thirty-year interval the city's non-clerical population had decreased by 122 *vecinos*, not a dramatic decline but a decline nonetheless.

The figure for the last census of the century, that of 1597 which listed 9,000 *vecinos*, does indicate a more dramatic decrease in population. In the six-year interval since the census of 1591, the population had decreased by almost 2,000 *vecinos*. However, given the city's reluctance to provide accurate census information in the last two decades of the century, it would be unwise to place too much confidence in these later figures.

A loss of population is not indicated by the curve in figure 1: the number of baptisms in 1598 is the second highest in the century and those of 1603 are the second highest in the figure. The city suffered bouts of sickness in the 1590s, but none to compare with that of 1578–80. Even in 1599–1600, when Toledo was struck by the plague that ravaged the whole of the Iberian peninsula, the baptismal rates do not show a great decline. Though the plague took its toll of victims in the Imperial City, it does not appear to have done as much damage as the crisis of 1578–80, nor did it strike Toledo with the same virulence as in some of the northern cities. The Toledo *corregidor* also judged that Toledo escaped lightly from the plague. In July 1599 he wrote to the Council of State, 'Considering the large number of inhabitants in this city and the many ordinary and extraordinary sicknesses extending through the greater part of these kingdoms, one can say that this city has almost no sickness or sick persons.'[17]

It is only in 1607 that the baptismal rates show a drop equal to that of 1579, and by 1620 they dwindled to a new low level that transformed the overcrowded, bustling city into the sleepy town of 5,000 *vecinos* recorded by Méndez Silva in 1645 (*Población general*, p. 10). The sharp decrease in the years 1606–7 reflects the effects of yet another subsistence crisis. One contemporary described 1606 as 'the most fatal year the peninsula of Spain has experienced in a lack of food and an excess of sickness', while another remembered it as the year 'when all over Spain people had to eat grass'.[18] In Toledo the price of wheat rose to new and dizzying heights,[19] and the hospitals were overwhelmed with patients. The city also lost population through emigration, both voluntary and forced. In 1621 the Toledo *arbitrista* Juan Belluga Moncada complained that 'since 1606 six

thousand *vecinos* [of Toledo] have gone to live at the court'.[20] Possibly
the limited bankruptcy of the city's rents and properties in 1605–6
and the *pósito* or grain reserve in 1608 encouraged people to reflect
upon the future fortunes of the Imperial City, while the return of the
court to Madrid in 1606 after its brief sojourn in Valladolid added yet
another attraction to a city that was relatively undertaxed compared
with Toledo. Between 1609 and 1614 Toledo also lost population
when the *moriscos* were expelled from the peninsula.

The depopulation of Toledo did not go unnoticed by contemporaries. From 1600 to 1630 depopulation and decline were
popular subjects for the Toledo intelligentsia, known collectively as
the Toledo School, who penned a bevy of treatises, memorials and
books in their effort to explain the causes and find solutions.[21] The
causes they gave to explain the city's decline were numerous: plague
and sickness; the growth of Madrid; excessively heavy taxation of
Toledo; unfair competition from cheap foreign textiles that undersold
those produced in Spain, thereby ruining Toledo's textile industries;
social values and financial conditions that encouraged the growth of
unproductive sectors of society (the church, the nobility and the
beggars) at the expense of the more productive ones (the merchants,
the peasants and the artisans). Modern research has begun to
document some of these causes,[22] but until a detailed study of the
city's economy and society is undertaken we shall not know exactly
what caused the spectacular decline of the Imperial City in the early
seventeenth century.

### RICH AND POOR IN 1561

Census figures are useful for determining the number of people who
lived in Toledo, but they shed little light on the character of the city or
its inhabitants. The only census which includes any information
about such matters is that of 1561, where the name of each *vecino* is
recorded in his appropriate parish and, in some instances, the title,
occupation or civil status of the *vecino* is noted.[23] Unfortunately the
Toledo census of 1561, actually a book of some 350 pages, has been
damaged, leaving the top portion of the last 100 pages partially
destroyed. The loss of individual names is regrettable, but since the
scribe recorded the number of *vecinos* at the bottom of each page, it is
possible to give an accurate total of the *vecinos* in each parish. Table 2
provides a list of the city's twenty-one parishes and their respective
number of *vecinos*.

Table 2. *Population of Toledo parishes, 1561*

| Parish | Vecinos | Inhabitants |
|---|---|---|
| S. Andrés | 450 | 2,250 |
| S. Antolín | 107 | 535 |
| S. Bartolomé | 321 | 1,605 |
| S. Cipriano | 520 | 2,600 |
| S. Cristóbal | 238 | 1,190 |
| S. Ginés | 99 | 495 |
| S. Isidoro | 664 | 3,320 |
| S. Juan Baptista | 116 | 580 |
| S. Justo | 590 | 2,950 |
| Sta. Leocadia | 544 | 2,720 |
| S. Lorenzo | 789 | 3,945 |
| Sta. María Magdalena | 641 | 3,205 |
| S. Martín | 348 | 1,740 |
| S. Miguel | 771 | 3,855 |
| S. Nicolás | 612 | 3,060 |
| S. Pedro | 378 | 1,890 |
| S. Román | 437 | 2,185 |
| S. Salvador | 129 | 645 |
| Santiago | 1,495 | 7,475 |
| Sto. Tomé | 1,727 | 8,635 |
| S. Vicente | 278 | 1,390 |
| Total | 11,254 | 56,270 |

The city of Toledo was, as it still remains, a maze of tortuous, narrow streets with buildings crowded into every available inch of space. Some idea of the complexity of the city streets is provided by the plan drawn by El Greco in the early seventeenth century, reproduced as figure 2.[24] The only point of orientation for the uninitiated is the cathedral, situated a bit east of the approximate centre of the city. The cathedral is flanked by the city hall and the archbishop's palace while the main business area stretches northeastward to the Plaza de Zocodover. Utilizing the plan of El Greco, the information given by Luis Hurtado in his 1576 history ('Memorial', pp. 481–576), and the eighteenth-century parochial divisions given by a modern historian,[25] an outline of the sixteenth-century parishes has been reconstructed and is reproduced as figure 3. Given the vagaries of sixteenth-century parochial divisions, when two parishes shared a public square, a street, or even a house, an exact repartition is nearly impossible, but the intention of the drawing is merely to give a general orientation to the location and size of the city parishes.

The disparity of size between the parishes underlines the need for

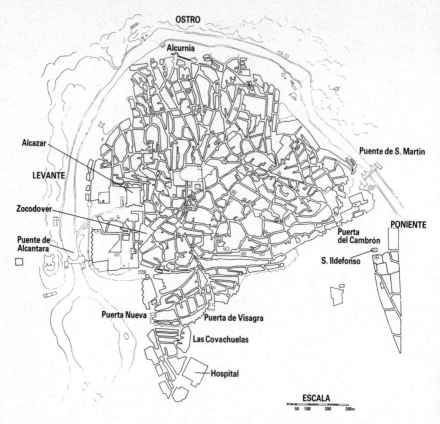

Figure 2. El Greco's plan of Toledo (first decade of the seventeenth century)

the parochial redistribution recommended by the Tridentine decrees
(sess. 21, caps. 4, 5), a proposal frequently reiterated in the Toledo
diocesan legislation,[26] though the redistribution apparently was not
realized until 1841. In terms of geographical extension and the
number of *vecinos*, the parishes of Santo Tomé and Santiago del
Arrabal were the largest in the city. The parishioners of Santo Tomé
ranged from the wealthy conde de Fuensalida, whose palace occupied
a sizeable portion of the parish, to the more humble artisans and
labourers who took up much less space by crowding into the remnants
of the old *Judería* or Jewish quarter, known in the sixteenth century as
the *Barrio Nuevo*. The parish of Santiago, situated at the northern edge
of the city, contained a more homogeneous population of artisans,

Figure 3. Toledo parishes in the sixteenth century

labourers and workers. Alongside these large parishes of some 1,500 to 1,700 *vecinos* were the tiny central parishes of San Ginés and San Juan Baptista which contained no more than five or ten streets, a parish church and 100 to 117 *vecinos*.

The 1561 census was compiled by the crown scribe, Miguel Mexia, from twenty-one lists drawn up by the parish priests of the city. Some parish lists, like that drawn up by the energetic chronicler Luis Hurtado for the parish of San Vicente, included the occupation, title or civil status of nearly all their parishioners. In other larger, less

Table 3. *Percentage of widows in Toledo parishes, 1561*

| Parish | Widows | Percentage in parish |
|--------|--------|----------------------|
| S. Andrés | 95 | 21.11 |
| S. Antolín | 11 | 10.28 |
| S. Bartolomé | 60 | 18.69 |
| S. Cipriano | 76 | 14.61 |
| S. Cristóbal | 47 | 19.74 |
| S. Ginés | 27 | 27.27 |
| S. Isidoro | 108 | 16.26 |
| S. Juan Baptista | 20 | 17.24 |
| S. Justo | 99 | 16.77 |
| Sta. Leocadia | 178 | 32.72 |
| S. Lorenzo | 225 | 28.51 |
| Sta. María Magdalena | 79 | 12.32 |
| S. Martín | 41 | 11.78 |
| S. Miguel | 128 | 16.60 |
| S. Nicolás | 93 | 15.19 |
| S. Pedro | 43 | 11.37 |
| S. Román | 101 | 23.11 |
| S. Salvador | 32 | 24.80 |
| Santiago | 252 | 16.85 |
| Sto. Tomé | 389 | 22.52 |
| S. Vicente | 74 | 26.61 |
| Total | 2,178 | 19.33 |

distinguished parishes, such as Santiago, San Isidoro and Santa María Magdalena, little more than the parishioner's name was recorded with an infrequent notation for the few distinguished citizens.

The only consistent notation made throughout the entire census was that of widow. Table 3 gives the parochial distribution and total percentage of these bereaved females, but these figures may be an underestimate because of the partially destroyed pages of six parishes: San Juan Baptista, San Justo, Santa María Magdalena, San Román, Santiago, and San Vicente. If the total percentage of widows in Toledo, 19.33 per cent, seems high, it is not startling when compared to other Castilian cities. In 1561 the number of widows in Medina del Campo amounted to 21 per cent of the population; in Burgos, 20.1 per cent; in Segovia, 19 per cent and in Valladolid, 15 per cent.[27] An abundance of widows was common to all Castile, perhaps because men died earlier, or perhaps because Castile's imperial obligations demanded a constant supply of manpower to fill the armies and garrisons of Europe and to conquer and settle the New World. Also, some men simply abandoned the wife and family and moved on to greener pastures. Three female patients who entered the Hospital of Tavera in 1571 reported that their husbands were absent: one was reported to have gone to the Indies while the other two had mysteriously disappeared without a trace.[28] Judging from the reproofs of the moralists and the verbiage of the Toledo diocesan legislation,[29] bigamy and desertion of one's family were not uncommon. The parochial percentages of widows reveals that they preferred the more stable, wealthy parishes of the city, perhaps because these parishes provided more security or charitable assistance.

Between the widows and the numerous females listed as alone or unmarried in the 1561 census, Toledo appears to have been a man-poor society, or, as Luis Hurtado observed, there was 'an excessive number and notable quantity of women' ('Memorial', p. 498). One consequence of this surfeit was the proliferation of female religious orders. In 1576 and 1591 the number of female religious was more than double that of the males, though many women included in these estimates did not take formal religious vows. It was not until 1582 that the pious congregations known as *beatas* were officially classified as tertiary religious orders[30] and some women lived a communal life of withdrawal without taking any formal vows. When Sixtus V ordered that no lay woman could reside in convents, Cardinal Quiroga founded Nuestra Señora del Refugio, a house where twenty-four lay women – widows, young women awaiting marriage or married women involved in divorce or other legal proceeding with their absent spouses – might live a cloistered life under the supervision of the Augustinian prioress of Santa Monica (Salazar de Mendoza, *Mendoza*, p. 309). Thus the figures for the female religious include many women and girls who devoted themselves to pious activities or who merely lived apart from the secular world, temporarily or permanently.

Aside from the widows, the other individuals who stood a good chance of consistent notation throughout the census are persons of wealth and social distinction. The total number and parochial distribution of these persons is given in table 4. The first column, the nobles, includes all the dons, doñas, señores, counts and marquis except those who were also clerics; thus don Juan de la Cerda, a

Table 4. *Distribution and percentage of persons of wealth and social distinction in Toledo parishes, 1561*

| Parish | Nobles | Regidores | Jurados | Professionals | Secular clergy | Merchants | Total | % of parish population |
|---|---|---|---|---|---|---|---|---|
| S. Andrés | 10 | 2 | 2 | 22 | 27 | 2 | 65 | 14.44 |
| S. Antolín | 3 | 1 | 1 | 5 | 13 | 0 | 23 | 21.49 |
| S. Bartolomé | 7 | 2 | 1 | 9 | 23 | 3 | 45 | 14.01 |
| S. Cipriano | 2 | 0 | 0 | 0 | 1 | 0 | 3 | 0.57 |
| S. Cristóbal | 5 | 1 | 0 | 0 | 3 | 0 | 9 | 3.78 |
| S. Ginés | 0 | 0 | 0 | 1 | 0 | 13 | 14 | 14.14 |
| S. Isidoro | 1 | 0 | 0 | 3 | 0 | 0 | 4 | 0.60 |
| S. Juan Baptista | 1 | 0 | 5 | 3 | 3 | 0 | 12 | 10.34 |
| S. Justo | 11 | 2 | 1 | 7 | 30 | 0 | 51 | 8.64 |
| Sta. Leocadia | 6 | 1 | 2 | 7 | 5 | 8 | 29 | 5.33 |
| S. Lorenzo | 8 | 0 | 5 | 19 | 28 | 2 | 62 | 7.85 |
| Sta. María Magdalena | 0 | 1 | 0 | 3 | 1 | 0 | 5 | 0.78 |
| S. Martín | 5 | 0 | 0 | 0 | 1 | 0 | 6 | 1.72 |
| S. Miguel | 1 | 0 | 1 | 5 | 10 | 0 | 17 | 2.26 |
| S. Nicolás | 0 | 0 | 8 | 2 | 1 | 0 | 11 | 1.79 |
| S. Pedro | 2 | 0 | 0 | 1 | 7 | 0 | 10 | 2.64 |
| S. Román | 5 | 1 | 6 | 9 | 12 | 0 | 33 | 7.55 |
| S. Salvador | 7 | 0 | 3 | 2 | 12 | 2 | 26 | 20.15 |
| Santiago | 0 | 0 | 0 | 7 | 0 | 1 | 8 | 0.53 |
| Sto. Tomé | 34 | 0 | 6 | 21 | 15 | 0 | 76 | 4.40 |
| S. Vicente | 3 | 2 | 2 | 6 | 7 | 80 | 100 | 35.97 |
| Total | 111 | 13 | 43 | 132 | 199 | 111 | 609 | 5.41 |

*Rank according to percentage*

1. S. Vicente – 35.97
2. S. Antolín – 21.49
3. S. Salvador – 20.15
4. S. Andrés – 14.44
5. S. Ginés – 14.14
6. S. Bartolomé – 14.01
7. S. Juan Baptista – 10.34

8. S. Justo – 8.64
9. S. Lorenzo – 7.85
10. S. Román – 7.55
11. Sta. Leocadia – 5.33
12. Sto. Tomé – 4.40
13. S. Cristóbal – 3.78
14. S. Pedro – 2.64

15. S. Miguel – 2.26
16. S. Nicolás – 1.79
17. S. Martín – 1.72
18. Sta. María Magdalena – 0.78
19. S. Isidoro – 0.60
20. S. Cipriano – 0.57
21. Santiago – 0.53

cathedral canon, has been placed in column 5 with the clerics. The census of 1561 listed only those people who lived in the city and some of the secular clergy, *regidores* and *jurados* resided elsewhere. Thus the totals for columns 2, 3 and 5 appear to be too low when compared with information taken from other sources. In addition, some municipal authorities had other titles and occupations under which they have been listed. For example, eight *jurados* in the parish of San Vicente were also merchants who appear in the figures for the latter column, and the conde of Cifuentes, who was a *regidor*, has been listed with the nobles. Persons included as professionals are those with a degree – *maestro, licenciado, médico*, doctor – and the scribes, notaries, *fiscales, procuradores* and *mayordomos*. The clerics range from the wealthy cathedral canons to the more humble parish priests, though none of the regular clergy were mentioned in the 1561 census, so this column is limited to the secular clergy. Those included in the last column, the merchants, are persons listed as *mercaderes*, not the small retailers (*tratantes*).

The total number of people listed in table 4 is 609 or 5.41 per cent of the 1561 population. While it cannot be said that every *doña* was wealthy, that every cleric achieved social distinction, or that every wealthy citizen of Toledo falls into one of the categories of table 4, it seems reasonable to assume that the table reflects a sizable portion of the city's wealthy and prestigious inhabitants. The largest group included in the table are the 199 secular clergy, though, considering that in 1549 Blas Ortiz counted 400 ecclesiastics in the cathedral alone, this is a small portion of the total number of clerics who derived an income from the rents of the Toledo archdiocese. While the secular clergy formed the largest group, it cannot be said that the city was overrun by churchmen, but the addition of the regular religious, who probably accounted for some 1,200 persons in 1561, gives the church a considerable representation. The second largest group are the professionals (132) who are followed by the equally distributed nobles and merchants (111 in each group). The sizable group of merchants indicates that Toledo was still an active centre of trade and commerce in 1561.

The parochial figures in the table suggest that persons of similar interest and social background clustered together. This is particularly true for the merchants who clearly preferred the parish of San Vicente, located close to the commercial centre of the city. These same parishioners also dominated the ranks of the city council, with

two *regidores* and ten *jurados* (including the eight listed as merchants on
the table). The combined total of the wealthy and prestigious citizens
in this parish, plus the fact that it had a small parish population of
only 278 *vecinos*, makes San Vicente the wealthiest parish of Toledo.

The parochial delimitations do not give an accurate picture of the
living pattern of the city, for the persons of means lived near two focal
points, the cathedral and the city hall, forming what might be termed
an inner core of wealth which overlapped parochial boundaries. In
the case of the six southern parishes, the wealthy *vecinos*, many of them
clerics, settled as close as possible to the cathedral, abandoning the
outer fringes of the parish to the poor. The northern parishes
presented a more solid front which extended from the cathedral to the
northern boundaries of the parishes of Santa Leocadia, San Vicente
and part of San Nicolás. An outline of this nucleus of wealth and social
distinction is given in figure 4.

To speak of an inner core of wealth is, of course, to simplify a very
complex living pattern. San Pedro, a parish that is centrally located,
was largely non-residential in character with the bulk of its space
occupied by the cathedral, the Hospital del Rey and the shops and
storerooms of merchants who lived in other parishes. Living space in
the city was at such a premium, however, that even the basements of
the shops and storehouses were occupied, presumably by those
persons who could not afford the luxury of light and fresh air. Nearly
all the parishes had pockets of poverty as the poor filled up any
available living space: they lived inside the city gates, in the porter's
lodge of monasteries, in the doorways of buildings such as the
carpentry shop and in the overcrowded sixteenth-century slums
known as *corrales*. Despite the omnipresence of the poor and the
inevitable palace that falls outside the limits described in figure 4, it is
still arguable that the majority of Toledo's most prestigious citizens
preferred to live in the area outlined in figure 4.

For the majority of the population, the 75 per cent not included in
tables 3 and 4, the 1561 census is not very informative. Only the
parishes of San Lorenzo, San Andrés and San Vicente contain
consistent notations as to occupation, and in some instances occupations are not given even in these parishes. For instance, in San
Vicente, with a population of 287 *vecinos*, there are 104 *vecinos* not
included in the earlier tables. Of these 104 *vecinos* only 63 are given an
occupation, with the remainder described as widowers or maidens
(*doncellas*) or not described at all because their name or occupation

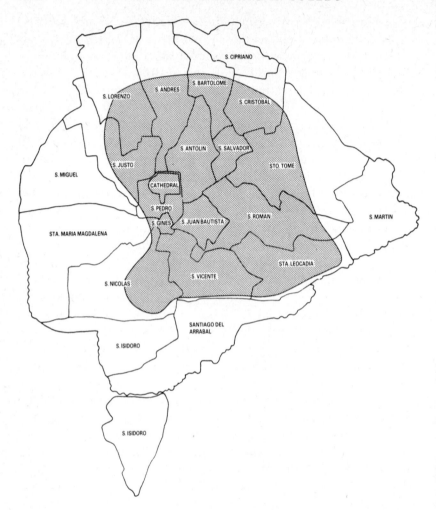

Figure 4. Nucleus of wealth in Toledo, 1561

has been lost in the destruction of the original document. Thus in all three parishes the total number of *vecinos* whose occupation is known amounts to 663.

Scant as this information is, it can be combined with the description given by Luis Hurtado in 1576 to provide some insight into the types of work that occupied the more humble citizens, those who sustained themselves by manual labour. As priest of San Vicente, the parish of merchants, Hurtado was familiar with the business affairs of the city, and his chronicle is full of observations about employment and prosperity or the converse, unemployment and poverty. Hurtado was probably concerned about such matters because 1576 was a bad year for business in Toledo, thanks to the crown's decision to suspend all its payments prior to the bankruptcy of 1578. The three enterprises mentioned by Hurtado as employers of the majority of 'the common people' were the manufacture of silk and wool, the retail business as practised by shopkeepers and tradesmen, and the work offered by *caballeros* and winegrowers.

The 1561 census gives a total of 265 textile workers: 100 weavers of velvet and silk, 85 weavers of unspecified material, 57 dyers, 19 spinners, 2 wool combers and 2 carders. While silk weavers are the most numerous group, the numbers are too small to allow any generalizations as to the relative importance of silk or wool. However, the seventeenth-century *arbitrista*, Damián de Olivares, reported that the Toledo silk industry had employed 20,000 people, a figure that accounts for nearly one-third of the city's population at its highest recorded level in 1571 and makes silk the largest industry of the city.[31]

Judging from Hurtado's narration, the silk industry was not flourishing in 1576. Originally silk was brought from Granada, Murcia and Valencia to Toledo where it was spun, wound, dyed and woven into velvet, taffeta, damask, satin and silk cloth. The Granada Rebellion of 1568 had cut off one important supplier of raw silk; the mulberry trees had been destroyed and the *moriscos*, who tended both the trees and the silkworms, had been resettled. To help fill the need for raw silk and possibly to employ the *moriscos* who came to Toledo and its province in 1571, some regions around the city attempted to produce silk, but this had not proven to be very successful. However, the void left by the decline of Granada's silk production was eventually filled by Valencia which became a large supplier of Toledo.[32]

Nor did the priest find the wool industry in a prosperous state, or at least that segment of the wool industry devoted to making woollen hats (*bonetes*). Hurtado reports that when Charles I visited Toledo 'a squadron of 3,500 bonnet makers were there to welcome him' ('Memorial', p. 525), while in his own day a mere 100 people were involved in the trade. Hurtado attributed this decline to a change in fashion – people of the 1570s preferred velvet caps (*gorras*) to woollen hats – and the inability of the Toledo merchants to find the fine wool that they used to buy in Segovia. Sebastián de Covarrubias confirms Hurtado's observations about the change in fashionable headwear and also mentions that many of Toledo's woollen hats were exported, possibly to the Moors in North Africa (*Tesoro*: 'bonete', 'gorras'). The shift from wool to velvet must have been well underway by 1561 because only thirty-six bonnet makers are listed in the 1561 census.

As for the small shopkeepers who lived by retailing, they were especially abundant in San Lorenzo which housed forty-nine tradesmen while the other two parishes had seven shopkeepers. For these people 1561 must have been a prosperous year, what with the presence of the court in Toledo, but in 1576 Hurtado noted that many shops were empty and closed because of 'large debts and little capital' ('Memorial', p. 575).

Hurtado's final group of employers were the *caballeros* and the winegrowers and few of the people employed by these two groups are included in the three parishes. Only the prestigious shieldbearers, who accounted for thirty *vecinos*, and four grooms are mentioned. Possibly the thirty-nine workers (*trabajadores*) of San Lorenzo worked in the vineyards, but they might have been employed in many places.

In addition to the large employers mentioned by Hurtado, Toledo had numerous small industries. One was leather which was made into saddles, bridles, halters, harnesses, winebottles, shoes and gloves. Some of the most beautiful choir screens in Spain are found in the Toledo cathedral and work in metals had a long tradition in the city; there were makers of armour, swords, pikes, lances, window screens and locks as well as cutlers. Those who worked in less base metals were the coin makers of the Casa de la Moneda and the silver- and goldsmiths. Wood was worked by sculptors, carpenters, turners and the makers of boxes, clogs and crossbows. Books and the Bull of the Crusade were printed in the city, and at the lower levels of the textile industry were the many tailors, stocking and lace makers, embroiderers and those who worked in esparto grass. Water carriers, porters and doormen were probably legion.

The construction industry flourished throughout the sixteenth century, but the 1561 census does not indicate that it employed nearly as many people as textiles; in the three parishes there were nine masons, eleven carpenters, three stonecutters and one peon. Nonetheless construction or remodelling of hospitals, chapels, churches and houses must have provided employment for many people. In addition to these private buildings were the public works programmes undertaken by the city. In the 1560s streets and squares were enlarged and in the 1570s, under the direction of *corregidor* Juan

Gutiérrez Tello (1570–8), an enormous public works project was undertaken.[33] The new *alhondiga* or grain exchange was built, and the city hall, jails, bridges, and walls were repaired, just to mention the larger projects. Until the 1580s Toledo utilized much of its abundant labour force in building projects.

The final group of people to be considered in 1561 are the poor. If information about occupations in the 1561 census is meagre, it is non-existent for the poor. Only Luis Hurtado has noted that three parishioners of San Vicente were poor and another begged alms. In May 1558, when the city was in the depths of one of its periods of famine and sickness, parish poor lists were drawn up to determine how many persons were in need of public assistance.[34] Unfortunately the actual lists have disappeared, but the number of needy persons counted in each parish has been preserved. Since only three years separate the poor lists of 1558 and the census of 1561, it seems reasonable to assume that the parish population did not undergo any radical change in such a short time. For the compilation of table 5, which indicates the percentage of needy persons in each parish, the 1561 parish population has been utilized, although the percentages have been figured on the basis of inhabitants rather than *vecinos* since the original poor lists included men, women and children.

The percentage of poor in each parish illustrates that the eastern side of the city, the area that housed many of the workers of the city, was the poorest. San Miguel, San Cipriano, the southern half of San Cristóbal, San Andrés, San Justo, San Bartolomé and San Lorenzo housed bonnet makers, weavers, spinners, dyers, leather tanners and drovers. Santa María Magdalena not only housed the poor, but also provided them with taverns, inns and eating houses. On the western side of the city was the extremely poor and populous *Barrio Nuevo* which extended from the western edge of Santo Tomé into the parish of San Román. Relegated to the perimeter of the city, the poor formed an outer fringe of crowded humanity which encircled the city's inner core of wealth and social distinction.

Two parishes that should be considered as among the poorest of Toledo are San Isidoro and Santiago del Arrabal, neither of which is ranked very high in the 1558 poor lists. Both these parishes are in the north, huddled under the shadows cast by the heights of the interior city. Luis Hurtado observed that the parish church of Santiago had so few chapels 'because the parishioners are poor and working people' ('Memorial', p. 529), while some years earlier, Sebastián de

Table 5. *Percentage of poor in Toledo parishes, 1558*

| Parish | Inhabitants (1561) | Number of poor (1558) | % of poor |
|---|---|---|---|
| S. Andrés | 2,250 | 398 | 17.68 |
| S. Antolín | 535 | 85 | 15.79 |
| S. Bartolomé | 1,605 | 492 | 30.65 |
| S. Cipriano | 2,600 | 573 | 22.03 |
| S. Cristóbal | 1,190 | 370 | 31.09 |
| S. Ginés | 495 | 38 | 7.67 |
| S. Isidoro | 3,320 | 154 | 4.63 |
| S. Juan Baptista | 580 | 64 | 11.03 |
| S. Justo | 2,950 | 555 | 18.81 |
| Sta. Leocadia | 2,720 | 508 | 18.67 |
| S. Lorenzo | 3,945 | 998 | 25.29 |
| Sta. María Magdalena | 3,205 | 723 | 22.55 |
| S. Martín | 1,740 | 232 | 13.33 |
| S. Miguel | 3,855 | 1,283 | 33.28 |
| S. Nicolás | 3,060 | 663 | 21.66 |
| S. Pedro | 1,890 | 251 | 13.28 |
| S. Román | 2,185 | 575 | 26.31 |
| S. Salvador | 645 | 76 | 11.78 |
| Santiago | 7,475 | 1,110 | 14.84 |
| Sto. Tomé | 8,635 | 1,719 | 19.90 |
| S. Vicente | 1,390 | 238 | 17.12 |
| Total | 56,270 | 11,105 | 19.73 |

*Rank according to percentage*

1. S. Miguel – 33.28
2. S. Cristóbal – 31.09
3. S. Bartolomé – 30.65
4. S. Román – 26.31
5. S. Lorenzo – 25.29
6. Sta. María Magdalena – 22.55
7. S. Cipriano – 22.03
8. S. Nicolás – 21.66
9. Sto. Tomé – 19.90
10. S. Justo – 18.81
11. Sta. Leocadia – 18.67
12. S. Andrés – 17.68
13. S. Vicente – 17.12
14. S. Antolín – 15.79
15. Santiago – 14.84
16. S. Martín – 13.33
17. S. Pedro – 13.28
18. S. Salvador – 11.78
19. S. Juan Baptista – 11.03
20. S. Ginés – 7.67
21. S. Isidoro – 4.63

Horozco, who related the Toledo festivities held in 1555 to celebrate the conversion of England to the Catholic faith, congratulated these parishioners for their contribution 'which they performed very well for such poor people'.[35] The parish of Santiago fell within the confines of the city walls as did a portion of San Isidoro, but the latter parish also included two extramural settlements known as Azucaica and Covachuelas.

In the second half of the sixteenth century San Isidoro was the fastest growing parish of Toledo. Comparing its baptismal rates with those of a more stable interior parish like San Justo, plotted in figures 5(a) and (b), the growth of San Isidoro is spectacular. But even comparing San Isidoro's baptismal rates with another poor parish, Santiago del Arrabal,[36] plotted in figure 5(c), San Isidoro's growth is impressive. In 1561 Santiago was the second largest parish in Toledo and perhaps for this reason the baptismal records for the early years of the century are non-existent or too poorly kept to be used with confidence. However, by utilizing the few reliable baptismal records of the 1550s and 1560s, it can be seen that the parish had a large population in these decades. It maintained a high level of baptisms in the 1570s and 1580s, but did not experience the spectacular increase of San Isidoro, which by the 1580s had an average baptismal rate of 168 as opposed to 105 in the 1560s, a 60 per cent increase. On the other hand both poor parishes were more productive in the last quarter of the century than the relatively wealthy interior parish of San Justo which achieved its highest baptismal rate in the 1560s. This difference can probably be explained by the high rate of immigration experienced by the poorer parishes in the last thirty years of the century.

The great expansion of San Isidoro is partially explicable in terms of the geographic location of Toledo. Perched on a hill with two-thirds of its perimeter surrounded by the deep, fast-flowing Tajo River, the northern extramural settlements were the only places the city could expand. As early as 1538 the city requested and was granted a royal *cédula* decreeing that no more hospitals, convents or monasteries be built within the confines of the city walls because of a shortage of living space.[37] In 1546, the architect–administrator of the recently founded Hospital of Tavera, Bartolomé de Bustamante, complained that he could find no building space within the city so he was forced to build outside the city walls.[38] When Philip and his court descended upon the city from 1559 to 1561, the Toledo poet, Sebastián de Horozco, complained:

> We have no room in our houses,
> And we suffer inquietude;
> We cannot walk in the streets should we want to,
> Such is the multitude. (*Cancionero*, pp. 182–3)

Philip's brief stay in the Imperial City probably convinced him of the unsuitability of Toledo as a permanent residence, for even without

Figure 5(a). Baptisms in the parish of San Justo

Figure 5(b). Baptisms in the parish of San Isidoro

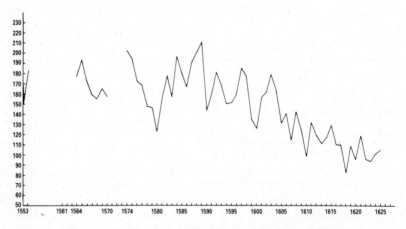

Figure 5(c). Baptisms in the parish of Santiago del Arrabal

the court Toledo was a very crowded place, awkward to provision and difficult to expand.

Thus the parish of San Isidoro, half outside the city walls, was a natural spot for expansion. For the most part the parishioners were humble persons who worked as gardeners, day labourers, water carriers and potters. Many of the remnants of Toledo's moorish population, the *mudejares*, lived in San Isidoro and many of the Granada *moriscos* settled there in the 1570s.[39] The parish received immigrants from all over the Iberian peninsula, especially poor persons from the north. Since the area was adjacent to the highways to the north, it did a great trade in provisioning and lodging travellers, yet it also suffered the hazards inflicted by a constant stream of the most unsavoury elements of society – the muleteers, peddlars, vagabonds and delinquents.

The city council used the parish as a convenient dumping ground for all the morally or physically suspect persons not welcomed in the city proper. The prostitutes, the young boys with contagious skin diseases, and the beggars were all housed in the parish of San Isidoro. When the plague struck in 1599, the San Lázaro, also located in the parish, was converted to a plague hospital. Though the actions of the city council would seem to indicate that they considered the parish as impermeable to physical contagion, it was San Isidoro that suffered the highest mortality rates from the plague.[40] While it is difficult to explain their low percentage in table 5, San Isidoro and its neighbour, Santiago del Arrabal, were two of the poorest parishes of the city and should be included in the fringe areas of poverty that surrounded the city in 1561.

How does the living pattern of Toledo compare with that of other Castilian cities and towns? In Medina del Campo, Segovia and Talavera de la Reina the poor were concentrated in peripheral areas as in Toledo, while in Valladolid, where the poor colonized central parishes, the pattern was distinct.[41] Spatial segregation between rich and poor characterized many cities of Europe. Whether the poor were relegated to peripheral parishes or managed to gain entry to the centre of the city, they lived in very crowded, insanitary and unhealthy conditions, while the more prosperous citizens enjoyed the luxury of space, fresh air and a modicum of sanitation.[42]

Can the poverty level of Toledo be compared with that of other cities? Comparing poverty levels of sixteenth-century cities is a tricky business unless the terms of comparison are defined. In Toledo the 11,105 people who received assistance in 1558 represent what one historian has termed the conjunctural poor.[43] These are the people temporarily in need of assistance because some crisis – a famine, an epidemic, or a work stoppage – threw them out of work or drove the price of grain so high that they could no longer afford to buy bread. A subsistence crisis also precipitated migrations as starving country people sought relief in the cities where charitable resources and grain supplies were more abundant, and these migrations added still more people to the city's relief rolls. In periods of abundant grain and employment these same people, whether artisans, apprentices, widows, unskilled labourers or outsiders, could eke out an existence, albeit on a subsistence level. In addition to the people who received temporary relief were the structural poor whom sixteenth-century society recognized as recipients of more permanent support: people unable to earn a living because of a physical defect, the aged, orphans, or impoverished widows.

Obviously these two groups overlapped; an artisan with yet one more child might fall from a position of subsistence to dependence. Still a distinction should be made because the 20 per cent poverty level of Toledo in 1558 is undoubtedly higher than it was in years of prosperity or good harvests. In fact the poverty level of 1558 was higher than it was in 1556 when the city compiled the first poor lists in what was to be a three-year battle against scarce grain and sickness. In December 1556 the city counted 10,608 needy people; in May 1558 there were 11,105, an increase of 497 people. Thus the poverty level of the city increased as the crisis continued. While the city of Toledo might keep records for the number of people in need of relief during a crisis, it did not compile poor lists in periods of normal harvests and good health. In these years relief was left to the numerous confraternities, hospitals and charitable endowments whose record books may or may not survive and may or may not contain some notation as to the number of people they assisted. For this reason it is difficult to give a figure for the number of structural poor in Toledo.

As for the poverty level of other Castilian cities, it is known that in 1561 Medina del Campo counted 8.89 per cent of its population as poor, Valladolid 9.54 per cent and Segovia 15.74 per cent, while in 1559 Málaga registered 22.60 per cent and in 1557 Trujillo counted 50 per cent.[44] The large variation in these figures, from 9 per cent to 50 per cent, gives one pause for thought. According to the history of Juan de Mariana, 1557 was a year of great scarcity in almost all Spain and in 1558 many people died of the plague: 'This illness began in Murcia, spread to the city of Valencia and, not long afterward, to the city of Burgos. It was some years before it was eliminated completely' ('Historia', p. 393). Is it possible that 1559 was a bad year in Málaga, for instance, as it was in Toledo, Valencia and the villages near Valladolid?[45] If this is the case the poverty level of Málaga would be artificially high as it represents the level during a period of sickness and scarce grain. This issue is worth considering if valid comparisons of poverty levels in Castilian cities are to be made, or if the Castilian figures are to be compared with those of other cities and towns of Europe such as Lyons, Verona, Worcester, Norwich and Warwick, where modern research has found the level of the conjunctural poor at between 20 per cent and 30 per cent and the structural poor at between 4 per cent and 8 per cent.[46] It can at least be said that the Toledo figure for 1558 fits in well with the percentages for the first group.

### THE RELIEF OF THE POOR

A discussion of poor relief in Toledo must begin with a question: did Toledo enact a poor law in 1540 as did many cities in Old Castile? Unfortunately, the minutes for the city council meetings, which would answer this question, are non-existent for this period. And in the correspondence of the archbishop of Toledo, Juan Tavera, only Madrid is specifically mentioned as having enacted a poor law, though the cardinal did say that in December instructions had been sent out to all the cities of the realm (see above, chapter 1, notes 31, 34). Salazar de Mendoza reports that the cardinal's accounts for 1540–1 showed a substantial expenditure for poor relief – 45,000 ducats and 33,000 *fanegas* of wheat – which was given to feed the people who lived within the cardinal's archdiocese as well as 'the Asturians and people from the mountains' who migrated southward in search of food (*Tavera*, pp. 230–2). The cardinal's gift was used not only to feed the poor, but also to place them in hospitals or specially designated houses: four in Toledo, six in Madrid, two in Talavera and Alcalá de Henares, and one in Guadalajara, Ciudad Real, and Alcaraz. According to this report, Toledo was one of many cities and towns in New Castile that implemented a poor law in 1540–1.

Cardinal Tavera was in Toledo in late December of 1540 which may be when the city was persuaded to adopt 'the new order' for relieving the poor, because by 1541 the city had proclaimed a poor law. This date is substantiated by a manuscript written by a Franciscan, Luis de Scala, in 1542 that defended the rights of beggars 'who had formerly walked about the city begging alms at doorways'. Unfortunately this manuscript appears to have been destroyed in the fire of the Toledo Franciscan monastery San Juan de los Reyes, but according to the records compiled by later friars it began with the observation, 'The past year of 1541 a provision was brought to Toledo. . . .'[47] In the same year the brotherhood that operated the small hospice of San Miguel reported that they had been ordered to take in poor beggars whose expenses for food and drink were paid by the city. The brotherhood was instructed to let no one leave the hospice 'to beg anything', and that if anyone left the hospice without a licence they need not be readmitted.[48] The small hospitals of San Miguel and the Virgen y Madre de Dios apparently served as two of the four hospitals mentioned by Salazar de Mendoza as places where beggars were housed in Toledo.

The fact that a Franciscan wrote a treatise opposing the Toledo poor law is no reason to conclude that the reform was unpopular with all the Toledo intelligentsia. The Toledo humanist and schoolmaster, Alejo Venegas, published two books that contained clear support for the new order. In *Agonía del tránsito de la muerte* (Toledo, 1537) Venegas accused healthy beggars of two sins: the first was the 'grave sin of laziness' and the second was theft because they took the alms of those who deserved relief.[49] In a later book, *Primera parte de las diferencias de libros* (Toledo, 1540), Venegas outlined a programme for eliminating healthy beggars that sounds very much like the programme defended by Juan de Robles in 1545. In addition, this book was written 'by special commission and order of the very illustrious Cardinal don Juan Tavera'.[50] Master Venegas was acquainted with other Toledo humanists. One was the cathedral canon, Doctor Juan de Vergara, summoned before the Inquisition for heretical opinions and his approval of Erasmian ideas, who, one can surmise, would favour the elimination of public begging.[51] Another was the cathedral dignitary Pedro de Campo, a friend to both Venegas and Vergara and a doctor of theology at the Toledo university.

The Toledo reform was similar to that of Zamora. Public begging was forbidden and those deemed deserving of relief were placed in hospitals or houses where they were provided with the necessities of life. No doubt alms were solicited from the Toledo parishioners, but, as in Zamora, no consolidation of charitable resources into one central fund occurred. Cardinal Tavera tried to effect at least a minor consolidation in Toledo. In March 1540 he received papal permission to found a large general hospital in Toledo and in February 1541 the emperor added his approval.[52] Within his new hospital Tavera hoped to include the rents of the small poorly run hospitals of the city, but the consolidation was never implemented, possibly because the pope would not give his approval for the reform.[53]

Cardinal Tavera was in Toledo again in March 1543 when another welfare reform was initiated. Directed towards improving the relief given to the parish poor, this reform included a written record of all the needy persons in the twenty-one city parishes.[54] The parish lists were compiled by the combined efforts of the cathedral chapter (one canon was assigned to each of the parishes), the parish priest and 'one or two honourable parishioners'. These parish visitors were in-structed to visit the needy in their homes and to record the following facts: the number of children or dependent people in each household; their 'manner of living', and if any person begged publicly. Based on these criteria the visitors were to determine how much bread each person should receive and to give the recipients a slip of paper that indicated the amount. As an obvious concession to the shamefaced poor, those persons who would not proclaim their need publicly, the bread was to be given to whomever appeared with the slip of paper; thus an impoverished doña could send a servant to collect her share of bread. The eventual collation of the information about the needy was known as the Book of the Poor.

After the persons in need had been inspected and counted, centres for distributing the bread were set up in every parish, and parochial distributions were made on a regular weekly basis. The twenty-one parishes were divided into seven groups with three parishes receiving their bread on each day of the week. Since the committee in charge of organizing the relief had 2,000 *fanegas* of wheat to distribute, they decided that 140 *fanegas* (142 *fanegas* were actually distributed) should be given out every week for 100 days from April to July, when the harvest would begin. The wheat was distributed in the form of bread and the two bakers appointed were ordered to be sure that the bread was 'well cooked and well seasoned'. The committee reckoned that each *fanega* of wheat contained 85 pounds of baked bread, which meant that 12,070 pounds of bread were given out each week, based upon the 142 *fanegas* actually distributed.

The 1543 Book of the Poor exhibits features common to most sixteenth-century welfare reforms. People in need of relief were counted and inspected, their needs assessed and, on this basis, the amount of bread they would need was determined. All these facts were recorded on paper, which enabled those in charge of distributing the relief to assemble an adequate amount of grain and to distribute it in a rational, orderly manner. The Toledo reform was organized, implemented and paid for by the church. Cardinal Tavera donated 1,000 *fanegas* of wheat, the cathedral canons gave 500 *fanegas* from the *mesa capitular*, and 500 *fanegas* were taken out of the cathedral account for building and maintenance (*obra y fábrica*). With the exception of the two honourable parishioners, who were probably city council members, ecclesiastics determined the recipients of relief, handled the distribution of bread, and paid for the relief. In Toledo, at least, the church was prepared to set an example to those who railed against its lack of concern for the poor. This must be seen as a voluntary completion of its mission, since no one was threatening to appropriate the rents of Castile's ecclesiastical hierarchy.

The paean of praise for the Toledo church must be qualified, however, because the 1543 reform did not become a permanent institution that functioned every day of every year. It was created to meet a short-term crisis caused by the bad harvest of 1542. By March 1543 the high price of bread and 'the little trade and means to earn one's bread' meant there were a large number of hungry people in the city. Assuming that a poor law was still in effect and public begging was prohibited, some means had to be found to feed these people. Though the original Book of the Poor remained a temporary expedient that operated in 1543 and again in 1545–6, the techniques and machinery it established for assessing the needy and distributing relief served the city for the next twenty years and probably much longer.

Possibly the Book of the Poor did not become a more permanent institution because the motivating force behind its creation, Cardinal Tavera, died in August 1545. It was probably the death of Tavera, in addition to the criticisms of Domingo de Soto, that spelled the end of Toledo's early attempts to eliminate public begging, for it was the money and grain of the cardinal that subsidized the reform in the archdiocese of Toledo. In addition, in February 1540 the cardinal gave 1,400 *fanegas* of wheat to the city and the university of

Salamanca (1,000 and 400 *fanegas* respectively), a gift that may have had something to do with Domingo de Soto's early acceptance of the reform in that city.[55] Tavera did not content himself with writing new legislation for relieving the poor, he also provided large sums of money and grain to assure that the poor were fed and housed. That he favoured a policy of eliminating public begging cannot be doubted, but he made every effort to assure that the poor received relief by other means, and he seemed to assume that it was the obligation of the church to provide this relief.

In 1543 the secular clergy of Toledo played an active role in organizing, distributing and paying for poor relief. However, the church did not assume responsibility for punishing those persons who broke the law by begging publicly. Punishment was the responsibility of the city authorities, a point that is well illustrated during the next subsistence crisis that struck the city in 1546. In January of that year the cathedral canons Juan de Salazar and Diego de Guzmán visited the city council to complain of 'the many beggars who have come to this city because of the good reputation it has for almsgiving'.[56] The large number of people in need of relief meant that the funds in the Book of the Poor were inadequate and 'the strangers take the alms while the natives die of hunger'. The canons urged the city council to consult the crown pragmatic about this subject (that is, the poor law of 1540, printed in 1544), and to do something about the number of foreign beggars in the city. Thus, in 1546 the initial impetus for the enforcement of the poor law came from two cathedral canons, but it was the city authorities that had the unpleasant task of enforcing the law and punishing offending beggars.

The large numbers of beggars who came to Toledo in 1546 was caused by two factors. In the winter of 1545 the province of Toledo was drenched by heavy rains, and in January the Tajo River flooded, causing much damage to property and crops. As early as 26 December the dean of the Toledo cathedral chapter, Diego de Castilla, reported that the severe weather had caused much sickness in the city and there were more poor people than ever before.[57] Also, when Cardinal Tavera died in August 1545, he left 12,000 ducats to be distributed among the poor of the archdiocese of Toledo, with 2,000 ducats designated for the city of Toledo. Possibly news of the cardinal's death and his generosity had spread and attracted prospective alms recipients to the city.

Because of some confusion in settling his estate, Cardinal Tavera's gift of 2,000 ducats to the poor of Toledo was slow in being paid. The administrators of the cardinal's estate, Diego Tavera, bishop of Badajoz, and Ares Pardo, marshal of Castile, began receiving letters of complaint from the Toledo cathedral chapter as early as September 1545. In February 1546 the paymaster of the estate recorded the payment of 2,000 ducats to the poor of Toledo, but the administrators had decided that some of this money should be used for purposes other than feeding the parish poor: 400 *fanegas* of wheat were to be distributed in the cardinal's new hospital and another 200 ducats would be given to the monasteries of the city.[58] This decision brought yet another letter from the deputies of the city and the cathedral who explained that they hoped to follow the system of 1543 and planned to buy 3,000 *fanegas* of wheat and distribute it in the parishes at a rate of 30 *fanegas* a day for a period of 100 days. If the amount of the cardinal's bequest was reduced, 'parochial distributions would cease almost as soon as they started, leaving the poor to starve'.[59] A compromise was reached when the administrators added 200 ducats more to the original donation, but the 400 *fanegas* of wheat for the hospital distribution still had to be taken out of the original gift.

Following the pattern set in 1543, the cathedral chapter added 250 ducats and 500 *fanegas* of wheat to Tavera's gift, making a total of 2,250 ducats and 100 *fanegas* (500 less the 400 to be given out at Tavera's hospital) available for parish distributions.[60] From April until the end of June, approximately 90 days, a total of 2,730 *fanegas* of wheat were distributed in the Toledo parishes at a rate of 210 *fanegas* per week. This is somewhat less than the 3,000 *fanegas* the canons had originally hoped to distribute, but the 400 *fanegas* given out at Tavera's hospital would make up the difference.

While Tavera's grain was being discussed and distributed, a Committee for the Relief of the Poor was formed.[61] This committee was composed of both secular and cathedral authorities. The city was represented by the *corregidor*, Pedro de Córdova; two *regidores*, Fernán Álvarez de Toledo and Hernando de Silva; and two *jurados*, Alonso Pérez de Villareal and Alonso de Alcocer. Ecclesiastics were also abundant; Gaspar de Ponte, the abbot of San Vicente, represented the interests of the new archbishop of Toledo, Juan Martínez Silíceo; Pedro de Campo, Fernando de Silva, Diego López de Ayala, Diego de Guzmán and Francisco de Guzmán represented the cathedral chapter. Not all these people attended all the meetings of the poor relief committee, but they were the most frequent in attendance.

One of the first acts of the committee was to write to the new prelate of Toledo, explaining the dire situation of the poor of the city and asking for a contribution. Best known for his opposition to the Jesuits and his imposition of a statute of purity of blood in the Toledo cathedral chapter, Cardinal Silíceo proved to be a generous patron of the poor.[62] On 10 April he wrote informing the committee that he would donate 5,000 ducats for poor relief, though he found himself in the embarrassing position of having no money because the receipts from the diocesan rent collectors had not yet arrived. He promised to send the money as soon as possible and, as testimony of his good intentions, sent the cathedral silver to the committee along with his permission to pawn it should the money be needed immediately. Impressed by the cardinal's saintly intentions, the committee decided not to pawn the silver and within a few days the 5,000 ducats arrived in a bewildering variety of coins.

Having received such a generous donation, the committee's next step was deciding how it should be spent. On 14 April the committee assigned four parish visitors to each parish: a *regidor*, a canon, a *jurado* and the parish priest (for some reason the parishes of San Pedro, San Justo and Santa María Magdalena did not have a *regidor* among their visitors). The canons assigned to each parish were the same persons already involved in the distribution of Cardinal Tavera's wheat, so they must have had a good idea as to the number and needs of the poor. Nonetheless the newly appointed visitors were instructed to visit the poor in their homes and record all pertinent information.

At the committee meeting on 19 April the *corregidor* decided that no final decision should be made about the distribution of Cardinal Silíceo's gift until the next day when the guardian of the Franciscan monastery, San Juan de los Reyes, the prior of the Dominican convent, San Pedro Mártir, and the eminent humanist, Dr Juan de Vergara, would be present. It should be remembered that public begging had been forbidden in the city, and possibly the *corregidor* was hoping to placate any open objections of the mendicant orders by including them in the decision-making process. Presumably Dr Vergara was invited as a counterbalance to the advocates of unrestrained begging. If disagreements occurred at the meeting of 20 April, and it is hard to believe they did not, they are unfortunately not included in the records. However, the regular religious fared well in the 1546 alms distribution: in addition to the 200 ducats they received from Tavera's estate, Cardinal Silíceo also ordered that they be given 100 *fanegas* of wheat from his donation.

It was decided at the meeting of 20 April that Silíceo's donation should be divided between the parish poor, who received 4,000 ducats, and the beggars, who received 1,000 ducats. The 10,729 parish poor received their gift in two repartitions: at the first one of 1 May they had a choice between 2 *reales* or an equivalent amount of bread. In the second repartition of 13 June only bread was distributed and the total amount given out was reduced because the committee felt that more money should be spent on caring for the sick.

For the conversion of money into wheat, the price of wheat has been established at 16 *reales* a *fanega*, the one price mentioned in the 1546 document, which also agrees with the prices given in Tavera's estate papers,[63] and the number of pounds of baked bread in each *fanega* has been established at 80, the figure given in the 1546 document which also represents an average of the weights taken from other sources.[64]

If the 4,000 ducats spent for the parish poor is converted into wheat, the committee could have distributed 2,757 *fanegas* of wheat. However, this amount must be reduced by 100 *fanegas* to account for the wheat given to monasteries, which leaves 2,657 *fanegas* or 212,560 pounds of bread. This is probably more bread than the parish poor received since the second repartition was reduced and it is likely that in the first distribution many people took 2 *reales* instead of bread. But assuming for the moment that all 4,000 ducats (less 100 *fanegas*) was spent on bread for the 10,729 parish poor, then each person would have received 10 pounds in each repartition, or a total of 20 pounds of bread. Adding the figures for the bread distributed from Tavera's gift to that of Silíceo's, some 430,960 pounds were given out (218,400 from Tavera and 212,560 from Silíceo), which means that for a period of 100 days each person received the equivalent amount of 0.4 pounds, or a bit less than a half pound of bread a day.

It is difficult to explain why the poor relief committee, which contained an abundance of cathedral canons who had been involved in the 1543 and the 1546 Book of the Poor distributions, decided to distribute Silíceo's gift in two large lump sums or to give the poor a choice between money or bread. The system used in the Book of the Poor, where small amounts of bread were distributed more frequently, was far superior, as later poor relief committees recognized. Possibly the fact that the poor were also receiving wheat from Cardinal Tavera's gift explains the decision to give the poor such large donations. According to the wages paid in the Hospital of

Tavera in 1549, 2 *reales* was the equivalent of two days salary for an unskilled worker (a peon), one day's salary for a carpenter, and 17 mrs less than the daily wage of a mason.[65] As mentioned earlier, it purchased the equivalent of 10 pounds of bread in 1546.

Throughout the 1546 document, a distinction is made between the parish poor and beggars. While it might have been clear to the 1546 committee exactly who was considered a beggar, it is difficult for the modern reader to discern. Beggars could have been those disabled people of Toledo who normally made their way by begging, had no home in the city and thus were excluded from the parish visits and assistance. It could also mean the half-starved peasants who came to Toledo in search of food, or the professional beggar who came to find alms. What is clear is that these people were not excluded from the relief given in Silíceo's donation, even if they got it on a less abundant scale than the parish poor.

Of those whom the committee termed beggars, the most comfortably housed were probably the 341 persons taken into private homes. The list of persons who took in the needy includes the most famous names of the city: Lope de Guzmán was most generous in housing ten beggars; the wealthy *converso regidor*, Diego de San Pedro, housed six; the conde de Cifuentes and Rodrigo Niño each took in five; the Inquisitor Valtodaño; the dignitaries, canons, and chaplains of the cathedral chapter; the *regidores, jurados* and one *alcalde* of the city; merchants, scribes and the prior of the Benedictines all housed one or two beggars. Though the number of titled and prestigious households is impressive, equally impressive are the names of the more humble *vecinos*. A potter, an apothecary, a dyer, an innkeeper, a stocking maker, a wax-chandler, a bonnet maker, a silversmith and an embossed leather maker all took in a beggar.[66] What made the 1546 undertaking a success was that people of all estates contributed to help the poor. Unfortunately the list of households that took in beggars is incomplete and records of only ten of the twenty-one city parishes are preserved. Assuming the eleven missing parishes housed an equivalent number of beggars, then 700 may have been lodged in private homes. Considering the medical beliefs of the time, which associated beggars with the spread of contagious diseases, the willingness of the Toledo *vecinos* to take these people into their homes is remarkable.

As hungry people continued to pour into the city, private homes were not adequate to house them all and many were lodged in the

Hospital of Tavera, the cathedral cloister, the archbishop's palace and in other city hospitals. Unfortunately the document contains no mention of the total number of beggars. The Hospital of Tavera distributed 200 pounds of bread a day ($2\frac{1}{2}$ *fanegas*), so there may have been 400 people at the hospital, assuming they were fed a half pound of bread a day. The committee's decision to give the parish poor 4,000 ducats and the beggars 1,000 ducats could indicate that there were four times as many parish poor as beggars, which would be the equivalent of 2,570 beggars, not an unreasonable estimate.

Considering the scarcity of bread throughout the region, the generosity with which beggars were treated, and the fact that the city had proclaimed a law prohibiting public begging, one wonders how the city limited the number of people it could assist. The documents contain no mention of limiting the number of poor who could enter the city, or of placing special guards at the city gates. Something was said about offending beggars however. On 21 April the committee appointed 'two good, charitable people' and a porter to go through the city streets and inspect any beggars they found there. Those who were ill were to be sent to a hospital, while those who were healthy were to be sent to the city jail 'because the *corregidor* ordered that they be punished there'. In ordering offenders to the city jail, the Toledo *corregidor* was merely following the directives of the 1540 Castilian poor law, which called for four days' imprisonment for the first begging offence, eight days in jail and two months' exile on the second offence, while the third transgression brought one month of enforced labour or sixty lashes and exile. Aside from a later order that the *alcalde mayor* should be sure the poor with ulcers were confined to a hospital, this is the only mention of punishment in the entire document so it cannot be said that it was a matter of great importance for the committee.

From the latter part of April until June the committee concentrated on increasing the bedspace in the city hospitals. Three of the larger hospitals – Santa Cruz, Santiago de los Caballeros, and the Misericordia – were asked to increase their bedspace, and the committee paid for the purchase of thirty beds that were placed in three small hospitals. For every pauper taken in, the hospital received between 20 to 25 mrs a day from the committee.

While the prelates of Toledo provided the vast majority of money for the 1546 relief effort, the committee solicited aid from all members of the community. All such assistance was given voluntarily, but there was a certain amount of social pressure involved. The four parish visitors called on all parishioners of means, who were offered the choice of housing a beggar or contributing to the poor relief fund. In view of the prestigious group of parish visitors and the fact that the parishioners' response was to be written down 'where it can be seen', it is doubtful that anyone could gracefully refuse to contribute something. Donations were also solicited from the guilds, and the tailors, hatters, stocking and halter makers all contributed a small amount. Even the papal nuncio Juan Poggio, who was in the city at the time, gave 200 ducats. Excluding the amount paid by those who housed beggars in their homes, the contributions raised by the city probably accounted for 1,000 ducats. This money, together with the 1,000 ducats given by Silíceo, was spent for the beggars and hospital care.

By July the start of a good harvest should have relieved the city of many outsiders who had sought help in Toledo, though the committee's bookkeeper continued to pay out money until December, possibly to the hospitals that treated sick patients, or possibly to those persons who usually made their way by begging and now no longer could.

The relief effort of 1546 was a unique experiment in Toledo's efforts to help the poor. There is a quality of idealism about the whole undertaking, especially in the committee's attitude toward beggars who were treated with such solicitude. In 1546 there is a complete absence of rhetoric associating beggars with the spread of contagious diseases or immorality. Instead they were taken into private homes and the entire city was turned into a hospital. This is a far cry from the reception a beggar would receive forty years later, when the city had established its beggars' hospital and the rhetoric against them had reached a pitch of near paranoia. Also, the inclusion of the mendicant orders in the committee's most important meeting suggests that the city hoped to form an alliance acceptable to even the most critical segments of the community.

The *vecinos* of Toledo also considered the 1546 relief effort as remarkable. In 1547, when Cardinal Silíceo began proceedings to impose a statute of purity of blood in the Toledo cathedral chapter, the *jurados* of the city wrote a letter of complaint to the crown. The letter began with a eulogy to the relief effort of 1546:

In the past year of great hardship and sterility, many lords, nobles, clerics and citizens, all in complete conformity and with great humanity and charity, devoted themselves to visiting the beggars and the parish poor, to taking in poor peasants who came to the city, to curing the sick and making hospitals in their own homes, and to giving money to succour all those in need.[67]

Ten years after the 1546 relief effort, Toledo was struck by a longer subsistence crisis that lasted from the harvest of 1556 to the harvest of 1559 and may have included an outbreak of plague. In December 1556 representatives of the cathedral chapter and the city council again formed a Committee for the Relief of the Poor.[68] One of the first acts of the committee was to meet with Cardinal Silíceo, who suggested that the church, the city and private individuals should jointly provide alms for the needy. The cardinal volunteered his support and again threatened to sell the cathedral silver and added the cathedral tapestries to the list of salable items if he could not raise the money by other means. Four visitors – a *regidor*, a cathedral canon, a *jurado* and the parish priest – were assigned to record the names and number of those in need, and in December 1556 they counted 10,608 people.

As in 1546, Cardinal Silíceo proved to be the most generous provider; he donated 9,000 *fanegas* of wheat, a sum that so impressed the city council that they placed a special sign commemorating his generosity in the city hall (Pisa, *Descripción*, vol. 1, fol. 262v). In addition, the cardinal donated 1,000 ducats from the cathedral account for building and maintenance to be spent in having beds and bedclothes made for the city hospitals. The cathedral hierarchy donated another 1,503 *fanegas* of wheat and approximately 400,000 mrs; the city council donated 2,000 *fanegas* of wheat that were to be paid for by the surplus of the *encabezamiento*; and nine private contributors (the most generous was the silk and wool guild which gave 100 ducats) gave 96,875 mrs and 83 *fanegas* of wheat.

The committee decided to distribute bread in the parishes twice a week at a rate that would give each person a little more than a half pound of bread a day, 'because if it is given in wheat or money, it would be spent in a short time and the poor would die of hunger the rest of the year'. The distribution was to last for six months, from mid-January to mid-July, meaning that the committee needed 12,000 *fanegas* of wheat. Since the committee had more than the necessary 12,000 *fanegas*, it was suggested that the prisoners and poor monasteries of the city should also receive wheat. Before any more worthy recipients could be found, one committee member pointed out that by May and June the number of needy persons in the parishes would increase and any extra wheat would be needed for them.

Having organized the parish bread distributions, the committee turned its attention to the task of augmenting the number of beds in the city hospitals. As Cardinal Silíceo had specified, 1,000 ducats were spent to purchase fifty beds and bedclothing. These beds were placed in three small hospices on grounds that the convalescents could be removed from the larger hospitals and placed in the smaller establishment, leaving the staff, equipment and facilities of the larger institution free to care for those who were more seriously ill. Since the convalescents required less care, they could be looked after by a non-professional staff and could also sleep two to a bed.

In the midst of the six-month distribution, Toledo lost one of its most generous supporters of the poor when Cardinal Silíceo died in May 1557. Silíceo's sentiments about the poor and his obligations to them are expressed in a letter he wrote to the parish priest of the village of Guardia during a period of famine.

You know that the wealth I possess can be called a deposit of the poor vested in me . . . in times of such extreme need all that we possess belongs to the poor. And if the 500 and more *fanegas* of wheat that I have ordered sent to you, together with the 500 *fanegas* I have already sent . . . are not enough, tell me so that you can take as much wheat as you need to kill the hunger of these poor villagers. And do not close the door to strangers who will come by chance, knowing that there are alms, because God gave us the large rents we have for everyone. . . . If you knew the spiritual gain we receive from the many paupers who come to us, you would make all haste to receive and welcome them. We do not know, nor begin to know, the mercy that God gives to the rich in offering them an opportunity to use their wealth so well. And I have ordered that my wheat, in all the places I have it, not be sold so that if all of it is necessary to remedy this calamity, I will use all of it. (Pisa, *Descripción*, vol. I, fol. 262).

Judging by this letter, Cardinal Silíceo did not favour a policy of limiting relief to natives and excluding outsiders. He sounds, in fact, like an exponent of Soto's dictum that 'mercy should succour everyone'. Both the letter and Silíceo's generous donations in 1546 and 1556 are evidence that he deserved his sobriquet 'Father of the Poor'. Possibly the prelate's humble origins explain his sympathy for the poor as well as his dislike of the Jesuits and *conversos*.

Soon after Silíceo died and before his successor, Bartolomé de

Carranza, was appointed in Brussels (February 1558), the city of
Toledo asked for and was granted permission by the crown to
prohibit public begging and to collect alms in the city parishes to
relieve the poor.[69] Judging by the convoluted and qualified assent
given by the crown, discussed in chapter 1 above, Tavera's policy of
eliminating public begging had been abandoned in Toledo and all
Castile. In addition to being without a prelate, Toledo was also
without a *corregidor*, the harvest of 1557 was very poor and there was
much sickness in the city. As the city council put it, 'of the many
people who have become sick, the greater part have died because
there is no way to feed or cure them'. What happened to the poor and
sick from November 1556 until June 1558 is unknown, because it was
not until June and July that the city managed to organize a
distribution of 4,000 *fanegas* of wheat for the 11,105 needy parishioners, an increase of 497 persons since December 1556.

Bartolomé de Carranza arrived in Toledo in October 1558 and met
with the poor relief committee in December, when a new bread
distribution was organized for 1559. Unfortunately the records for
this distribution are woefully incomplete; they include the number of
needy in only five of the city's parishes and give no indication of the
amount of bread that was distributed. In early 1559 the new
archbishop left Toledo to visit his archdiocese and in July he was
arrested by the Inquisition, which may explain the incompleteness of
the records for poor relief.[70] However, the city's mid-century
subsistence crisis was terminated by the good harvest of 1559, and
possibly the arrival of the king and the Cortes offered the city some
consolation for the loss of their prelate.

From 1543 to 1558 a great deal of bread was distributed to a great
many Toledo parishioners, and this information has been sum-
marized in table 6. Unfortunately the lists of the recipients have not
survived for any of the distributions, only the total number for the last
three distributions and in 1546 and 1558 the numbers for each parish.
This loss is particularly sad for 1543, where the information is limited
to the total amount of wheat available, the amount of bread given out
per week and the length of time the distribution lasted. However,
judging by the daily amount each person received in the three later
distributions, approximately a half pound of bread was the established quota. If the 1543 committee also decided to give each
person the equivalent of a half pound of bread a day for 100 days, then
3,400 persons received relief, making the crisis of 1543 minor

Table 6. *Parish bread distributions in Toledo, 1543–58*

| Year | Number of recipients | Fanegas (pounds per fanega) | Pounds of bread | Number of days of distribution | Daily amount of bread per person |
|---|---|---|---|---|---|
| 1543 | 3,400(?) | 2,000 (85) | 170,000 | 100 | (12,070 pounds per week) |
| 1546 | 10,279 | 5,387 (80) | 430,960 | 90 | 0.45 |
| 1557 | 10,608 | 12,000 (80) | 960,000 | 180 | 0.50 |
| 1558 | 11,105 | 4,000 (80) | 320,000 | 60 | 0.48 |

compared with the three later ones. Overall, it is obvious that the poor were best provided for in 1557, thanks largely to the generosity of Cardinal Silíceo; they were given more bread over a six-month period, the longest of all the distributions.

The poor lists of 1546 and 1558 include the number of needy persons in each parish, and these figures are given in table 7. Also included in this table are the figures for the pounds of bread distributed in each parish in 1543, and the five parishes mentioned for the 1559 distribution. The 1558 figures were used to determine the poverty level of the city, established at 19.73 per cent. It is impossible to figure the poverty level for 1546 unless some parish census information comes to light, but in view of the city's assumed population expansion from 1546 to 1558 it is difficult to explain the very minimal increase (376) in the number of people who received relief. Possibly the crisis of 1546 was more severe. From 1540 to 1546 the city seemed to suffer from intermittent grain shortages, and the five years of scarce and expensive grain may have made the poor more susceptible to hunger and disease in 1546. In any event it cannot be said that the figures on table 7 indicate that the problem of poverty had increased from 1546 to 1558.

Concentrating on the parish figures for 1546 and 1558, it is tempting to sketch a picture of increasing poverty in the poorer parishes and of decreasing poverty in the wealthier parishes; in other words, more segregation between rich and poor. Certainly the sizable increase in the number of poor in the parishes of San Lorenzo, Santa María Magdalena, San Miguel and San Nicolás is impressive, as is the decrease or near stability in San Andrés, San Antolín, Santa Leocadia and San Salvador. Unfortunately, other parishes do not fit

Table 7. *Number of persons receiving relief in each Toledo parish,*
*1543–59*

| Parish | 1543 (in pounds of bread per week) | 1546 | 1558 | 1559 |
|---|---|---|---|---|
| S. Andrés | 680 | 471 | 398 | 475 |
| S. Antolín | 170 | 150 | 85 | |
| S. Bartolomé | 340 | 546 | 492 | |
| S. Cipriano | 425 | 534 | 573 | |
| S. Cristóbal | 255 | 300 | 370 | |
| S. Ginés | 85 | 26 | 38 | |
| S. Isidoro | 935 | 456 | 154 | |
| S. Juan Baptista | 170 | 115 | 64 | |
| S. Justo | 340 | 536 | 555 | 640 |
| Sta. Leocadia | 850 | 750 | 508 | |
| S. Lorenzo | 765 | 752 | 998 | |
| Sta. María Magdalena | 680 | 437 | 723 | |
| S. Martín | 510 | 216 | 232 | |
| S. Miguel | 1,020 | 819 | 1,283 | 1,293 |
| S. Nicolás | 595 | 438 | 663 | 685 |
| S. Pedro | 255[a] | 178 | 251 | |
| S. Román | 1,020[b] | 434 | 575 | |
| S. Salvador | 255 | 74 | 76 | |
| Santiago | 1,190 | 1,466 | 1,110 | |
| S. Tomé | 1,360 | 1,931 | 1,719 | 1,780 |
| S. Vicente | 170 | 100 | 238 | |
| Total | 12,070 | 10,729 | 11,105 | |

[a]Includes the prison of the archbishop.
[b]Includes the royal prison and the perpetual prison.

into this neat pattern: in the wealthy parish of San Vicente there is an increase, while in the poor parishes of San Isidoro and Santiago there is a decrease.

The fact is that without more information about the recipients of relief and the actions of the church, city, and charitable institutions, conclusions about increasing or decreasing levels are hazardous. It may well be that by 1558 many more of the Toledo *envergonzantes* were receiving relief from confraternities and thus were not included on the public relief rolls. And in 1558, what happened to the very prominent beggars of 1546? Surely Toledo contained as many beggars – whether natives or hungry immigrants from neighbouring villages – in 1558 as in 1546, but they are not mentioned in the documents. Were they included as part of the public relief dole, or were they housed in the city hospitals, the cathedral cloister and the archbishop's palace and their relief paid for by other means? As for the parish of San Isidoro, the large amount of bread given out in 1543 is impressive, especially bearing in mind that the parish had not yet begun its period of such remarkable growth (see figure 5(b)). The 1546 figures for this parish may be too low because, while the parish bread distributions were carried out, the Hospital of Tavera was also distributing wheat. The hospital's daily distribution of 200 pounds of bread was not limited to the parishioners of San Isidoro, but they were the closest to the hospital and proximity probably counted for a great deal in determining who got bread. Can it be that the hospital also distributed bread in 1558, thereby leaving the 1558 committee to concentrate its resources in other parishes? More investigation might answer some of these questions, though it is doubtful that the actual poor lists still survive.

The decade of the 1560s was one of reform and innovation for the charitable foundations in Toledo. Inspiration for the most ambitious new foundation came from Gómez Tello Girón (d. 1569), appointed governor of the Toledo archdiocese during the early years of Archbishop Carranza's imprisonment. The governor hoped to institute throughout the archdiocese of Toledo an Arca de Misericordia y Monte de Piedad, as recommended by a papal bull of the Lateran Council and supported by many 'pious and zealous persons in this city'.[71] Since the city of Toledo was to serve as a proving ground for the new pious work, the governor sent a copy of the foundation statutes to the members of the city council, asking for their approval, recommendations and participation.

The new foundation, called here the mercy chest, a shortened and literal translation of its long name, was to serve as a collection and distribution centre for money and grain. The collection process was fairly simple, though it required much recordkeeping on the part of the *mayordomo*. Persons inspired to donate money or jewels to the mercy chest could take their donations to the *mayordomo* at the collection centre, or they could deposit them in one of the special poor boxes to be conspicuously hung in all the parish churches. Anyone who chose to donate grain to the foundation could take it to a special place in one of the city's grain storage areas where it would be weighed, recorded and stored. All depositories were guarded by the three-key system that seemed to be the sixteenth-century equivalent of a modern bank vault: the chest or box was fitted with three different locks and the key for each lock was kept by a different person, who was one of the administrators. In the case of the mercy chest, the vicar-general of the Toledo diocese, a deputy of the cathedral chapter, and a deputy of the city council each had a key.

The distribution system of the mercy chest was somewhat more complicated than the collection. At the beginning of each year, the parish priest, a *jurado* and a deputy of the cathedral, the key holders of the parish poor boxes, were to compile a list of all the needy persons in their respective parishes. In addition to names, the list was to include 'the quality of the person, the form of their need and the type of relief that would best meet their needs'. The people on these lists would receive one-tenth the total amount collected by the mercy chest in the previous year.

The greatest amount of the mercy chest's reserve, nine-tenths, was to be loaned in the form of grain. These loans would occur twice a year: in September for sowing, and in April or May so that people would have enough to eat until the next harvest, 'because this is the time when the greatest need for bread occurs even for those who are not poor'. The amount loaned depended upon the judgment of the three administrators and the reserves of the mercy chest. Special provision was made for lending grain to the *envergonzantes*. To any person who appeared with a special paper from the three deputies, the *mayordomo* was to give grain 'with the least possible noise and demonstration because many people who receive this charity will be embarrassed to accept it in any other manner'.

The mercy chest also loaned money, though exactly how it had the resources to do this is not explained. Prospective borrowers needed adequate security or they had to give a suitable obligation and find a guarantor who would cover the debt.

All in all, the mercy chest was a very ambitious undertaking. Not only did the governor order that similar reforms be effected in all the settlements of his archdiocese, he also believed that within a few years the reserves of the mercy chest in the city of Toledo alone would be so abundant that they could be extended to include the villages within the jurisdiction of the city. To this last suggestion the city council wisely remarked, 'it is not necessary to put this in now until experience shows what should be done'. It might be said that Governor Tello hoped to accomplish through the creation of a new charitable institution what only God could provide: enough grain to feed all the people in New Castile. He seemed convinced that after three years the mercy chest would have a reserve ample enough to accomplish all the goals he suggested. To ensure that it received the maximum number of donations, all priests, confessors and public scribes drawing up last wills were urged to remind their charges of the new institutions.

The governor's original proposals also mentioned two other methods of collecting enough grain to achieve the grandiose aims of the mercy chest. In times of scarcity the foundation would sell grain and bread in the city at a cheap price. This would help to feed the poor, to drive down the price of grain and to bring in a profit to the new foundation which would be reinvested in buying more grain. Secondly there was the daring proposal that all individual deposits of grain left by charitable givers for the poor should be consolidated into the mercy chest. The city council objected to both these proposals because both menaced the city's own grain reserve, the *pósito*. Founded in 1507 by the *regidores* to provide cheap bread for the poor of the city, the Toledo *pósito* was sanctioned by a papal bull and received its largest donation of 20,000 *fanegas* of grain from Cardinal Cisneros in 1512.[72] Clearly the governor's new foundation threatened to absorb the city council's *pósito*. As with the hospitals, no one who was destined to lose his particular foundation was enthusiastic about consolidation.

Scattered references testify that the mercy chest was founded soon after 1561 and it seems to have functioned largely as a lending institution. In 1566 the three administrators reported that the foundation had no money, 'having loaned all it had to poor and miserable persons from whom it cannot be collected at this time'.[73] Somehow the foundation must have replenished its reserve because it was functioning in 1577 when grain for sowing was loaned to peasants in the Toledo archdiocese.[74] And in 1581 the *regidor* Pedro de Silva accused the foundation of lending money to the wrong people instead of 'the needy people, workers and widows' it was supposed to assist.[75] He also stated that the *mayordomo* could not collect the money that had been loaned, and that the greater part of the foundation's income was spent in paying salaries to officials instead of helping the poor.

The threat of losing its *pósito* prodded the city council into reforming the institution. As the 1561 proposals of Governor Tello pointed out, 'some grain deposits left by pious persons . . . have been lost and others have diminished greatly through the negligence of those persons encharged with conserving them'. In 1561 the Toledo *pósito* was devoid of money and grain, a depletion that may have occurred during the long famine of 1556–9. Nor could the *pósito* stocks be replenished quickly since the presence of the court in Toledo from 1559 to 1561 placed great strain on the local grain supply and grain prices soared. In March 1562, the city published new 'Bread Ordinances', which included a recompilation of the bull of Julius II and added a few more officials to supervise the *pósito*,[76] but in essence the institution remained unchanged.

The Toledo *pósito* did not give grain away and was prohibited from doing so by its constitution; rather, the *pósito* grain was sold to the bakers of the city who in turn sold the bread at a fixed price established by the city council. The selling price of *pósito* bread fluctuated with the current selling price of wheat and was usually pegged a few *maravedís* or *reales* below the open market price. Thus, if *pósito* grain had been bought at 10 *reales* a *fanega* and grain was selling at 20 *reales* a *fanega* six months later, the *pósito* grain might be sold for 19 *reales* a *fanega*, clearly bringing a tidy profit to the *pósito*. All the profits made through selling *pósito* wheat were, of course, to be reinvested in the institution so that it would become, as its founders had suggested, a self-perpetuating institution.

In theory the *pósito* should have made enough money to be self-perpetuating, but in practice it frequently lost money. During the famine of 1546, for instance, the *pósito* ran out of grain and was forced to buy more at the very high price of $16\frac{1}{2}$ *reales* a *fanega*.[77] Then the price of grain dropped as it became apparent that the next harvest would be abundant; persons who had hoarded grain, hoping to sell it at a higher price if the next harvest failed, were now selling, forcing the price of wheat down to 9 *reales* a *fanega*, while the *pósito* remained with a sizable amount of grain purchased for $16\frac{1}{2}$ *reales*. As the *corregidor* pointed out to the city council, it was inevitable that the *pósito* would lose money, but in order that it lose as little as possible he recommended that the city sell off the remaining grain at $10\frac{1}{2}$ *reales* and decree that everyone in the city must buy it so it would be used up as quickly as possible. Despite the objection of one *jurado* that the poor were being forced to pay more for their bread than the current market price, the recommendation of the *corregidor* was accepted.

The city could have stored the grain until the next famine, but this course of action never seemed to occur to any of the city council, perhaps because of the inadequate storage facilities of the city. Until the new *alhondiga* or grain exchange was built in the 1570s, the city kept its grain scattered about in four distinct locations, known as *alholies*, each of which had to be guarded. Also there were complaints that the grain had been spoiled because of water seepage and dampness or through the effects of some sort of a grain weevil.[78]

If the city *pósito* had a money-losing year, its stocks might be replenished by the gifts of generous donors or by utilizing some of the income the city collected in taxes. Until 1561, one of the largest sources of income for the city of Toledo came from the *alcabalas*. Each Castilian city paid the crown a certain sum for the *alcabalas*, known as the *encabezamiento*, but the city of Toledo collected a bit more than it owed the crown, a sum known as the *sobras* or the surplus of the *encabezamiento*. Philip II gave Toledo permission to spend 8,000 ducats of the 1561 surplus to replenish its *pósito*,[79] so the institution was once again solvent. But a surplus in taxes became rarer after 1561 when the crown increased the *alcabala* rate to 5 per cent, and in 1576, when the impost was raised to 10 per cent, Toledo was barely able to pay the amount it owed the crown much less collect any surplus. The *pósito*, which did not prosper despite the 1561 refunding, was forced to borrow from the Episcopal See: 20,000 ducats in 1568 and 100,000 ducats in 1577.[80] The scanty harvests that occurred periodically in the 1560s and the 1570s, combined with the city's population expansion and the growth of the nearby city of Madrid, explain some of the *pósito*'s financial difficulties. The city had more people to feed and less grain to feed them.

Beginning in 1575 the city council became more and more concerned about the number of poor persons in the city, especially 'the Galicians and the people from the mountains'. In June the *corregidor* mentioned that there were more than 300 sick people who could not be admitted to the already overcrowded city hospitals and thus they were left 'to die in the streets'.[81] As for the new arrivals who were in good health, the city had already ordered what should be done with them. Unfortunately the municipal books do not say exactly what the city did order, but it is very likely that the new arrivals formed part of the large labour force that rebuilt and repaired many of the city's public buildings and monuments from 1573 to 1578.

The problem of an abundance of sick and poor people in the city continued for the remainder of the 1570s. In 1576 Luis Hurtado grumbled about the crowded conditions of the city's hospitals and blamed the 'moriscos, Galicians and Asturians who have brought so much poverty and sickness to this city' ('Memorial', p. 554). The person who complained most frequently about the number of paupers in the city was Pedro de Silva, *alferez-mayor* of Toledo, señor del termino del Corral, knight of the military order of Santiago, and the father of eleven children.[82] Pedro de Silva inherited his titles from his father, Fernando de Silva, a younger son of the marqués de Montemayor, Juan de Silva y Ribera. In 1561 don Fernando had purchased the recently created office of *alferez-mayor* of Toledo from Philip II, a title that seemed to confer upon the bearer a position of leadership in the city council. In 1577 Pedro de Silva, complaining about the beggars who took the alms of the non-begging poor and the danger of contagious diseases spreading in the city, suggested that the city council meet with the cathedral chapter to remedy these two problems.

This is the last book of records for the city council until 1581–2, but the severity of the 1578–80 subsistence crisis, outlined in figure 1, indicates that there was some justification for Pedro de Silva's concern. The crisis of 1578–80 provoked forceful policies on the part of the city authorities who sought to isolate those persons thought to be detrimental to the prosperity, morality and health of the city. Successful implementation of these policies required new institutions or a refashioning of the old ones.

By the mid-1560s the city council of Toledo supported various officials and institutions devoted to helping the poor or enforcing the poor laws. These included the solicitor of the poor, chosen from the ranks of the city council, two *padres de los mozos*, who supervised the activities of the male teenagers of the city, an *alguazil de vagabundos*, loosely translated as a bum bailiff, and a college of the Niños de la Doctrina. In 1568 the Toledo college took in thirty young, poor boys who were fed, clothed, housed, instructed in the Christian doctrine and eventually placed in service.[83] The city council appointed the rector, who was a cleric, and contributed to the upkeep of the boys through regular donations taken from the city's tax receipts. The college also received support from fines collected by the city and the church for legal infractions and from private donations.[84] In 1579 the cleric Sancho de Moncada, uncle of the famous *arbitrista* with the same name, was appointed rector and the clientele of the college was enlarged. In addition to poor boys, the college took in, 'the lost, vagabond and vicious persons who were in the city, women as well as young boys and girls'.[85] The city council viewed this new college as a great achievement because 'many vices and sins had been avoided' and the entire undertaking had been supported by 'alms and that which was acquired through the industry, work and occupation of the people confined'. In other words, the college had become a place where unsavoury females and young boys and girls were confined, put to work and no doubt given frequent sermons on the Christian doctrine. Despite public donations and the work projects of those confined, the new college was not self-supporting, because in 1586 Sancho de Moncada reported to the crown that he was 264,947 mrs in debt. With expressions of approval for the new pious work, the crown determined that the city of Toledo should pay 190,800 mrs of the rector's debt.

Shortly after Sancho de Moncada took over the reformed Niños de la Doctrina, Toledo founded its more famous beggars' hospital. Officially proclaimed in January 1581, the new foundation was supported by the prelate, Cardinal Quiroga, the *corregidor*, don Fadrique Portocarrero, the city council and the cathedral chapter. The actual administration of the hospital and also the collection of alms in the city parishes devolved upon a Hermandad de Caballeros which included Cardinal Quiroga and 'the greater part of the lords, knights, cathedral dignitaries and canons, and the principal persons of the city'.[86] The theorist of the beggars' hospital, Miguel Giginta, remained in Toledo until May 1581 when he requested and was granted permission to leave the city. Cardinal Quiroga, who was frequently in Toledo from 1580 to 1583 because of the various diocesan and provincial synods convened during this period, supplied the bulk of the financial support for the new foundation and offered his constant moral support. The Jesuits, enjoying a new-found acceptance in Toledo thanks to Cardinal Quiroga, preached in favour of the hospital, with the provost, Father Juan Manuel, giving a special sermon in the cathedral.[87]

One of the most ardent and most verbal supporters of the new foundation was, of course, Pedro de Silva, who gave long and impassioned speeches to the city council about the importance of the hospital. Another contingent of supporters came from the wealthy Franco family. Mentioned by Hurtado as the founder of a hospital in the parish of San Nicolás in 1575–6, Hernán Franco served as rector in the beggars' hospital in 1583.[88] The *regidor* Hernán Suárez Franco testified in favour of the beggars' hospital in 1583 and, when he served as a *procurador* in the 1588 Castilian Cortes, offered constant support for Miguel Giginta.[89] And yet another Franco, Diego Sánchez Franco, served as rector in the beggars' hospital in 1585. Dr Francisco de Pisa, *catedrático* of Holy Scriptures at the University of Toledo and a chronicler of the city, was also a partisan of the new hospital.[90]

When Toledo officially opened its hospital, public begging was forbidden, a prohibition the city could morally justify on grounds that it offered the beggars in the hospital 'everything necessary for their body and soul as well as the liberty to come and go as they pleased'. Not all the beggars in Toledo got into the new hospital however. Giginta claimed that when he came to the city there were one thousand beggars, but since the opening of the hospital, 'the greater part of the poor have left this city and others have taken a master or other means of sustaining themselves; those who are confined do not amount to more than 330'. Some of the beggars preferred to return to their place of origin (*tierras*) 'with some succour given them for their journey'. In addition to eliminating many beggars, the supporters of the hospital promised that the new foundation would:

free the republic from a great number of dissolute and licentious persons who disturb and infect it . . . a seminary of robbers and dishonest young men and women who deceive and carry after them the children of good and poor parents by their evil words and even more evil deeds . . . and remove the present danger of contagious diseases which are spread and transmitted by these poor people. . . .[91]

Despite all the advantages of the beggars' hospital and its prestigious list of supporters, the project did not prosper. Feeding and housing 330 persons was a considerable expense and the hospital was continually short of funds. The original foundation consisted of two private houses in the parish of San Nicolás: one, which housed the men, belonged to don Pedro de Sandoval and was rented for 2,000 *reales* a year; the other, where the females were installed, had previously housed the Beatas del Espíritu Santo and cost 882 *reales* a year. In 1582 the city council decided that it could save nearly 3,000 *reales* a year paid out in rent if it built a new hospital on property belonging to the city. Also, if the beggars had their own hospital they would receive more financial support and charitable donations, 'which are not given now because it is thought that by not having a building, the hospital and the confinement cannot continue'.[92] As a convenient site for the new hospital, the city council suggested a

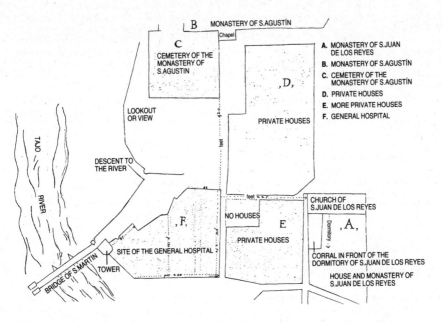

Figure 6. Proposed location for the Toledo General Hospital of Beggars, 1582
(AGS, MPD xii-108)

property it owned known as the *rastro*, located in the southwest corner
of the city in the parish of San Martín.

The Royal Council was persuaded by the city council's plans and
in April 1583 recommended that a licence should be granted for the
construction of the new hospital. But sometime between April and
June, before the licence had been granted, the complaints of the
Franciscan and the Augustinian Orders reached Madrid. The
Toledo *corregidor* was ordered to hold a hearing about the new
hospital, to record the testimony of the friars and persons who
supported the foundation, and forward the results to Madrid. For
some reason the Augustinians did not appear at the hearing, but the
case for the regular religious was ably argued by the Franciscans.

Friars Francisco Castañoso and Luis de Castro held that the
proposed new hospital would ruin the view of their monastery, an
important consideration since the only recreation available to the
religious of San Juan de los Reyes was the contemplation of the
currents of the river and the freshness of the irrigated lands adjacent
to the Tajo. The city presented measurements and diagrams, one of
which is reproduced as figure 6, to demonstrate that the monastery
was a good distance from the proposed hospital site and was situated

on much higher ground so that its view would not be restricted.

Deprivation of visual recreation was not the only complaint of the friars. They argued that the persons housed in the hospital would disturb the tranquillity of the neighbourhood:

Since the poor who are to be confined in the hospital are always the scourge of the people and the most turbulent, they will have continual quarrels, differences and altercations and will make so much noise that the divine offices, continual orations and other spiritual exercises carried out in the monastery will be disturbed.

Furthermore, when the beggars left their hospital they would come to the small squares near the monastery 'making much noise and dirt' which would be very offensive to the important persons who came to hear mass.

Finally, the Franciscans suggested that proximity of the new hospital represented a threat to the good health of the friars.

The hospital would be located in the part from whence the winds come to the monastery, winds that blow the greater part of the year with much fury; if such a hospital should be founded there, where ordinarily three hundred and up to four hundred persons are confined, and who are all, or almost all, always sick with contagious diseases, their vapours would rise to the winds, infecting and corrupting them so that of necessity the friars would be infected by the contaminated air and contract various illnesses.[93]

The threat to the health of the monastery was further increased by the fact that Franciscans were putting in a new, larger choir window through which still more contaminated air would enter. To support their arguments, the friars presented four Toledo doctors, all of whom confirmed the dangers to the health of the monastery.

One might wonder what Saint Francis would have thought of the testimony presented by the Toledo friars, but such sentiments about beggars were not unique to the Order of Saint Francis. The proclamation published in 1581 to announce the opening of the new hospital had urged that the beggars should be confined in the interests of public health and morality. Also, it is possible that the Franciscans had merely plagiarized the arguments of the 1581 proclamation as an opportune means of subverting the hospital. This was what one witness, Juan de Segovia, suggested when he testified, 'it is public knowledge that the friars do not want the hospital there or in any other place because they opposed it even before it was founded'. It was a Franciscan, Luis de Scala, who wrote a treatise against the

Toledo poor law of 1541 and the Order of Saint Francis had been active in opposing such schemes in the Netherlands. As a Mendicant Order, the friars could hardly feel comfortable about the city's attempts to eliminate public begging, even though the 1581 proclamation said nothing about the regular religious. Whether the Franciscans feared the loss of health, tranquillity and their scenic view, or merely hoped to subvert the project to confine the beggars, they were successful in thwarting the city's plans to build a new hospital in the parish of San Martín.

While the Franciscans presented their objections, the city council found other means to pay for the beggars' hospital. By 1584 the Toledo *pósito* had become an institution of public investment which paid 7.14 per cent interest on 42 million *maravedís* worth of *censos* (a type of mortgage rent).[94] From July 1584 to July 1585, the *pósito* sold 153,979 *fanegas* of grain, the equivalent of 12,318,320 pounds of bread, to nearby villages, private individuals, monasteries, and the bakers of the city, who sold it in the public squares of Toledo. Exactly how such a system of public investment affected the *pósito*'s status as a 'pious' institution is not known. Grain was sold to monasteries and the city bakers at 10 *reales* a *fanega* less than it was to other individuals or corporations, while the beggars' hospital and the Niños de la Doctrina frequently received grain free of charge, so the *pósito* still fulfilled its obligation of providing the poor with cheap bread. Several Castilian cities resorted to the expedient of selling *censos* to investors in order to maintain their *pósitos*. In the face of ever increasing crown taxation and rising cereal prices, it was the only means the cities could find to raise the money necessary to buy an adequate supply of grain. If this recourse offered a temporary solution to the problem, it eventually led to disastrous results as the cities sold off more and more *censos* and got further and further behind in their interest payments. The Toledo *pósito* was forced to declare bankruptcy in 1608,[95] but in the meantime the resources of the *pósito* helped to sustain the city's institutions of confinement.

The amount of grain sold by the Toledo *pósito* in 1584–5 was unusually large because of a famine in La Mancha, the region south of Toledo which ordinarily served as a granary for New Castile. The Toledo *pósito* sold grain to villages from which it normally purchased, and many of the peasants of these villages migrated to Toledo in search of food. The number of persons in the beggars' hospital increased to 500 and the city council sent out pleas for financial assistance to Cardinal Quiroga and the Royal Council. These letters intimated that Toledo was in danger of another epidemic because of the poor health of the immigrants, 'who through the lack of bread and work have been forced to eat such bad food as to cause grave concern for the health of this kingdom of Toledo'.[96] Cardinal Quiroga was the most responsive of the prospective donors. He gave 10,000 ducats: 7,000 for the beggars' hospital and 3,000 for the parish poor. The Royal Council gave the city permission to donate 1,000 ducats from the profits of its *pósito*, if there were any profits, an expedient the city had already utilized in 1583 without crown permission.[97]

When the last of Cardinal Quiroga's donation was spent on the beggars' hospital in January 1586, the city was left in the all too familiar position of trying to raise money to support the foundation. The Royal Council unhelpfully suggested that the city council propose a series of money-raising schemes or *arbitrios* that might yield enough income to keep the hospital functioning. As these money-raising projects were to be taken out of the city's rents and properties, well overspent as early as 1570,[98] the committee appointed to study the matter had to exercise some ingenuity.

The Committee of Arbitrios, headed by the most fervent supporter of confining beggars, Pedro de Silva, presented its report in March 1586.[99] It recommended that all the city's institutions of confinement – the beggars' hospital and Sancho de Moncada's enlarged Niños de la Doctrina – should be housed in the San Lázaro, conveniently located outside the city walls. Since the city council had some control over the appointment of the San Lázaro rectors, and the building could easily be enlarged, it appeared to be the ideal site. At the time the San Lázaro was occupied by the eighty young boys with contagious skin diseases who were treated by the Confraternity de las Angustias and their rector, Alonso de Ribera, but the commissioners were confident that none of these parties would object to having additional residents in the hospital; rather, the new inmates would be an embellishment to the confraternity and the rector. The committee reasoned that if all these undesirable groups were housed together outside the city walls, the city council would eliminate the expense of maintaining separate staffs and buildings, bookkeeping would be simplified and the health and morality of the city would be much improved.

To raise money to support this new undertaking, the commissioners presented a list of seven schemes.

1. The city's donation to the Niños de la Doctrina should be increased from 400 to 500 ducats.
2. A new tax should be imposed on meat. For every sheep slaughtered, the entrails would be sold for 20 mrs, 10 of which would go to the beggars' hospital.
3. The city would give 1,000 ducats from the profits of its *pósito*.
4. The San Lázaro would open a theatre where comedies were performed and all the proceeds would be given to the hospital.
5. A new tax would be imposed on the sale of wine, two-thirds of which would be given to the hospital.
6. The small hospitals and some of the confraternities of Toledo would be fused into the San Lázaro.
7. His Majesty should donate 2,000 mrs in *juros* invested in the Casa de Contracción in Seville.

As the wealthiest and most generous supporter of the beggars' hospital, Cardinal Quiroga was consulted about the recommendations of the committee, and the city council emphasized the desirability of a hospital consolidation. In his response of 7 July 1586 the cardinal expressed enthusiasm about giving the beggars a permanent building of their own, 'because without it, everything is in the air and without root'. The prelate also urged that some effort be made to limit the number of beggars in the city 'since the people, especially those who are not rich, tire of seeing so many alms collectors and so many beggars'. As to the hospital consolidation, the cardinal's response was vague and non-commital. He reminded the city that 'His Holiness had committed this consolidation to the prelates . . . and if it is not executed by them, I do not know what validity it would have'. Further discussion of this matter was deferred until the cardinal's impending visit to Toledo when the remains of Saint Leocadia were to be transferred to their new resting place in the Toledo cathedral.

Considering that the city council supported a hospital consolidation, that Cardinal Quiroga was one of the staunchest supporters of the Toledo beggars' hospital, and that the crown had sent letters to both parties urging the reform,[100] it is difficult to explain why a hospital consolidation did not occur in Toledo. At least one small hospice in the city did contribute something to the beggars' hospital. In 1581 the brotherhood that operated the Hospital of San Miguel decided to give the hospital's beds and bedclothing to the new general hospital.[101] However, the brotherhood seems to have made this decision on its own volition, it lost none of its rents, and the old hospital building was not sold off at auction. Possibly some of the other hospices of the city donated, or were forced to donate, their beds to the beggars' hospital, but Toledo witnessed no hospital consolidation on the scale it was carried out in Seville or Madrid.

The city did eventually receive permission to enact the first three of its seven *arbitrios*, and in December 1587 the city proclaimed the establishment of the beggars' hospital in the San Lázaro.[102] At the same time a new list of regulations about begging and the administration of the beggars' hospital was drawn up. One or two *alguaciles de vagabundos* were appointed to see that no one begged except those persons appointed to solicit alms for the beggars' hospital and those confraternities which offered some assistance to the poor and sick. Any unauthorized beggar, male or female, would receive 100 lashes. The Hermandad de Caballeros seems to have dissolved; the new rector of the beggars' hospital, Alonso de Ribera, was to be assisted each month by one of the twelve commissaries appointed by the city council.

Despite all the proclamations, *arbitrios* and Cardinal Quiroga's promise of continued support for the hospital, the institution was no longer functioning in 1589 because of a lack of funds. The operational costs of the hospital varied according to the price of bread and the number of persons in residence, but under normal conditions the average cost per month was 500 ducats or 2,250,000 mrs a year. The city council estimated that the *arbitrios* yielded a total of 713,500 mrs in 1589; 250,000 mrs from the comedies (the beggars' hospital received a portion of the money taken in at the comedies presented at the Mesón de la Fruta), 51,000 mrs from the meat tax, 37,500 mrs from the increased donation to the Niños de la Doctrina and 375,000 mrs from the *pósito* profits. This left nearly 4,000 ducats which had to be raised every year through private donations. Undoubtedly the first flush of enthusiastic support among the Toledo parishioners, if it ever existed, had long since passed, just as the Hermandad de Caballeros had given way to twelve city appointees. In addition to the usual operational costs of the hospital was the expense of the materials needed to enlarge the San Lázaro, estimated by one *jurado* at 6,000 ducats.[103]

Pedro de Silva delivered another of his frenzied speeches about the dangers of poor persons wandering through Toledo and the need to confine beggars in 1589.[104] What provoked his speech was the fact that Toledo was being inundated by beggars from Madrid, where a new system of expelling unsavoury non-residents had been initiated. Madrid's efficiency drove these persons to other places, especially to Toledo which was conveniently close at hand. So the Toledo beggars' hospital was resurrected, or the city sought funds to resurrect it. The only outside donation, given by Cardinal Quiroga, amounted to a mere 1,000 ducats. Despite the paucity of the gift, it was scrupulously divided between various charitable institutions of the city: two confraternities that visited the poor and the sick in their homes each received 75,000 mrs; another 126,000 mrs was given to three hospitals to buy more beds; the remaining 99,000 mrs went to the beggars' hospital. The city council admitted that this was not much money for the beggars, but it was hoped that the rector might be able to raise more money privately.

Since the beggars' hospital was functioning, yet another list of rules about begging was promulgated, though little was changed from the earlier ones. In imitation of Madrid, the city council initiated a system of closer supervision of beggars; fourteen *porteros* were appointed to assist the *alguacil de vagabundos* and to see that no unauthorized persons begged in the city. The punishment for begging was augmented to banishment in addition to 100 lashes, and special attention was given to those persons who had left the beggars' hospital with the promise to leave the city and never beg there again. These persons, 'who, forgetting their promise, return to the city to beg as before, dissimulating and hiding themselves from the *alguaciles* and porters', were to be taken to prison and punished 'in such a manner that they do not return to begging in the city'.

No one wanted the beggars, who apparently wandered about from place to place, their peregrinations dependent upon the degree of police surveillance in the cities and towns. The spectacle of migrating beggars brings to mind the 1545 Robles–Soto debate. One of Soto's severest strictures against the 1540 poor laws was that foreign paupers were excluded from permanent relief, an exclusion the Dominican interpreted as a violation of Christian charity which was to succour all persons no matter what their point of origin or their ailment. In 1589 the cities of Madrid and Toledo chose to disregard Soto's precept, and the following year Toledo received a royal letter ordering that only natives and residents of the city should be admitted to the beggars' hospital (see below, chapter 2, note 78). The same year Valladolid also received a crown order to expel all poor strangers from the city,[105] so it is very likely that all the larger urban centres of

Castile received similar instructions. The crown letter of 1590, which excluded all foreign beggars from public assistance in Toledo, was more severe than the Zamora poor laws of the 1540s which promised all travellers three days' food and lodging. Thus, for at least one year, the frequently repeated observation that Castilian poor relief always remained open to all persons must be modified,[106] though it should be added that the crown's order pertained only to the poor relief directed by the municipal authorities. Private institutions, or at least the Hospital of Tavera in Toledo, continued to admit strangers and non-residents.

The final blow to Toledo's beggars' hospital came in 1592 with the legal proceedings between the church and the crown concerning the visitation rights in the San Lázaro. In 1587 the San Lázaro was full of people: the beggars, the Niños de la Doctrina, the eighty boys with skin diseases were all housed there under the supervision of the Confraternity de las Angustias and their rector, Alonso de Ribera. It was not the surfeit of inhabitants in the hospital that provoked the confraternity's appeal to Madrid, but the issue of episcopal visitation, discussed in chapter 2 above. Also, the brothers were vexed by the last will and testament of their rector.

In 1587 Alonso de Ribera drew up a will leaving 4,200,000 mrs to the San Lázaro and named the city council as executor of his bequest.[107] The money was to be spent in feeding and clothing the young boys with skin diseases and, if any money remained, it was to be given to the beggars and the Niños de la Doctrina. The confraternity argued that the money donated by the rector belonged to them and 'the poor children of San Lázaro who acquired it through begging alms in the city and through their own labour'.[108] There is no doubt that the boys in the San Lázaro worked; the vicar-general testified that they and the beggars had carried out all the building repairs in the San Lázaro. Yet even if the boys worked and were hugely successful in begging alms it is doubtful that they could have raised 4 million mrs. Since Alonso de Ribera had given all the money to the hospital, the confraternity must have been insulted because it had been excluded from the administration of the money.

Whatever the brothers of the Confraternity de las Angustias hoped to achieve when they appealed to Madrid, they were the losers. On 15 October 1592 the Toledo San Lázaro was declared a hospital of the Royal Patrimony and the king appointed Alonso de Ribera as rector, while the confraternity was reduced to appointing two persons to take accounts along with the *corregidor* and two *regidores*. Five days later, obviously piqued by their treatment, the confraternity took all its signs, insignias and the rest of its paraphernalia and relocated in the Dominican convent of San Pedro Mártir.[109] As a parting shot, they opened the archive of the San Lázaro, took out all the title deeds and contracts and published certain letters of the nuncio in all the churches of the city. It would be interesting to know more about the contents of the nuncio's letters, but the whole affair was hushed up by the crown which ordered that the *corregidor* investigate the matter as quietly as possible and that no censures be published against the confraternity.

Alonso de Ribera, a dedicated, devout priest who hoped to retire to a life of contemplation, was scandalized by the confraternity's actions; he died shortly after the incident in May 1593.[110] His demise spelled the end of the beggars' hospital for no suitable replacement could be found. Master Cristóbal Palomares, a close friend of Alonso de Ribera, suggested to Licenciado Tejada of the Royal Council that Sancho de Moncada would be a suitable successor since he possessed great charity and patience in caring for the poor and 'seems an angel he is so tireless and vigilant'.[111] However, Sancho de Moncada had abandoned the poor to devote himself to the business affairs of his brothers and Master Palomares doubted that he could be persuaded to give up his new vocation. Out of the deluge of petitions for the vacant rectorship, the Cámara appointed the brother of Alonso de Ribera, Licenciado Diego López de Soto in July 1593.

The appointment of a rector did not end the adventures of the Toledo San Lázaro. In August 1594 the city council asked the king to let the brothers of John of God, who specialized in treating convalescents, move into the institution.[112] It was the city council's belief that the hospital was large enough to house convalescents as well as the people suffering from contagious skin diseases, and the brothers were willing to treat both types of patients.

The brothers of John of God had been in Toledo for a long time. In 1549 Blas Ortiz mentioned that John of God had visited Toledo to ascertain if the people of the city 'were inclined to help the poor and miserable'.[113] Apparently they were, because the vicar also mentioned a recent foundation that he called the Hospital of Fernando. According to another chronicler, in 1569 doña Leonor de Mendoza left the brothers a church and a 'house for curing convalescents' (Pisa, *Descripción*, vol. II, p. 72), and in 1586 the brothers received permission to enlarge their hospital, known as Corpus Cristi.[114] Presumably the city council was hoping to transfer some of the brothers from their old hospital to the San Lázaro.

On 23 August the city sent out yet another letter to the king, whose answer was delayed because he felt it necessary to ask the opinion of the archbishop of Granada, Pedro de Castro.[115] What Philip asked the prelate was whether he thought the brothers were capable of governing the hospital on their own or whether they should have an administrator to supervise them. Archbishop Castro was unwilling to offer any opinions about the Toledo San Lázaro, but he did add that 'it seems these brothers of Joan are encharged with more than they can administer, being of the quality they are. I have here petitions for them from Lisbon, from the cardinal in Seville and the abbot of Alcalá la Real and I have sent them to all these places.'[116] Possibly Pedro de Castro's judgment had something to do with the crown's decision to retain an administrator who acted as a supervisor in the Toledo San Lázaro.[117]

The person who persuaded the city council of Toledo to give the San Lázaro to the brothers of John of God was Brother Baltasar, the same person who had persuaded the crown to give the Córdoba San Lázaro to his congregation. In Toledo, Brother Baltasar was also placed in charge of the Niños de la Doctrina, an appointment that earned him the admiration and respect of the city council until his death sometime before February 1598.[118] However, the brothers of John of God stayed on in the San Lázaro, now known as the Hospital of the Convalescents, and continued serving even when the hospital's clientele was changed again in August 1599, this time to plague victims.

The last decade of the sixteenth century was not a happy one for Toledo. The search for an adequate amount of grain to feed the people of the city seemed to reach a new intensity, while to pay for the grain the city sold off more and more censos backed by its depleted rents and properties and the profits of its pósito.[119] The search for grain was probably complicated by a 1589 crown order forbidding Toledo to buy grain 12 leagues to the south and west of Madrid (towards the Mancha and Toledo) and 20 leagues to the north and northeast of the capital (towards Sigüenza and Old Castile).[120] In addition to the reduced buying area, many of the harvests of this decade were scanty and the quality of the grain was poor. Combined with the shortage of grain was an abundance of sickness. In 1591 there were so many sick people that the hospitals were full; to help the poor and sick, the city sought money from its most generous supporter, Cardinal Quiroga, and received crown permission to donate grain from its *pósito* for poor relief.[121] In his history of Spain Juan de Mariana mentions that in the autumn of 1590 many people died from a sickness that struck especially hard in the villages and the countryside, and the large number of poor and sick people in Toledo in 1591 was probably a result of this sickness ('Historia de España', p. 406). In 1594 the city claimed it had 6,000 poor people to feed 'without counting those who beg', who probably counted for another thousand.[122]

On 4 March 1598 a sizable complement of the city council, including the vigorous *corregidor* Francisco de Caravajal, convened a meeting of all the beggars in the city.[123] The 356 beggars were gathered in the Hospital of Santa Cruz where they were inspected to determine whether they should be given a begging licence, confined to a hospital, or expelled from the city. The cause of this inspection is not explained in the document; it might have been a response to the threat of plague or to the 1597 crown 'instruction' urging the Castilian cities to found an albergue. In 1597 similar inspections were held in Seville, where 2,000 beggars turned up, and in Valladolid, where 310 beggars were retained in the city.[124] These inspections were probably the first step the Castilian cities took before deciding that they could not afford to found an albergue. At least this is what the city of Seville concluded, unless the crown consented to giving the albergue some of the rents from the new consolidated hospitals.[125]

Of the 356 beggars who appeared in the Hospital of Santa Cruz, 187 received a begging licence and 169 were banished, though the exiles received a small donation for their journey. The infirmity and sex of the 187 individuals who qualified for a beggars' licence is given in table 8. Nearly all the licensees suffered from some sort of a physical handicap: the men, who outnumbered the women two to one, seemed prone to the loss of limbs, paralysis and syphilis; the women predominated in the categories of old age, sickness and as widows or mothers. As for the 169 persons who were banished from the city, there seems to be no rhyme or reason to the committee's decisions for expulsion. On the whole, women received more sympathetic treatment than the men: only 33 females were expelled compared to 136 males. Yet 45 of the exiles had some infirmity which should have entitled them to a begging licence; more than 30 men were crippled, old or infirm and 12 women were elderly or had children. Possibly

Table 8. *Sex and infirmity of 187 persons issued a begging licence in Toledo, 1598*

| Infirmity | Male | Female | Total |
|---|---|---|---|
| Fevers | 16 | 4 | 20 |
| Epilepsy | 1 | 1 | 2 |
| Shivers | 3 | 0 | 3 |
| Syphilis[a] | 18 | 4 | 22 |
| Asthma | 0 | 1 | 1 |
| Leprosy | 7 | 4 | 11 |
| Bad heart | 1 | 1 | 2 |
| Blind or loss of vision | 8 | 6 | 14 |
| Speech impediment | 7 | 3 | 10 |
| Wound | 0 | 1 | 1 |
| Lame or missing a limb | 21 | 1 | 22 |
| Paralysis | 20 | 8 | 28 |
| No teeth | 2 | 1 | 3 |
| Sick | 1 | 13 | 14 |
| Old | 4 | 12 | 16 |
| Widow | 0 | 5 | 5 |
| Woman with child | — | 4 | 4 |
| Not given or illegible | 9 | 0 | 9 |
| Total | 118 | 69 | 187 |

[a]Persons who were sent to the Hospital of Santiago have been classified as syphilitics since that was the disease this hospital treated.

those banished were non-residents of Toledo, yet individuals who had been born in France, Portugal and Galicia did receive a licence. It is also possible that some persons left the city of their own volition, tempted by the travel allowance that was usually 1 or 2 *reales*, though women with children received up to 4 *reales*. Considering that the parish poor of Toledo had received a gift of 2 *reales* in 1546, 1 *real* in 1598 does not seem particularly generous, but a beggar might take it and try his luck elsewhere, go home to his family if he had one, or try to sneak back into Toledo at a later date when the authorities were not exercising such close surveillance.

The majority of the persons banished from the city were men and boys who had nothing wrong with them. At least the scribe did not record any physical ailments and listed them according to their physical maturation (bearded, no beard, old). With the exception of four children and sixteen old men, the remaining applicants presumably qualified as healthy beggars and, according to the 1565 poor laws of Castile, should have been considered as vagabonds and sent to the galleys. However, in all the numerous decrees against public begging proclaimed in Toledo from 1546 to 1589, offending beggars had been threatened with jail, banishment and public whippings, but never with galley service. Only after the licensing programme of 1598 was completed did the city proclaim that any person who begged in the city without a licence would be punished with 200 lashes, in addition to ten years' galley service for the males and six years' exile for the females. It is doubtful that such severe penalties were enforced, but they might have served as a temporary deterrent to unlicensed begging.

Not long after the beggars were inspected, the city began preparing for the plague. Little has been said about the measures taken in Toledo to combat the plague, but they were similar to those employed in other parts of southern Europe.[126] Basically the city tried to seal itself off from any outside contamination and the entrance of 'people, merchandise, and clothes' from the outside was prohibited.[127] Guards were placed at all the city gates and bridges, and anyone of 'quality' who hoped to enter needed a written testimony that they came from a plague-free area; no poor person, whether they carried a testimony or not, was admitted. Given Toledo's geographic location and the strong walls and gates, the city could probably control the movement of population reasonably well. The one weak point was the area outside the city walls, Covachuelas, and in June 1598 the Committee of Health discussed this area and sent representatives to see if there was any way to protect it. Apparently there was not: Covachuelas suffered the highest mortality rates during the plague, and it was also the area where the city chose to locate its plague hospital.

Periods of plague were particularly difficult for the poor. Not only did they suffer the highest mortality rates, but the ban on bringing in outside merchandise meant there were no raw materials to supply the textile industries, so many people were without work and thus without money to buy food. This meant that there were still more people in need of relief. In December 1598 and in January 1599 there were complaints in the city council about the number of poor and sick people and the need to confine beggars, but the city had no means to pay for poor relief. In March 1599 came another complaint about the poor 'who wander through the streets, begging and sick; because they find no relief and nowhere to sleep, many die in the streets without confession or the rest of the sacraments' It was only in April that the city managed to find 400 ducats for poor relief, a very small amount in view of the many who were in need.[128]

In addition to the efforts made by the *corregidor* and the Committee of Health, the hospitals and confraternities also helped to meet the crisis. The royal hospital, Santiago de los Caballeros, was given permission to feed and house thirty poor persons for four months beginning in February 1599, 'in order to avoid finding them dead in the streets as is usually the case'. In August of the same year the hospital was permitted to admit and treat five or six plague victims and to spend 4,000 *reales* for the relief of sick people in the parishes of San Miguel and Santa María Magdalena.[129] In July 1599 the Hospital of Tavera prepared six beds for 'the sick people brought from the countryside infected by plague',[130] and the hospital staff was given a special mixture known as *soliman* (corrosive sublimate, mercuric chloride) to carry as a defence against the plague. The confraternity of the Santa Caridad overspent its income in 1599 in making visits to the sick and poor in their homes, and the confraternity of San Roch took a vow to build a hermitage to their patron, thought to be a protector against the plague, in Covachuelas.[131]

One would like to conclude that all the assistance given by Toledo's charitable institutions and the precautions taken by the Committee of Health helped to control the plague. However, in view of the fact that the plague was spread by fleas carried by brown rats, one must come to the more mundane conclusion that the city was lucky in having either inactive or small numbers of rats and fleas. This is not to say that Toledo escaped unscathed: the curve in figure 1 shows 1599 to be the lowest point in the 24-year interval between 1581 and 1605. However, compared with other subsistence crises in the sixteenth and early seventeenth centuries, Toledo was not hit hard by the 1599 plague.

Reflecting upon sixty years of poor relief in Toledo, what can be said about the city's policies? First of all it is obvious that Domingo de Soto did not carry the day in the Imperial City. In the early 1540s and again in the 1580s the city tried to eliminate public begging, and in the second attempt, which witnessed the foundation of a general hospital for beggars, Toledo led the way in Castile. Neither of these efforts enjoyed permanent success, but the city fought long and hard to maintain its beggars' hospital, making it clear that sentiments about eliminating public begging were not lacking in the city. Focussing upon attempts to eliminate public begging should not obscure all the positive actions taken to help the poor. Whether it was the distribution of bread in the parishes, the sale of cheap bread by the *pósito*, the loans made through the Arca de Misericordia y Monte de Piedad, or the money and beds given to hospitals, the city attempted to provide for the poor so they did not need to beg in the streets.

What characterized all these relief efforts was the involvement and cooperation of the secular clergy and the city authorities. It is true that in Toledo the church played a very important role in poor relief. The prelates were the first persons to receive a plea for help and they usually responded with great generosity. They were also instrumental in determining the city's policy toward public begging since it was the wealth and moral support of Cardinals Tavera and Quiroga that enabled the city to try and eliminate public begging in the 1540s and 1580s. Notwithstanding the important role played by the archbishops, the group that organized and distributed poor relief was usually a carefully balanced coalition of secular clerics and city authorities.

This is not to say that harmony prevailed within the church on all the issues of poor relief. The Franciscans of Toledo objected to the elimination of public begging, while the Jesuits supported the policy. These discords reflect the various sectors of opinion within the church, but it is worth noting that the objections of the Franciscans did not thwart the city's efforts to maintain its beggars' hospital, though they may have discouraged donations from some charitable givers.

It appears that the attitude towards public beggars grew harsher as the century progressed. Certainly the punishments for beggars became more severe and the public officials devoted to enforcing these punishments increased. And the treatment of beggars in 1546, when they were lodged in private homes and there seemed to be no limit to the number of needy persons the city would admit, contrasts sharply to the beggars' hospital, which was founded to eliminate morally and physically suspect people and in 1590 admitted only Toledo residents. Possibly this harsher attitude can be explained in terms of the city's increased population, diminishing resources, and deteriorating health; or possibly it was an expression of the *nouvelle vague* of Counter-Reformation charity that permeated much of Catholic Europe.

A great deal of Domingo de Soto's message was ignored in sixteenth-century Toledo, but the Dominican posed problems the city could not overcome. One had to do with the sources of income that could be used to maintain the beggars. It seemed to be an accepted fact that the Toledo beggars' hospital had to be financed through voluntary donations, whether they were collected in the city parishes or given by Cardinal Quiroga or a citizen in his last will and testament, or by indirect taxes, such as a tax on meat, a portion of the entrance fees for the comedies, or for certain fines. None of these voluntary gifts or indirect taxes was adequate to sustain the beggars' hospital.

Another problem posed by Soto was the question of liberty of movement for the poor. While in 1590 the Toledo beggars' hospital was closed to persons who were not born in or did not reside in Toledo, the fact that the crown gave permission for such a move implies that this was not the normal policy. This meant that under normal circumstances the beggars' hospital remained open to all deserving paupers, no matter what their point of origin. Toledo may have been one of the wealthiest cities in sixteenth-century Castile, but it was not in a position to maintain all the deserving paupers of the realm. It is likely that Soto's precept about liberty of movement for the poor and open charity for all those in need was a more effective deterrent to the elimination of public begging than the voluntary nature of almsgiving.

Toledo's experience with the poor and their relief is not very different from other areas of Catholic Europe, most notably Italy. In so far as the charitable institutions remained decentralized throughout the century, a beggars' hospital was founded in the later years of the century, and secular and ecclesiastical authorities adopted a similar policy toward the poor and their relief, there are parallels between Toledo and Venice. However, in contrast with Venice the church of Toledo played an active role in initiating and subsidizing welfare reforms. To find comparable clerical activism, one must look to such Italian cities as Verona, where Bishop Giberti attempted to introduce welfare reforms in the 1530s, and to Brescia, where a beggars' hospital was founded in 1577 by a city that acted upon the advice of Cardinal–Archbishop Carlo Borromeo.[132] Whether it was Cardinal Tavera's welfare reforms of the 1540s or Cardinal Quiroga's beggars' hospital of the 1580s, Toledo also experienced the new forms of philanthropy emerging from the Catholic Reformation and the Counter-Reformation.

# 4

## Private charitable institutions

This chapter focusses on the primary institutions of poor relief, the hospitals and the confraternities. Though these were the most important institutions, they were by no means the only ones. For instance, in the cathedral cloister bread was distributed on a daily basis to some thirty poor people and the 600 *fanegas* of wheat that comprised this gift was paid for by the cathedral chapter, the prelate and the account for building and maintenance; the cathedral chapter administered two bequests that provided dowries for poor girls;[1] and the respective heads of the Franciscan and the Dominican monasteries of the city were responsible for distributing 1,000 ducats to the poor in fulfilment of a bequest left by the countess of Ribagorza.[2] It is very likely that other monasteries, convents, churches and chapels were responsible for fulfilling similar charitable obligations. A study of all the charitable relief in the city would require another approach and another book to record the results.

Even if the discussion is limited to confraternities and hospitals the task is not so simple, for in 1576 Luis Hurtado listed some 27 hospitals and 143 confraternities, impressive figures in a city of 60,000 inhabitants.[3] Of course the fact that a charitable institution existed does not necessarily mean that it provided charitable assistance. The six hospitals of Martín Múñoz, which admitted no patients before the 1570 consolidation, serve as a reminder that many institutions survived only in name. No doubt this is true of some institutions listed by Hurtado, although 1576 probably represents a high point in the activities of the city's charitable institutions since many of them were still solvent and some of the older hospitals had been reformed in the 1560s.

In the sixteenth century Toledo was recognized as a hospital centre where patients could find treatment for a variety of diseases,

Table 9. *Hospitals and hospices in Toledo and their approximate bed space, 1576*

| Hospitals | Treatment given | Approximate bed space |
|---|---|---|
| 1. Santa Cruz[a] | Foundling children and general | 220(?) |
| 2. San Lázaro[b] | Skin diseases | 80 |
| 3. Misericordia | General | 60 |
| 4. Nuncio[c] | Insanity | 46 |
| 5. Rey[d] | Incurable | 100 |
| 6. Santiago de los Caballeros[e] | Syphilis | 105 |
| 7. Tavera[f] | General | 100 |
| Hospices | | |
| 8. Santa Ana | | 13 |
| 9. San Andrés | | 6 |
| 10. San Antón (extramural)[g] | | 19 |
| 11. San Antón (parish of San Miguel) | | 5(?) |
| 12. Candelaría | | 5(?) |
| 13. Concepción | | 6 |
| 14. Corpus Cristi | | 15(?) |
| 15. San Cosme y San Damián | | 5(?) |
| 16. San Ildefonso | | 8 |
| 17. San Justo y Pastor | | 13 |
| 18. San Lorenzo | | 10(?) |
| 19. Madre de Dios | | 12 |
| 20. San Miguel | | 30 |
| 21. San Nicolás | | 30 |
| 22. Nuestra Señora de la Estrella | | 6 |
| 23. San Pedro | | 25 |
| 24. Private house (no name given) | | 10(?) |
| 25. Santana | | 7 |
| 26. Santiago | | 15 |
| 27. San Sebastián | | 5(?) |
| Total bed space | | 956 |

[a]ADHT, Santa Cruz, Libro de registro de los niños expositos, 1570. In 1570, 120 foundling children were admitted; the number of other patients is unknown.
[b]AGS, PE, leg. 40.
[c]BL, Eg. 1882, fol. 194. According to Blas Ortiz, the Nuncio housed 33 insane people and 13 old people, 'who at one time had been rich but had become needy and impoverished'.
[d]AGS, PE, leg. 174.
[e]AHN, Órdenes militares, 1086c, fol. 179.
[f]AHT, LD, 1576.
[g]AGS, CR, leg. 115-7.

sicknesses and infirmities. The twenty-seven hospitals of the city, the ailments they treated and their approximate bed space in 1576 are given in table 9. This table is based largely upon the information given by Hurtado, but two of the hospitals he included have been eliminated (the infirmary in the prison and the bread distribution at the cathedral), and the Hospital of Corpus Cristi, operated by the brothers of John of God, has been added. Information taken from other sources has been noted in the table.

These institutions have been divided into two groups, the larger well-endowed hospitals that offered regular medical and spiritual attention, and the small not so well-endowed hospices that usually served as little more than a dormitory for poor persons who could not afford the price of space in the local inn. Two of the institutions classified as hospices, Corpus Cristi and San Nicolás, did occasionally offer medical attention but it was sporadic and dependent upon the wealth and dedication of the brotherhood in charge. For the most part the institutions classified as hospices provided little more than sleeping space.

The seven larger hospitals were each dedicated to treating specific types of ailments. The Hospital of Tavera and the Misericordia handled all types of non-contagious ailments such as wounds, dislocations, toothaches, stomach and intestinal maladies, and the multitude of fevers that afflicted sixteenth-century society. Santiago de los Caballeros, a hospital of the military order of Santiago, cared for syphilitics. The Hospital del Rey admitted persons suffering from contagious or incurable diseases, what would today be described as terminal patients; as Luis Hurtado observed, 'those who go there very rarely survive' ('Memorial', p. 558). Persons with contagious skin diseases were admitted in the San Lázaro, and the mentally disturbed were housed in the Nuncio. The Hospital of Santa Cruz was originally founded in 1495 as a general hospital that cared for non-contagious ailments, foundling children and distributed money to persons in need. In 1625 Salazar de Mendoza mentioned that Santa Cruz had abandoned all its activities except the care of foundling children, a change that must have occurred in 1608 or 1621,[4] but in 1576 the hospital still served all the purposes prescribed by its founder, Cardinal Mendoza.

Under normal circumstances the hospitals offered treatment in accordance with the provisions of their constitution and in keeping with their income, but during periods of subsistence crises the poor relief committees asked the hospitals for assistance. In 1546 the committee asked the hospitals of Santa Cruz, Santiago de los Caballeros and the Misericordia to increase their bed space. In 1556 fifty new beds for convalescents were given to the hospices of Santa Leocadia (twenty-four beds), the Madre de Dios (sixteen) and San Andrés (ten) so the larger hospitals could admit more sick people.[5] In

1580 the cathedral chapter discussed adding beds to the Hospital of Santa Cruz to help in the treatment of the numerous sick people in the city.[6] In 1589 the hospitals of Santa Cruz, the Misericordia and San Nicolás were asked to increase their bed space, a step the Hospital of Tavera had already taken,[7] and in 1599 Santiago de los Caballeros and Tavera agreed to take in plague victims (see below, chapter 3, notes 129, 130). The confraternities usually escaped the attention of the poor relief committees, but in 1589 the *mayordomos* of two confraternities that visited the poor in their homes – the Santa Caridad and the Madre de Dios – were called before the committee and given money to increase their home visits. During periods of crisis the city did attempt to coordinate the activities of the most important charitable institutions, and at such times it is probable that more than a thousand persons were treated in hospitals.

The foundation of Cardinal Tavera's hospital in 1541 marked the end of the era of large hospital foundations in Toledo. Not many small hospitals were founded after this date either, and those that were did not involve the construction of a new building but rather the conversion of an old building to serve as a hospital. Efforts were directed toward improving old hospitals, especially in the 1560s when there was a flurry of hospital improvements. The Confraternity of San Miguel increased the bed space in its hospice and purchased new blankets for the beds.[8] The old hospital of San Nicolás was taken over by the Confraternity of Jesus which offered to care for persons suffering from lengthy illnesses, such as dropsy and consumption, not treated in any of the other city hospitals.[9] The Hospital of San Antón, in a state of great deterioration, was rebuilt by the cathedral canon, don Pedro González de Mendoza, in the 1560s.[10] The San Lázaro, which had previously offered no hospitality, began to take in patients in the 1560s and by 1580 it housed eighty persons. Even though the city did not experience a surge of new hospital foundations after 1540, more persons could be cared for in 1576 than heretofore because of the improvements in the old institutions.

As for the supervision of the hospitals, the absence of records for the visits carried out in sixteenth-century Toledo makes generalizations difficult, but it is doubtful that many charitable institutions escaped diocesan inspection. In October 1544 Cardinal Tavera ordered a general visitation of his archdiocese and his instructions to the visitors were lengthy and specific. They were to visit all parish churches, hermitages, hospitals and confraternities and other pious places, to correct all things worthy of correction, to check all accounts and to compel whoever was in charge – heirs or executors – to spend any money they had to repair the building or to augment the purpose of the pious work.[11] Thus in 1544 the diocesan visitors had a mandate to visit both confraternities and hospitals, although whether this was accomplished throughout the city is another matter.

Three Toledo hospitals fell clearly within the jurisdiction of the crown: Santiago de los Caballeros, the San Lázaro and the San Antón. Throughout the sixteenth century the first hospital was visited with impressive regularity. The San Antón and the San Lázaro were each visited at least once in the late sixteenth century by the *corregidor*.[12] Possibly he made other visits, though it is doubtful that this overworked crown official was as punctilious in his hospital inspections as were the special visitors of the military order of Santiago. The legal proceedings concerning the Hospital del Rey have been discussed in chapter 2 above, but one result of the hospital's unclear jurisdictional status was that it escaped inspection by the church and apparently also by the crown. At least it escaped until 1632 when the diocesan visitor remarked, 'The first thing to be noted is that this hospital has not been inspected by the visitor-general of this city until now (August 1632); its rents and properties are confused and no older papers or books can be found except a register made in 1609.'[13]

For the remaining larger hospitals – Santa Cruz, the Nuncio, the Misericordia, the Tavera – the cathedral chapter provided visitors who inspected the hospitals regularly. As for the smaller hospitals of the city, it is doubtful that they escaped the inspection of the church. Attempts to escape required a good cause, such as foundation by a crowned head, and a great deal of money to defend one's cause in the courts, and the smaller hospitals possessed neither of these prerequisites.

The charitable organizations that proliferated in sixteenth-century Toledo were the confraternities. The majority of the brotherhoods were founded prior to 1550, but new groups were organized throughout the second half of the century. It was in 1536 that the Toledo diocesan synods warned of the dangers of so many confraternities, and in 1549 the vicar-general of Toledo, Blas Ortiz, counted some 115 brotherhoods in the city. In 1576 Hurtado counted 143, an increase of twenty-eight brotherhoods in the 27-year interval, but the majority of confraternities were in existence by 1550.[14]

For ecclesiastical purposes Toledo possessed twenty-seven parishes, the twenty-one Latin parishes plus the six *mozárabe* parishes that were largely depopulated in the 1570s. Neither Ortiz nor Hurtado mentioned two of the *mozárabe* parishes, so the results of both authors are based upon twenty-five parishes. Of the twenty-five parishes, seven experienced no change in the number of confraternities, thirteen experienced an increase of one, while in five parishes there was an increase of two or more. In this latter category were the parishes of San Isidoro, Santa María Magdalena, San Miguel, San Martín and Santa Leocadia, for the most part the poorest and fastest growing parishes. Those that remained unchanged were the more stable and wealthier parishes of San Andrés, San Antolín, San Cipriano, San Juan Baptista and San Lorenzo.

The brotherhood that experienced the greatest increase in the 27-year interval was the Confraternity of the Souls in Purgatory, known simply as the *ánimas*. In 1576 there were twelve new branches of this parochial brotherhood that buried the dead, visited graves, and celebrated masses and vigils for the souls of the dead.[15] Increasing concern for souls of the departed was, of course, a trend of the Counter-Reformation. As Hurtado put it, 'The people of Toledo are punctilious in celebrating the fiestas of Our Lady, the Holy Sacrament, and the Souls in Purgatory in order to show the splendour of their faith against the three principal errors of the Lutherans' ('Memorial', p. 566). Toledo did not experience an increase in the confraternity of the Holy Sacrament because all but two of the parishes had this confraternity in 1549. The parochial branches of these two confraternities accounted for fifty of the brotherhoods listed by Hurtado.

Another popular new cause were the brotherhoods of discipline which practised flagellation. In 1576 Toledo boasted four of these confraternities – Vera Cruz, Nuestra Señora de la Soledad, Nuestra Señora de las Angustias and Santo Nombre de Jesús – and the last three were not mentioned by Blas Ortiz.[16] These brotherhoods attracted large numbers of brothers, 600 to 2,000 according to Hurtado, who came from all backgrounds and estates. The increasing popularity of the penitents in sixteenth-century Castile runs counter to events in Venice but in accordance with the recommendations of Carlo Borromeo.[17] Hurtado waxed enthusiastic about these large confraternities and their acts of mortification, but some diocesan authorities had reservations. In 1592 the vicar-general of Toledo gave the following explanation as to why the confraternity of the Angustias should not be involved in the government of San Lázaro:

Although it is true that there are some brothers of ability and talent, because it is a brotherhood of discipline there are brothers of all conditions and there is much confusion. It is not known that they have helped the hospital in any way except with certain alms that they beg at Christmas and give to the hospital, which amount to 600 *reales*. And they use this to take advantage of the hospital for their impediments of discipline, heaps of things that occupy many rooms.[18]

It is likely that another fifty of Toledo's confraternities were those composed of people who shared a common profession. The gardeners, the silk weavers and spinners, the hat makers, the blind, the winegrowers, the porters, are but some of the groups that had their own confraternity. Though these brotherhoods adopted a patron saint and offered their brothers mutual assistance, they were probably more concerned with activities usually associated with guilds than with spiritual or pious ends. These are the brotherhoods that Hurtado wanted to eliminate because, 'instead of meeting to dedicate themselves to pious works, they meet to conspire against the common good of the republic' ('Memorial', p. 560). In suggesting that these particular brotherhoods should be eliminated, Hurtado was expressing a prejudice common among the affluent, who feared any association of artisans or workers. Also, since these confraternities were composed largely of laymen, it is questionable whether they were included within the purview of the church. Hurtado's recommendation, that they be absorbed into the parochial branches of the Holy Sacrament and the Souls in Purgatory, would certainly have placed them under close supervision of the church.

Of the 143 confraternities of the city, there were some twenty that practised open charity, as opposed to charity limited to the members of the brotherhood, and included in this estimate are the brotherhoods that operated, or at one time operated, a hospice. Of the twenty, four offered charity on a large scale: the brotherhood of the Misericordia, which operated a hospital of the same name; Nuestra Señora de la Paz y Corpus Cristi, which operated the Hospital del Rey; and the Santa Caridad and the Madre de Dios, which offered home relief in all the city parishes, though the Madre de Dios also operated a hospice. On a lesser scale, home relief was provided by the confraternity of San Miguel.

This was the situation in 1576, but it changed later in the century.

By 1589 the Santa Caridad and the Madre de Dios had curtailed their home visits and in the same year a new confraternity, that became known as El Niño Perdido, was organized by the Jesuits.[19] The new brotherhood began relieving the poor in their homes, took in poor people they found in the streets and gave them food and a place to sleep, and visited patients in the Hospital del Rey. However, by 1614 El Niño Perdido was complaining of its debts, asking the city council for a donation, and limiting its home visits to the parishes of Santo Tomé, San Isidoro and Santiago, 'where there are so many poor and sick people that the brotherhood could not sustain them all even if it were rich'.[20] Thus the amount of home relief offered by the brotherhoods changed with the years.

Hurtado criticized the brotherhoods that offered home relief on grounds that they were disorganized in selecting their recipients ('Memorial', p. 564). There was constant and acrimonious rivalry between the Madre de Dios, founded in 1505 under the auspices of Cardinal Cisneros, and the Santa Caridad, an older brotherhood. Their disputes, usually about matters of privilege or preeminence, frequently ended in litigation that cost the brotherhoods much money. Possibly this rivalry carried over to the distribution of relief, leaving some persons with too much and others with none at all, which is what Hurtado claimed. However, it is worth noting that Hurtado became involved in litigation with the Santa Caridad over the question of whether the parish cross or the Santa Caridad's cross should have preeminence in the burial of a parishioner of San Vicente, and Hurtado did not win his case.[21] This might have influenced the priest's judgment of these brotherhoods, and it might also explain another of his criticisms, that the brotherhoods performed 'spiritual works that should be exercised by clerics . . . and they treat clerics like apprentices' ('Memorial', pp. 560, 564).

The records for the Santa Caridad indicate that the diocesan authorities kept watch over some of the activities of the charitable brotherhoods. In September 1535 Dr Diego de Naveros, the visitor of the city of Toledo appointed by Cardinal Tavera, inspected the books and accounts of the Santa Caridad, and in February 1587 Dr Juan López also inspected the books and accounts.[22] After 1564 diocesan authorities regulated the begging activities of the brotherhoods and kept close watch over the execution of pious bequests. In 1613 the diocesan Council of Government handed down a provision approving an agreement between the four major brotherhoods that offered home relief, the Santa Caridad, the Madre de Dios, the Niño Perdido and San Josefe. This agreement formally limited the number of parishes for which each brotherhood assumed responsibility, and the Santa Caridad provided home relief in only four parishes of the city.[23]

Another grudge Hurtado bore the confraternities might best be described as their impious behaviour. Membership in a confraternity bestowed upon the brothers a sense of corporate identity and social prestige that they were willing to fight to defend. During a general procession, held to celebrate great events or welcome important personages to the city, all the confraternities were represented with their emblems, crosses and staffs. The exact location of one's confraternity in the procession was an issue that led to verbal and physical abuse, the 'blows and desecrations' bemoaned by Hurtado. Martin de Elcano, a *vecino* of Zarauz who acted as a representative of both the *corregidor* and the bishop of Pamplona in inspecting the hospitals of Guipúzcoa, recommended that all the confraternities of that province be merged with the Holy Sacrament so that encounters of rival confraternities would be avoided.[24]

The brothers also spent a lot of money on food and drink, and sometimes their banquets got out of hand. Martín de Elcano urged that all meals in churches or hermitages be stopped because they led to 'deaths, questions, jealousies and other depravities'. Ecclesiastical authorities continually railed against the more secular activities of the brotherhoods. The Toledo diocesan synods of 1622 ordered that the brotherhoods were not 'to run bulls, hold comedies, or celebrate profane feast days because none of this is in service of God or in honour of His saints'.[25] Judging by the continual reiteration of these proscriptions in the diocesan constitutions, the church had little success in eliminating the more secular activities of the brotherhoods, probably because the banquets, dances, theatrical displays and the like were considered by contemporaries as an important aspect of the fraternal spirit.

There is some evidence that more forceful attempts to regulate begging in Toledo were taken after the Council of Trent. In February 1564 the cathedral chapter decided to petition the governor of the archdiocese that the man who begged alms for the foundling children of the Hospital of Santa Cruz not have his begging licence renewed; the canons hoped that the hospital rector could raise money by other means.[26]

The 1568 Toledo diocesan constitutions decreed that all institutions and persons who solicited alms were to be licensed by the diocesan authorities 'except those who are truly poor or who beg for the wax and lamp of the Holy Sacrament and the Souls in Purgatory'.[27] The hermitages, confraternities and hospitals that received begging licences frequently appointed persons to beg for them known as *demandores*, a custom discouraged by the Tridentine decrees (sess. 21, cap. 9), though it seems to have continued unabated in Castile. Not only did it continue, but in 1601 the *demandores* extended their field of activity to selling crosses, images and relics causing 'great scandal and indecency' to the faithful.[28] Considering the number of institutions that solicited alms in Toledo, not to mention the individuals who might or might not have a begging licence, competition for alms must have been fierce. The Confraternity of the Santa Caridad was exultant in 1600 when the diocesan authorities determined that it should be the first confraternity to beg during Holy Week, though the fact that such matters were discussed by the brothers indicates that stronger efforts were being made to control begging in the city.

It does not appear that the diocesan authorities exercised great care in issuing begging licences to pious and charitable institutions during the first half of the sixteenth century. When in 1545 the city authorities compiled a list of recommendations for the diocesan synod Cardinal Tavera had scheduled for the following year, one of the city's recommendations was that the vicar-general should be more scrupulous in dispensing begging licences since many were given to young boys who abused this privilege.[29] The Hospital of San Antón was largely sustained by alms. In 1583 the hospital employed five young boys to solicit alms in Toledo and two men to beg in nearby villages; between them, these persons collected 75,000 mrs, more than two-thirds of the hospital's income.[30] It has been mentioned that the San Antón was in a state of collapse until it was rebuilt in 1562, but its licence to beg alms was renewed by Cardinal Tavera in 1545 and Cardinal Silíceo in 1552.[31] Possibly there was some reason why the San Antón qualified for a begging licence, but it was not on grounds of the sick people treated in the hospital.

### THE HOSPITAL OF TAVERA

The career of Cardinal–Archbishop Juan Tavera has been discussed in chapter 1. As archbishop of Toledo, inquisitor-general of Castile, and a trusted servant of the crown, the cardinal was not only one of the most influential personages of the realm, but also one of the wealthiest. Some of the profits of Tavera's years of service to the Castilian crown were to be invested in the hospital he founded in Toledo, a hospital which the cardinal stipulated should be 'large and sumptuous'. The building was barely underway when the founder died in 1545, but before his death he had made efforts to ensure that his fledgling foundation would prosper. In 1540 he obtained a bull from Paul III recognizing and approving the foundation of the new hospital, and three years later he received another bull confirming the permanent annexation of two ecclesiastical benefices to the hospital.[32] The cardinal had named his two nephews, Diego Tavera, bishop of Badajoz, and Ares Pardo de Saavedra, marshal of Castile, as executors of his will. The latter was officially named as patron of the hospital but the two nephews acted jointly in supervising the construction and increasing the endowments of the new hospital. When Diego Tavera died in 1560 as bishop of Jaén, he left the hospital a sizable endowment, but the most lucrative of the hospital's rents acquired after the cardinal's death was permanent annexation of six more benefices confirmed by a bull issued by Pius IV in 1560.[33]

Ares Pardo, the eldest son of the cardinal's eldest brother, Diego Pardo de Deza, was chosen to carry on the fortunes of the Tavera–Pardo family. As marshal of Castile and heir to considerable property in Seville, Ares Pardo was not lacking in wealth or social distinction. What the family aimed for, however, were the upper echelons of the Castilian aristocracy where they might enjoy the prestige of a title and the economic benefits of founding a *mayorazgo*, an unbreakable entail that would ensure the transmission of property intact from one generation to another.[34] In order to found a *mayorazgo* the family needed landed wealth, and when Charles V began to sell off some of the property of the military orders, Ares Pardo was able to satisfy this deficiency. In 1542 he purchased the village of Paracuellos, now practically a suburb of northeast Madrid, and six years later he bought the village of Malagón, some thirty kilometers north of Ciudad Real. After the purchase of Malagón, the Pardo family transferred its residence from Seville to Toledo. Finally, in 1556 the emperor gave Ares Pardo permission to found a *mayorazgo* and the title of *señor* of Malagón. When the lord of Malagón died in 1561, the estate consisted of the two villages purchased in the 1540s, a mansion in Toledo, 6,000 *fanegas* of grain in the *tercias* of Seville and the patronage of the Hospital of Tavera.

The Pardo family was more successful in acquiring property than in producing successors. The first marriage of Ares Pardo was childless; his second marriage to doña Luisa de la Cerda, a daughter of the duke of Medinaceli, was more fruitful, though, unfortunately, of the seven children born only one lived beyond the age of fifteen. This lone survivor, doña Guiomar de la Cerda, married three times and in 1599 was awarded the title *marquesa* of Malagón by Philip III, but she remained childless. The estates of the house of Malagón reverted to the branch of the family founded by one of Ares Pardo's sisters, Guiomar Tavera, and her husband, Juan de Ulloa Sarmiento, lord of Villalonso and Villafarces. The third generation of the Tavera–Ulloa family produced Diego de Ulloa, who was responsible for finishing the hospital church in 1624. The long list of titles and names of Cardinal Tavera's distant cousin is impressive: he was known as Prince Diego Pardo de Ulloa y Tavera, marques of Malagón, count of Villalonso, knight of the military order of Alcántara, *comendador* of Belvís and Navarra, and *mayordomo* of Philip IV.[35]

The patron of the hospital exercised great control in the government of the institution. The two most important officials, the administrator and the receiver-general or treasurer, were appointed by the patron, who also reserved the right to remove any official. After the death of her husband in 1561, doña Luisa de la Cerda, an intelligent and extremely wealthy widow, became patron of the hospital. Doña Luisa took a great interest in religious affairs. She persuaded Saint Teresa of Jesus to found a convent of her order, the Discalced Carmelites, in Malagón and continually offered the saint moral and financial support.[36] Doña Luisa also took a great interest in the hospital; it was she who appointed the most famous of the hospital's administrators, Pedro Salazar de Mendoza, who served as administrator from 1587 to 1615.

After the death of doña Luisa in 1596, the house in Toledo was sold, quite suitably, to the Discalced Carmelites, and her daughter, doña Guiomar de la Cerda, built a residence in Madrid. The transfer of the patron from Toledo to Madrid does not mean that the hospital was totally neglected, but an absentee patron was less likely to inspire devotion to duty or to ensure that the hospital was adequately supervised. Perhaps for this reason the quality of the administrators deteriorated until in 1629 the administrator Fernando Montero was placed in prison.[37] The chain of authority which had animated the hospital seemed to break after the long twenty-eight year reign of

Salazar de Mendoza. The most visible expression of the lack of direction and supervision is the degeneration of the hospital's account books which became progressively more chaotic and, in some cases, inaccurate.

As for the hospital building, it was, as Cardinal Tavera had specified, large and sumptuous.[38] The Hospital of Tavera, also known as the hospital of San Juan Bautista, was not unique in its monumental size: the Hospital of Santa Cruz was equally as large. But construction in Tavera continued for nearly seventy years and the building was never completed in accordance with the original plans. Perhaps because the construction continued for so many years, or perhaps because money for poor relief was in ever shorter supply, the founder and the architect of the Hospital of Tavera became targets of criticism. Salazar de Mendoza wrote an 'Apology' to satisfy these critics, who suggested that the original architect, Bartolomé de Bustamante,[39] would be subjected to an exceptional amount of heat in purgatory for the immense plan he drew, and that the interests of the poor would be better served if prelates gave more of their copious wealth to the poor who were living rather than investing it in stone. Salazar de Mendoza, himself a great builder and never at a loss in argument, maintained that Cardinal Tavera had given adequate alms to the poor during his lifetime (*Tavera*, ch. 52). As to the size and elegance of the building, he stressed that it conformed to the wishes of the founder and it also helped the poor indirectly since the constant construction in the hospital provided them with employment.

Even if a great deal of Cardinal Tavera's wealth was invested in stone, the hospital did care for many poor persons. Originally the hospital treated convalescents, patients with long-term ailments or those discharged from other hospitals who were not yet able to return to work. Since Santa Cruz and the Misericordia were both general hospitals catering for non-contagious ailments there was hardly a need for another hospital to do the same thing. However, in 1569, perhaps because of the increasing number of persons in need of hospital care, new constitutions were written for the Hospital of Tavera which stipulated that it was to treat any type of non-contagious ailment except 'long and difficult ones', while persons suffering from contagious diseases, defined as 'the sickness of San Lázaro and San Antón, leprosy and syphilis',[40] were not to be admitted to the hospital. Thus, in 1569 Tavera began operation as a general hospital, although it was not until 1570, when many of the deported Granada *moriscos* passing through Toledo on their way to their prescribed destinations were temporarily housed in the hospital, that it began operation on a full scale.

Figure 7 traces the hospital's activity from 1569 to 1625. The figures for this graph and all those dealing with the number of patients in the hospital at any one time have been taken from a series of books kept by the *despensero*, the official who was responsible for buying and distributing all the food consumed in the hospital. The *Libros de Despensa* include detailed menus of the meals provided in the hospital, the exact cost of each item and the total number of patients who were fed every day.[41] Since the *despensero* was accountable for every *maravedí* he spent, these are an extremely accurate set of books, at least until the 1620s when they suffered in the general deterioration of the hospital's accounts.

Figure 7 has been compiled by adding the number of persons fed every day at the evening meal, the *cena*, according to the notations of the *despensero* and is, therefore, a record of the number of meals provided in the hospital every year. It does not record the number of patients admitted to the hospital, as the same patient may have been

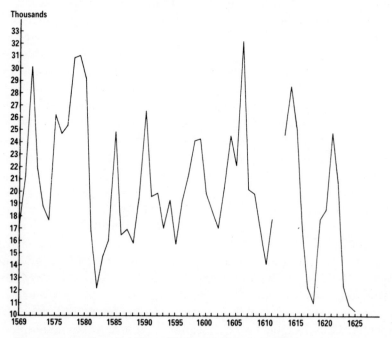

Figure 7. Number of patients fed by the Hospital of Tavera, 1569–1625

fed for three days, three weeks or even three months, depending upon the nature of his ailment. It is difficult to figure with accuracy the total number of patients admitted each year despite the series of books, the *Libros de Recepción de los Enfermos*, in which a scribe was to record the name and other details concerning each patient when he was admitted to the hospital.[42] It appears that the *Libros de Recepción* were not kept with great precision. For instance, on 27 September 1595 the *despensero* recorded that forty-eight patients had been fed and on the following day that fifty-seven patients had been fed, an increase of nine patients; but the *Libros de Recepción* record the admission of only four patients on 28 September. It seems far safer to rely on the figures of the *despensero* since all records dealing with money received the strictest attention. Unfortunately the *Libro de Despensa* for 1612 is missing, which explains the interruption in the line of figure 7.

Though the hospital's most active period extends from 1570 to 1625, patients were, of course, admitted before and after this interval. Before 1570, when the hospital admitted persons suffering from lengthy illnesses, the number of patients rarely exceeded fifty a day (7,771 meals were provided in 1555 and 9,751 in 1561); the same is true after 1625 when the hospital's shrinking income forced a limitation of the number of patients who could be admitted. After the third decade of the seventeenth century, the number of meals provided dwindled – 14,473 in 1630, 8,710 in 1643, 5,839 in 1653 – until by 1693 no more than 3,000 meals were served and the hospital was caring for fewer than ten patients a day. When new constitutions were written in the eighteenth century they stipulated that the hospital was to treat no more than thirty patients a day,[43] but earlier constitutions had set no limitation on the number of patients except to mention that the hospital was to treat as many persons as possible 'according to the possibilities of its rents'.

Salazar de Mendoza explained that the hospital adapted its bed space to meet the needs of the time and the fluctuations in the curve of figure 7 support his remark (*Tavera*, p. 287). However, an even more graphic illustration of this remark is given by figure 8, which includes the curve of the hospital's activity (figure 7) and the curve of the parish baptismal rates (figure 1). From 1569 to 1592 these two curves are in opposition: as the baptisms decrease, the hospital's activity increases; and as baptisms increase, the hospital's activity decreases. This pattern is interrupted from 1592 to 1597, which may mean that

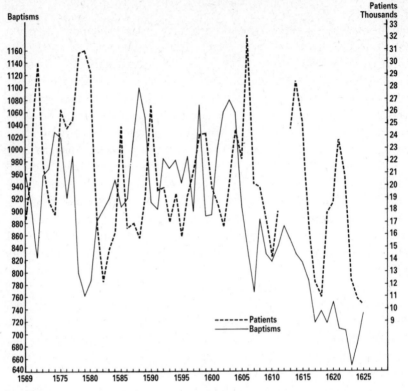

Figure 8. Toledo baptisms and patients fed by the Hospital of Tavera,
1569–1625

there were no epidemics in this five-year period. But the opposition of
the two curves begins again in 1598, with the hospital curve
demonstrating the effects of plague sooner than the baptismal curve,
and it continues until 1608, at which point there seems to be little or
no correlation between the two curves. Both 1614 and 1621 were
years of sickness in Toledo, as indicated by the curve of hospital
activity, but this is difficult to discern from the baptismal rates which
from 1609 onward never recover even the average level from 1569 to
1605. If the opposition of the two curves were to follow the pattern set
from 1569 to 1605, the increase in baptisms that begins in 1608 should
continue through 1609 and 1610; the same is true of the increase in
1616, which should continue until 1619. The obvious reason why this
does not occur is that the city no longer had the population to sustain
a large increase in baptisms. Looking at the figure, it appears that the
baptismal decrease in 1606 and 1607 reflects the first substantial loss
of population, whether through sickness or depopulation, since the

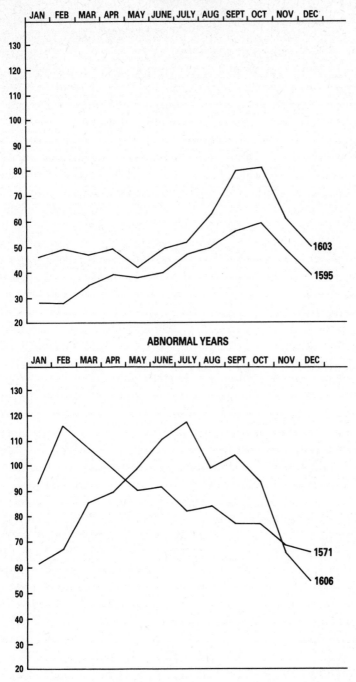

Figure 9. Monthly average of patients fed each day by the Hospital of Tavera

baptisms never rise above the 882 attained in 1608. Depopulation seems even more obvious in 1615, 1616 and 1617, when the hospital's activity is decreasing and so too is the curve of baptisms. From 1608 to 1625 the curve of the hospital's activity appears to be a more accurate indicator for the health of the city than the curve of baptisms, a conclusion which demonstrates that the Hospital of Tavera did respond to crises by caring for an increased number of people.[44]

The figures for the total number of meals provided every year do not give any idea of the monthly variations in the hospital's activity, for, according to the medical beliefs of the time, certain months were thought to be more conducive for curing illness than others (Hurtado, 'Memorial', p.544). During a normal year, when no unusual sicknesses were abroad, the hospital cared for the greatest number of patients in September and October. Figure 9(a) gives some idea of the average number of patients cared for every day during each month of two normal years. Medical theory concerning the salubriousness of September and October probably had a great deal to do with climatic and economic considerations. These were two of the most temperate months in Castile, when a patient would not suffer from extremes of heat or cold. Also, they were the months of the lowest operational costs for the hospital; no heat was necessary for the infirmaries, and grain, food and wine prices were at their lowest level. Finally, these were the months when many people were on the roads, whether vagrants, pilgrims, migrant workers, or peasants travelling to the city to buy their winter provisions. The normal pattern of hospital activity suggests that either the hospital dealt with chronic medical ailments which could be postponed until certain months of the year, or that the hot summer months caused an increase in disease, possibly typhoid fever. During years of epidemics the pattern of admittance was more chaotic and erratic, as the hospital attempted to cope with the increased demands for its services. Figure 9(b) traces the level of activity during two of the hospital's busiest years, 1571 and 1606. The maximum number of patients treated in the hospital occurred during these two years: for three days in January 1571, 126 patients were treated, and for twelve days in June 1606, there were 124 patients.[45]

The Tavera patients stayed in the hospital for a fairly long period of time, at least until the 1580s when the scribes still recorded both the date of admission and the date of departure for each patient. In a sample of 120 patients taken in 1571, the average length of stay was twelve days, while in a sample of the same number of patients taken in 1579, the average length of stay was fifteen days. Some patients stayed three weeks and some up to two months but, unless they died shortly after their arrival, no one stayed in the hospital for only one night. Perhaps the Tavera patients remained in the hospital for unusually lengthy periods because of the constitutional stipulation that no one was to be discharged until he had fully convalesced from his ailment.

Of course it is possible that the ailments treated in the hospital required a long time to cure, but the exact ailment of each patient must remain a mystery. When a patient was admitted to the hospital, a scribe recorded the nature of his complaint in the admittance book. If the scribe was new and still energetic, his notations were diverse and informative and might include such entries as toothaches, dislocations, burns, stomach and intestinal maladies, heart sickness, eye difficulties, tumours, bruises, broken bones, wounds, melancholy and weakness.[46] As a general rule, however, the scribes recorded nothing more enlightening than fevers, a diagnosis covering a multitude of ailments, so the hospital documents are of little use in determining the exact type of illness treated in the hospital.[47]

Although the hospital cared for more patients in times of sickness or epidemics, it should be noted that the number of patients in the hospital at any one time never exceeded 126. This restriction was probably imposed by limitations of bed space, personnel and income. As a private institution catering for non-contagious diseases, Tavera did not suffer from the overcrowding typical of some of the other city hospitals, nor was it burdened by the most unpleasant and lethal of diseases; under normal conditions the yearly mortality rate remained at about 17 per cent (see table 21 below).

On the other hand, the Hospital del Rey, which treated contagious and incurable diseases, probably had a mortality rate of close to 100 per cent. Luis Hurtado provides a grisly description of the conditions in this institution: 'at times, two or three boys and girls are placed in one bed . . . . one day I saw two poor persons who, for lack of beds, were placed in a bier and another two were on the covers of the same bier . . . . the bodies removed every day are so numerous that sometimes three and four biers leave together' ('Memorial', p. 558). When the San Lázaro was converted to a plague hospital in 1599, conditions in that institution were probably as bad as those of the Hospital del Rey. However, the conditions of these two hospitals do not necessarily reflect those of the other hospitals. Hospitals usually gained notoriety during times of great sickness when many of them were immensely overcrowded, a fact which has led historians to exaggerate the number of persons usually treated in these institutions. Generalizations about the quantity of patients and the quality of care given by Castilian hospitals depend very much upon the health of the year and the rents and the purpose of the hospital, but Tavera may serve as an example of a private institution that offered its patients a fair chance of survival.

Judging from Salazar de Mendoza's account (*Tavera*, chs. 49, 50), largely confirmed by the various record books of the hospital, the patients of Tavera were well treated. Officials were admonished to treat the patients with charity and compassion even if they were vexatious and peevish, 'since each one of them represents the person of Jesus Christ'. A record of the fines imposed upon the staff members by the administrator indicates that they did not always achieve the desired degree of patience,[48] but at least efforts were made to enforce the instruction.

When admitted to the hospital, the patient's name and a list of his clothes and possessions were recorded in a book. His clothes were taken from him, he was given a hospital gown, had his hair cut, his toe- and fingernails trimmed and was placed in some sort of a bed, what Salazar de Mendoza describes as 'a well-covered box' in the winter and 'a bed placed between the window niches' in the summer (*Tavera*, p. 393). The beds must have been fairly substantial because the hospital paid a carpenter to dismantle them, presumably in anticipation for the slacker months of the year.[49] Sebastián de Covarrubias mentions that workers and poor persons usually slept on nothing more than a blanket over straw or dried grass (*Tesoro*: 'Frazada'), so the sleeping accommodation of the hospital must be considered as more than adequate, especially bearing in mind that it was adorned with sheets and blankets.

All four of the infirmaries and the surgery room had a name and above each bed was a letter painted on the wall, while a tablet, attached to the bedstead, contained vital facts about the patient – his name, the date he entered, his illness and whether he had a *bulla de cruzada*. The doctor was to visit the patients twice a day, but the most important visit took place in the morning at five or seven, depending upon the season. The doctor was accompanied by a fleet of minor officials: the *botiller*, who recorded the patients' diets; the pharmacist, who noted his pharmaceutical needs; the barber, who was in charge of bleedings; the surgeon, who assisted with dislocated or broken

Figure 10. The *mayordomías* of the Hospital of Tavera

bones; and the assistant nurse, who did most of the physical work necessary in caring for each patient. Probably more salutary to the patient's health than the doctor's prescriptions were the two meals served every day, one at nine in the morning and another at five in the afternoon. When it was determined that a patient had fully recovered, his possessions and clothes were returned to him, the latter having been washed and mended.[50] Some attempts were made to maintain hygienic conditions in the infirmaries: before meals the patients' hands were washed with a damp cloth, the infirmaries and urinals were scrubbed every day and the beds were made daily.

Hospital care was not limited to physical and medical attention. It comes as a surprise to a modern reader to find that a list of patients 'cured' in a hospital includes those persons who died, but according to contemporary opinion, a patient who had confessed, received the last rites and was properly buried had been cured, spiritually if not physically. It might be argued that spiritual care was considered more important than medical care. The Toledo diocesan constitutions of 1536 ordered that 'in the first visit, the doctor called upon to treat a patient should admonish and persuade him to confess and do all that is fitting for a good Catholic'.[51] Any doctor who neglected these spiritual obligations was threatened with excommunication. This injunction did not pertain to the doctors in the Hospital of Tavera since the hospital employed an ample number of priests who were responsible for visiting every patient to see that he had discharged all his spiritual obligations. If a patient was close to death, the priests were to help him draw up a will, though they were stringently forbidden to influence the patient to leave anything to the hospital, 'if he does not do so of his own free will'. Every Wednesday and Sunday the patients took communion and if any patient was dying, a portable altar was brought to his bedside where he was given the last rites.

The services offered by a large general hospital like Tavera required substantial income. Since Castile had no mortmain laws, the hospital was free to purchase, or to receive through testaments, real estate and property. The most lucrative investment of the hospital was the income derived from the six *mayordomías*, which consisted of ecclesiastical benefices annexed to the hospital, lands purchased by the hospital, and the income received through rents and interest payments. The villages that comprised the six *mayordomías* – Talamanca, Alia, Ciempozuelos, Cazorla, Prado, and Fiñana – and their location in Spain are given in figure 10, although the village of Valdelosantos, included in the largest *mayordomía* of Talamanca, has not been located and does not appear on the map.

One of the most distant *mayordomías* was Fiñana, where the hospital owned a large house and held some 250 *censos*, a total that must have accounted for every parcel of land held by the villagers of Fiñana. In the remaining *mayordomías* the hospital collected a variety of ecclesiastical tributes, such as the first fruits, six-sevenths of 'the feet of the altar', a tribute which should have been given to support the priest of the village, the *préstamo*, a portion of the tithe, and the tithe itself. The tithe seems to have been made in two payments, one in specie and the other in grain which was apparently sold off shortly after it was collected. In the event, the hospital recorded two separate payments in its account books and the largest was always for the sale of grain. In 1589 the *mayordomía* of Alia, the most lucrative of the outside estates, brought the hospital 306,640 mrs in cash and 728,045 mrs for the sale of 2,140 *fanegas* of grain, while in the *mayordomía* of Talamanca, 40,770 mrs were collected in cash and 157,552 mrs for the sale of 462 *fanegas* of grain.[52] Ecclesiastical tributes were not the only source of income in the *mayordomías* for the hospital also collected rents on *censos*, tributes and property it owned, but this accounted for only 70,000 mrs in the *mayordomía* of Alia, a small sum compared to the other income.

Even though the profits from the outside estates varied greatly according to the harvest and the selling price of grain, the *mayordomías* provided the hospital with the largest percentage of its yearly income. In 1589 they brought in 2,543,321 mrs out of the hospital's total income of 4,678,580 mrs, nearly 65 per cent of the yearly income. According to an estimate made by the visitor who took the hospital's accounts in 1626, the six *mayordomías* accounted for 70 per cent of the total income.[53]

The *mayordomos* who collected the rents and administered the estates of the hospital were salaried officials, their income varying from 20,000 to 40,000 mrs a year, depending upon the size of the estates where they were employed. The *mayordomo* had to be a person of some property, for when he accepted the position he pledged his property as surety against negligence and fraud. If a *mayordomo* fell too far behind in his payments, he was subject to legal action by the hospital. In 1556 Blas Gómez, a cleric who had served as *mayordomo* of Alia and owed the hospital 326,115 mrs, was forced to cede the hospital 111 *fanegas* of his own land, one half a house and to sign a note for 190,000 mrs. His predecessor, Nicolás de la Serna, was less fortunate in as much as he ended up in jail in Talavera while the hospital distrained all his property.[54]

If the hospital kept close watch on its *mayordomos* in the mid-sixteenth century, the situation had changed by the seventeenth. In 1609 the total debt of the *mayordomías* amounted to nearly 2 million mrs: the village of Prado owed 437,157 mrs, Cazorla owed 228,487 mrs, Fiñana some 737,248 mrs and Talamanca and Alia were close to 600,000 mrs behind in payments.[55] The *mayordomía* of Fiñana was particularly hard hit because many of its *censo* holders had been *moriscos* who were deported after the 1570 uprising and the new inhabitants of the village were not prepared to honour the debts contracted by their predecessors.[56] It is doubtful that the hospital was any more lenient towards the *mayordomos* in the seventeenth century, but simply that collection was becoming increasingly more difficult in the face of disastrous harvests, financial confusion and an overtaxed and indebted peasantry. After 1609 the accounts for the outside *mayordomías* are chaotic with the hospital's receipts in arrears five years or more. By 1637 the hospital recorded the sale of only 1,264 *fanegas* of grain in its *mayordomías*, less than half the 3,889 *fanegas* sold in 1589, an indication that one of the hospital's most profitable sources of income had diminished.[57]

Another large and regular source of income for the hospital was the yearly interest it collected on its *juros*, a government bond that paid a stipulated annuity.[58] Charitable institutions usually purchased the low interest paying perpetual *juros*. In 1555 charitable and ecclesiastical institutions held all the perpetual *juros* issued on the *alcabalas* of Toledo, in addition to a few of the higher interest paying life and redeemable *juros*.[59] By 1626 the Hospital of Tavera owned thirteen *juros*, eleven purchased between 1545 and 1579 and the remaining two in 1606 and 1614, which represented a capital investment of 23,842,870 mrs. Nine *juros* were invested in the *alcabalas* of Toledo, while the other four were in the *alcabalas* of Seville, Ciudad Real, Uceda, and Ajofrín, a village near Toledo. The bulk of these *juros* were the lower interest perpetual *juros* that paid from $2\frac{1}{2}$ to 7 per cent interest. In 1589 the hospital collected 1,245,978 mrs on its *juros*, while in 1611, despite the fact that another *juro* had been purchased in 1606, only 890,087 mrs were collected.[60]

The hospital's diminishing receipts reflected the financial straits of the crown which in 1608 had reduced the interest payments on all perpetual *juros* to 5 per cent. The crown's financial difficulties had caused the hospital losses in the sixteenth century as well. In 1563 Philip II had reduced the interest payable on all perpetual *juros* to 7.1 per cent, and during periods of crown bankruptcies the hospital collected very little money; when the crown suspended all its payments in 1576, the hospital received only 61,871 mrs for its *juros*.[61] If the hospital occasionally lost money in the sixteenth century because of the crown bankruptcies and reduction of interest rates, these expedients became common practice in the seventeenth century. In 1621 the crown reduced interest payments on all *juros* to 5 per cent and in 1635 it appropriated one-third of the interest payable on all *juros* held by natives of Castile (foreigners lost one half). At the top of a lengthy list of hospital debts drawn up in 1637, the scribe recorded that only 591,326 mrs had been collected from *juros* because 'His Majesty has borrowed one-third of the annual payment.'[62]

The hospital also loaned money at interest in the form of *censos* and tributes.[63] Wherever the hospital had property it held a few *censos*, though, with the exception of Fiñana, the hospital did not encourage an abundance of small *censos* in the distant *mayordomías* as they offered little profit and were tiresome to collect. The hospital preferred to lend larger sums of money in the form of redeemable *censos* which, in as much as the interest rate was higher, yielded a greater profit. A great deal of money was loaned to villages in the *mayordomías* or close to Toledo and also to the city of Toledo itself.

Such *censos* could be highly profitable as long as the municipalities were able to meet their payments, but in the early decades of the seventeenth century, many cities and villages were in acute financial difficulties. In 1611 the hospital distrained the properties and rents of the village of Almorox because it had defaulted on its *censo* payments.[64] At least some recompense could be gained from Almorox whereas in the case of the city of Toledo, which owed the hospital 1,625,405 mrs in 1611, the hospital was not so fortunate. Shortly after 1606 Toledo declared a limited type of bankruptcy known as a *concurso de acreedores*. A *concurso* entailed a meeting between the debtor and his creditors in the chancery courts where a judge determined in what order the creditors should be paid by grading all debts in order of priority.[65] The city's debt to the Hospital of Tavera, graded number seventeen, had not been paid in 1626 at which time the hospital sent a piteous letter to the municipal authorities, begging them to pay the debt because of the dire needs of the hospital.[66]

If the municipalities had difficulties meeting payments, so too did individuals. The hospital distrained houses, lands, and vineyards belonging to defaulting *censo* or tribute holders in Toledo, Alia, Cabañas, Illescas, Burguillas and Toro.[67] This is not to say that the goal of the hospital's money-lending activities was to acquire property. Distrainment involved costly legal expenses and after the property was acquired the hospital was obliged to meet the payments for any other *censos* on the property, to keep the property in repair, find a suitable tenant and collect the rent. It was far simpler to collect the yearly interest on a *censo* or a tribute. In one instance of a house in Illescas the hospital decided it would not take possession because the house was old and burdened with *censos*.[68] The hospital distrained property when it was justified in doing so and when it was financially profitable, but the accumulation of property does not seem to have been the goal of its money-lending activities. Rather, it sought the maximum cash return on its investments with the minimum amount of bother.

Considering the population expansion of sixteenth-century

Toledo, it is not surprising that rents in and around the city soared. The rents the hospital collected on property owned in Toledo rose unremittingly: in 1559 the hospital collected 91,766 mrs, in 1589 some 133,586 mrs and in 1609 a total of 242,748 mrs.[69] This increase is somewhat distorted, however, because the hospital continued to accumulate more property. But the rent collected on one individual property, the hospital's *mesón* or tavern, shows an equivalent increase; it rented for 15,750 mrs in 1559 and for 70,000 mrs in 1609. After 1609, however, the rise in rents was halted. The *mesón* still rented for 70,000 mrs in 1637, but the tenant was 243,621 mrs behind in his rent payments.[70] In this same year other Toledo properties that the hospital usually rented out showed no income. If population expansion made sixteenth-century Toledo a haven for the property owner, the setbacks of the seventeenth century reversed the trend as property values plummeted and solvent tenants were few and far between. In so far as the hospital derived a very small percentage of its total income from property rents in Toledo, it was not so drastically affected as were some of the smaller charitable institutions which did not possess such diverse and copious rents. Nonetheless, defaulting tenants and empty houses in Toledo deprived the hospital of one more source of income at a time when it was hard pressed to make ends meet.

Besides the real estate in Toledo, the hospital owned grain lands in five villages not far distant from Toledo.[71] The hospital had purchased these lands with the thought that they would supply a portion of the hospital's annual grain needs; since they were all close to Toledo the grain could be transported at a reasonable price. These lands were rented out to tenants on a sharecropping basis. The percentage of grain the tenants retained is unknown, but it cannot have been much since the sum total of the lands amounted to 583 *fanegas* and the hospital usually collected 400 *fanegas* of grain.

By the second decade of the seventeenth century, all the hospital's sources of income had diminished and the Hospital of Tavera had begun what was to be a long period of financial reverses. It is true that the hospital had suffered some very bad years in the sixteenth century, but in those days the hospital still possessed a reserve of money in its deposit chest – more than 6,500,000 mrs in 1589[72] – which could tide it over a bad harvest, defaulting tenants and a crown bankruptcy. By 1626 the reserve had been spent. Totally dependent upon the shrinking income of its investments, the hospital was reduced to

Table 10. *Daily quantity of meat given to Tavera Hospital patients (in ounces)*[a]

|       | 1557 | 1569 | 1579 | 1589 | 1599 | 1605 | 1619 | 1629 |
|-------|------|------|------|------|------|------|------|------|
| A.M.  | 8.0  | 7.0  | 7.8  | 6.5  | 6.5  | 6.1  | 6.4  | 6.2  |
| P.M.  | 6.0  | 6.8  | 5.6  | 4.3  | 5.0  | —    | —    | —    |
| Total | 14.0 | 13.8 | 13.4 | 10.8 | 11.5 | 6.1  | 6.4  | 6.2  |

[a]AHT, LD, meals provided on 1 Sept. in 1557, 1569, 1579, 1589; meals provided on 18 Sept. in 1599, 1605, 1619, 1629.

selling the silver on its altar,[73] writing woeful letters to the city of Toledo and hoping for an abundant harvest.

Diminishing income dictated a cutback in the hospital's expenses. One economy measure was a reduction in the quantity of food provided for the patients. Patients received two meals a day, the larger meal, the *comida*, was served at nine or ten in the morning, the later meal, the *cena*, was served at five or six in the afternoon. Each patient was placed on a special diet according to his ailment. From 1557 to 1599 the first meal consisted of meat, fish, chicken and, in special cases, eggs or sardines. At the evening meal those patients on a meat diet were given a type of stew known as *verde*, which consisted of lettuce, spices and meat, while patients on a chicken diet received further supplements of fowl. All patients received a pound of bread a day no matter what their diet, and occasionally they were given such delicacies as apples, oranges, pears, cherries and raisins.

Assuming that a patient was on a meat diet, the quantity of meat he would have received from 1557 to 1629 is recorded in table 10. These figures have been taken from one of the meals provided in September and include the quantity of meat served at the *comida* and in the *verde*. With the exception of fresh fruit, usually served only in season, the hospital provided the same food all year round. In 1605 meat was served only at the early meal and for the *cena* the patients received either a broth made of chicken giblet or liver, or eggs. Until 1599 patients on a chicken diet had received a total of one whole chicken (*pollo*) or one half a hen (*gallina*), the varying proportions presumably had to do with the size of the fowl; by 1600 the rations had been reduced by half and these patients ate the same evening meal as the others. Eggs came to play a larger part in the diet after 1599, probably because the hospital kept its own flock of chickens so eggs remained a

Table 11. *Expenditure by the Hospital of*
*Tavera for patients' food rations*[a]

| Year | Number of meals provided | Cost of food (in mrs) including bread |
|------|------|------|
| 1579 | 30,978 | 507,660 |
| 1589 | 19,419 | 614,258 |
| 1600 | 19,875 | 831,782 |
| 1606 | 32,177 | 1,425,282 |
| 1609 | 17,100 | 689,147 |
| 1619 | 17,760 | 716,687 |

[a]AHT, LD and LB for the relevant years.

Table 12. *Hospital of Tavera expenditure in 1589 and 1626 (in mrs)*

|  | 1589 | 1626 |
|------|------|------|
| 1. *Mayordomías* | 330,738[a] | 188,000 (salaries only) |
| 2. Legal | 319,190[b] | 65,000 (salaries only) |
| Subtotal | 649,928 (16.71%) | 253,000 (4.97%) |
| 3. Staff |  |  |
| Salaries | 710,097 (43 persons) | 961,400 (52 persons) |
| 150 *fanegas* of grain for administrator | 11,900 | 76,500 (*a la tasa*) |
| Rations | 380,251 | 548,607 |
| Bread | 145,800 | 594,528 |
| Wine | 92,000 | 184,552 |
| Subtotal | 1,340,048 (24.15%) | 2,365,587 (46.20%) |
| 4. Patients |  |  |
| a) Drugs, wax, sugar, oil, cloth, wood | 805,314 | 596,700 |
| b) Food | 614,258 | 752,914 |
| Subtotal | 1,419,572 (25.59%) | 1,349,614 (26.55%) |
| 5. Construction | 2,137,228 (38.53%) | 998,902 (19.65%) |
| 6. Debts |  | 116,105 (2.28%) |
| Total | 5,546,776 | 5,083,204 |

[a]Includes *excusado*, repairs and transport.
[b]Includes collection of *censos*, litigation, notaries.

fairly cheap item. Bread rations began to dwindle in 1619 until by 1649 the patients received only a half a pound a day.[74] Concentration upon the decreasing rations fed to the hospital patients should not obscure the fact that they ate well. Considering that in the bread distributions of the 1540s and 1550s the parish poor were given a half pound of bread a day, the hospital's diet is luxurious.

The cost of feeding the patients was not usually one of the hospital's major expenses, though during times of epidemics it could be considerable. Table 11 gives some indication of the amount of money the hospital spent to feed its patients in certain years from 1579 to 1619.[75] When the hospital cared for a large number of patients, as in 1579 and 1606, the costs increased appreciably. Even when the hospital began reducing the quantity of the patients' rations, as it did in 1599, the ever increasing price of food kept the cost high; in 1589 the hospital provided 2,319 meals more than in 1609 at less cost.

A comparison of the hospital's total expenditure in 1589 and 1626 is presented in table 12. The figures for 1589 are taken from various hospital books, while those of 1626 are based on a diocesan visit made in this year.[76] Unfortunately the diocesan visitor figured the costs of construction and feeding the patients as one lump sum (1,751,816 mrs), so the costs of feeding the patients in 1626 have been taken from the hospital account books, and this figure has been subtracted from the visitor's total figure to get the costs of construction.

Gazing over the table and the percentages given for the subtotals in 1589, it is clear that the greatest single expense was construction, which accounted for 38.53 per cent of the hospital's expenditure. This high percentage may explain why Salazar de Mendoza felt compelled to justify the hospital's building programme on grounds that it provided employment for the poor. The second largest expense was the patients, followed closely by the expenses for the staff of forty-three people, about equally divided between those who provided medical services, those who provided spiritual services, and those who kept the accounts and made purchases for the hospital.[77] Some of the staff received salaries, and they were all fed at the expense of the hospital. The administrator received a salary of 100,000 mrs in addition to a gift of 100 *fanegas* of wheat, although by 1626 the grain was no longer a gift but sold to the administrator at the selling price of wheat established by the crown, known as the *tasa*.

By 1626 the percentages for expenditure have changed, in some cases dramatically. A new addition in the 1626 column is the hospital's debt. The figure given by the visitor must be limited to the expenses the hospital incurred in trying to collect its debts, because according to the hospital administrator, Joan Francisco de Santiago, the hospital had a debt of 30,000 ducats in 1626.[78] Large-scale construction ended when the hospital church was completed in 1624, but maintenance and repairs continued, and in 1626 they accounted for 20 per cent of the total expenditure, a decrease of nearly half the 1589 figure.

The expenses for the patients continued at about the same level, despite the fact that the hospital provided some 10,000 meals less in 1626 than in 1589; the increased cost of food kept the percentages about equal. Where the increased cost of food is most visible is in the expense of feeding the staff; in 1626 the staff accounted for 46.20 per cent of the hospital's total expenditure, a million mrs more than in 1589. The hospital could do nothing to control the cost of food, of course, but in 1626 there were nine more staff members than in 1589, and a staff of fifty-two was larger than the total number of patients in the hospital except for the busiest days in August and September when the patients numbered sixty.

In view of the hospital's financial difficulties, curtailment of expenditure was essential. Since the hospital constitutions stipulated that the hospital was to treat patients 'according to the possibilities of its rents', there was some justification for the reduction in the number of patients and the amount of food they were given, but a concomitant reduction in the number of the staff would certainly seem equally justified. A superabundance of officials who cared for a minimal number of patients was a common failing of hospitals. From the Council of Vienne to the Council of Trent the church had censured this malfeasance and Vives had complained bitterly of it in 1526. Whenever a hospital was beset by financial difficulties, the first item disposed of were the patients, while the staff lingered on to consume the available income in its own rations. The expense of maintaining a professional staff probably explains why many hospitals were operated by confraternities, whose members assisted in caring for the patients, and it may also explain the popularity and success of the hospital orders, like the brothers of John of God and the followers of Bernardino de Obregón who, for the most part, demanded no salary for their services. If by the third decade of the seventeenth century the Hospital of Tavera did degenerate into the common dereliction of hospitals, this should not overshadow the fact that for at least sixty years it had fulfilled its purpose at a very high level.

## THE CONFRATERNITY OF THE SANTA CARIDAD

Compared to the Hospital of Tavera, the welfare activities of a confraternity, even a wealthy and prestigious one like the Santa Caridad, seem somewhat meagre. The brothers of Santa Caridad did not offer to house, clothe and treat the poor in a large, fully-staffed hospital, but instead carried their relief to the poor in their own homes or wherever else they might need assistance. This type of relief did not entail the expense of maintaining a large, well-furnished building or of feeding, paying and housing a staff. Except for the officials who received a small salary, the members of the brotherhood offered their services free of charge as a part of the charitable obligations they sought to fulfil when they joined the confraternity.

Unfortunately many of the earliest documents of the Santa Caridad were destroyed by a fire in 1525, but according to the testimony presented by the brothers in the chancery court of Valladolid in 1557–8, the confraternity was founded in 1085 shortly after the reconquest of Toledo by Alfonso VI.[79] It was instituted to provide the Christians of the city, known as the *mozárabes*, with a decent Christian burial, to succour them in times of need and to ransom persons held in captivity by the Moors. After a period of inactivity the brotherhood was revived in the fourteenth century and transferred its residence twice before it finally settled in the *mozárabe* church of Santa Justa.

If the early history of the brotherhood remains somewhat nebulous, by the sixteenth century it counted among its members the most prestigious personages of Toledo. The marqués de Malpica, the conde de Cifuentes and the marshal of Castile were among the more illustrious brothers, but cathedral canons, city magistrates and many of the educated elite of the city belonged. The historian and hospital administrator, Pedro Salazar de Mendoza; the *arbitrista*, Juan Belluga de Moncada; the poet, Sebastián de Horozco; the lord of Higares, don Hernando de Toledo; and the *alferez-mayor* of Toledo, don Pedro de Silva; are only a few of the confraternity's most famous brothers.[80] The roster drawn up in the year 1609 included twelve *regidores*, twenty *jurados*, ten scribes, seventeen *letrados* and thirty-five clerics.[81]

Females were also admitted, although, according to the 1530 constitutions, they were to be limited to 'thirty *beatas* and widows'.[82] The convents of Santa Isabel, San Pablo, Sante Fa and Santa Clara, which housed the daughters of some of the wealthiest families of

Castile, provided the confraternity with a galaxy of famous names, many of them preceded by the title of *doña*. Elvira de Mendoza, Teresa de Carrillo, María de Guzmán, Isabel Dávalos and the very illustrious Constanza Niño de Ayala were all members. The *beatas*, a more humble group than their sister nuns, came from the Vida Pobre and the Casa de la Reyna. Widows of deceased brothers could join the confraternity when their husbands died if they desired to do so. The nuns, who are not mentioned in the 1530 constitutions, presumably qualified for membership because they were widows of deceased brothers.

The confraternity also admitted 'poor and honourable' persons, but it is difficult to determine how many members fell into this category. Since these members were excused from paying the 306-mr entry fee, they were not recorded in the account books when they joined; nor were they distinguished in the membership lists, which included special mention only for the rich and famous and left the names of the more ordinary individuals unadorned by any remarks concerning occupation or social status. In 1531 when the confraternity distributed its yearly gift of a gown to persons in need, some forty poor brothers and sisters received a gown[83] signifying that, in a society whose membership was limited to 200, the poor comprised 20 per cent of the confraternity.

It has been suggested that the Santa Caridad became the exclusive preserve of the wealthy by the seventeenth century, and that the trend to exclude the less affluent began in the mid-sixteenth century.[84] If this change did occur it is difficult to document because of the lack of information about the poorer brothers. As late as the 1570s the brotherhood received bequests from two widows whose husbands had been brothers: in 1571 Madalena Capoche, who had been married first to a silk weaver and then to a turner, named the Santa Caridad as executor of her will and left the brotherhood half her estate; and in 1575 Ana Hernández, the widow of a halter maker, left the brotherhood a bequest for the fulfilment of spiritual obligations.[85] In theory at least, the eldest sons of these two women could have taken the place of their deceased fathers as brothers of the confraternity. The entry fee was increased from 306 mrs in 1530 to 3,000 mrs in 1583, a sum that would discourage any poor person from joining the brotherhood. But this fee applied only to new members: poor brothers and sisters were exempted from paying it, and the eldest son of a deceased brother paid only a nominal entry fee of 1 *real* for the scribe and the porter and the cost of a pound of wax.[86] While it is certain that by the 1580s the brotherhood cut back on the relief it offered to needy outsiders, it appears that at least until the first decade of the seventeenth century relief continued to be given to those poor and needy persons who were members of the brotherhood.[87]

The fact that the brotherhood admitted females and poor people in limited numbers does not mean that it was a democratic organization. The government and administration of the society were controlled by the elite group of officials who kept all the accounts, supervised the daily activities and made all the important decisions in their frequent and closed meetings. At the annual meeting that was open to all the members, the officials for the new year were announced to the assembled group, having been chosen by the old incumbents with the assistance of 'four or five of the oldest and wisest brothers'.[88] Since the number of officials continued to increase throughout the sixteenth century – from eight in 1524 to thirty-four in 1600 – it might be argued that the confraternity expanded its circle of directors, but it was a horizontal rather than a vertical expansion, for the officials continued to be chosen from the ranks of the *regidores*, *jurados* and the wealthy elite who dominated the brotherhood. The increasing number of officials does not mean that the confraternity was performing any more charitable works at the end of the century than it did in 1524. A proliferation of officials and the lengthening of titles were phenomena common to all Castile by the end of the century.

The first three-quarters of the sixteenth century were golden years for the Santa Caridad in terms of the quantity and variety of its charitable activities. The brotherhood continued to serve as a burial society. All the brothers and any member of his immediate family, delimited by the constitutions to any relative or child over seven who was maintained in the home of a brother, were entitled to burial. The brothers also interred any citizen of Toledo who paid the stipulated fee of 1,000 mrs necessary for a 'commended' burial (*entierro encomendado*), though the costs were higher for people of 'quality'.[89] Since burial by the Santa Caridad was considered a social necessity for those who could afford it or did not belong to another burial society, the confraternity accompanied the funeral procession of many wealthy persons of the city. Some people were buried free of charge as part of the brotherhood's charitable obligations. Any poor person who did not belong to a burial confraternity or possess property or money; any prisoner who died in Toledo, whether on the gallows or in the prison; and any person who met his death by drowning, were buried at the expense of the brotherhood, although alms were solicited on these occasions to help defray the costs. Judging from the record books of the Santa Caridad, more persons met their death in Toledo through drowning than they did in the prisons. A surprising number of people were fished out of the deep, fast-flowing Tajo river each year, especially during the warm months from May to September.

Every year the confraternity appointed six visitors who were to visit the poor and sick in their homes and provide them with food, medicine and clothes. Each of the visitors was responsible for three or four of the city's twenty-one parishes and in each parish some five or six persons received assistance. Parish relief was not limited to members of the confraternity, but the majority of persons who received parochial relief were women and many were widows of deceased brothers; in October 1524 twenty-six of the thirty weekly recipients were females and fifteen of these were widows.[90] One of the parish visitors also included the three city prisons in his rounds, and in the largest of these establishments, the Royal Prison, the brothers paid a 'Mistress of the Prison' who regularly attended to the medical needs of the inmates.

Supplementing these daily activities were the three annual feast days celebrated by the confraternity at Christmas, Easter and Pentecost, when meat, bread and wine were distributed to the poor brothers and sisters, the parish poor, the persons in the Hospital del Rey and the inmates of the city prisons. The quantity of food and wine distributed varied in accordance to the prices of the year and the finances of the brotherhood, but they included a substantial amount of food. The 1530 constitutions suggested that between 1,000 and 1,500 one-pound loaves of bread should be baked, and in 1531 between twenty and thirty sheep were slaughtered for each of the banquets.[91] At Easter the brothers gave gowns to all persons in need, whether they were brothers or not, and the city prostitutes, forbidden to practise their trade during Holy Week, were given a small donation of one half a *real* so that 'they can buy food and do not sin'.

With the exception of the commended burials, all the welfare activities of the brotherhood were to be financed through alms begged by the brothers. Earlier constitutions had forbidden the confraternity from holding rents, 'in order to imitate the holy apostles

Table 13. *Income and expenditure of the*
mayordomo de finados *of the Santa*
*Caridad[a] (in mrs)*

| Year | Income | Expenditure |
| --- | --- | --- |
| 1524 | 259,088$\frac{1}{2}$ | 272,012 |
| 1531 | 260,191 | 289,284 |
| 1548 | 178,193 | 180,453 |
| 1555 | 251,284 | 214,078 |
| 1566 | 263,362 | 261,197 |
| 1576 | 142,855 | 132,100 |
| 1600 | 213,456 | 280,292 |
| 1622 | 203,523 | 184,213 |

[a]ADPT, Libros de finados, 'Cargo' and 'Descargo'
for the relevant years.

of Christ who did not have wealth or property and maintained
themselves by alms from good people',[92] so all the welfare activities
had to be financed by alms. While this prohibition was changed,
apparently in the first decade of the sixteenth century, all the
brothers, no matter what their social status, were under oath to beg
alms as part of their obligations to the confraternity. Some persons,
probably poor brothers, did nothing but beg alms continually,
bringing in the so-called continual demands (*demandas continuas*).
Other brothers made less frequent but more lucrative sallies; alms
were brought in weekly by different brothers who usually went in
pairs to beg in certain parishes. The most profitable collections were
made before the three annual feast days when the entire confraternity
made house-to-house visits throughout the city.

The income received through alms and the commended burials,
and the money paid out for all the confraternity's various welfare
activities were recorded daily by the *mayordomo de finados* (the steward
of the dead), one of the most important officials of the brotherhood.
Hardly a day passed that the *mayordomo* did not record the receipt of
alms, whether from the charity burials, the continual demands, the
poor boxes hung at the prisons, or from the periodic collections made
by the brothers. By the 1570s, however, the *mayordomo*'s records show
a notable diminution in daily alms receipts. Whereas in 1524 the
*mayordomo* recorded at least one donation a day and frequently more
than one, by 1586 the donations were reduced to fifteen a month, by

1600 to an average of seven a month and by 1622 to a mere two a month.[93]

The decrease in alms receipts is not reflected in the total yearly income recorded by the *mayordomo*, outlined in table 13, which remained remarkably stable from 1524 to 1622. This stability is somewhat deceptive, however, for the primary source of income had shifted from the daily alms receipts to the revenues from the expensive commended burials. In 1531 approximately 210,000 mrs or four-fifths of the total intake of 260,191 mrs had come from alms; in 1576 it accounted for less than half the yearly income; in 1622 only 50,000 mrs were collected and nearly all that came from the three annual house-to-house collections.

The expenditure of the *mayordomo de finados*, also given in table 13, remained as stable as his income which, in so inflationary an era as the hundred years in question, indicates a decreasing activity on the part of the brotherhood. In 1531, when the brothers purchased 1,200 *baras* (one *bara* equals 33 inches) of cloth to make the gowns for its annual gift to the needy, the cost was 18,000 mrs, while in 1566 only 580 *baras* cost 46,400 mrs.[94] This custom seems to have been abolished in the 1570s. In 1524 the average cost of a charity burial was 36 mrs: 24 mrs for the two priests who said mass and 12 mrs for the porter who carried the body. In 1600 a charity burial cost 400 mrs and included the payment of three priests (108 mrs), six paupers who accompanied the funeral procession (72 mrs), the grave digger (136 mrs), the sacristan (50 mrs) and the porter (34 mrs).[95] Perhaps because of the rising costs the confraternity undertook fewer charity burials: in 1524 some 181 paupers, prisoners and persons were buried; in 1600 some 15; and in 1622 only 23.[96]

By 1589 the brotherhood had almost ceased its open parish relief, although the poor of the confraternity still received assistance.[97] However, in 1598–9, probably in response to pleas from the municipal authorities who sought to utilize all available resources against the plague, the Santa Caridad again offered relief throughout the city and as a result went heavily into debt, 'because of the great sum of money spent to combat the attack of pestilence'.[98] By 1613 the Santa Caridad was responsible for relieving the poor in only four of the city parishes – San Román, San Bartolomé, San Cristóbal, and San Salvador.[99]

It is clear from the figures given in table 13 that the brotherhood frequently spent more money than it collected; in five of the eight years included in the table expenditure exceeded income. The documents are silent as to how the brothers managed to balance their books. It is possible that the officials and the wealthier brothers made up the difference out of their own pockets. Also, by 1560 and probably earlier the brotherhood kept a special reserve account from which it might have borrowed money to pay any debts.[100]

In some areas the Santa Caridad continued and even extended its activities. The three annual feast days were celebrated despite the increasing costs of bread, meat and wine. The brothers maintained their interest in the Royal Prison not only by paying the nurse who helped the sick, but also by appointing six brothers, each of whom devoted two months of the year to serving in the infirmary, and, in the 1590s, by putting the brothers of John of God in the infirmary. In 1594 the confraternity complained to the city council of the unusually large number of sick and wounded prisoners, many of whom were dying in the institution because of the overcrowded conditions.[101] The city prostitutes also received increased attention. By 1576 the Santa Caridad had appointed four 'commissaries to confine the prostitutes during Holy Week'. These four officials assisted when the prostitutes were transferred from their usual residence in La Casa de la Mancebía to the Hospital of San Ildefonso where, as Luis Hurtado explained, 'the strumpets are sheltered, fed, rebuked and persuaded to abandon their infamous and sinful lives' ('Memorial', p. 557). In 1600 the Santa Caridad spent a total of 7,820 mrs to reimburse the *alguaciles* who supervised these women, to move all the beds and blankets from one building to the other, to pay the euphemistically entitled 'Father and Mother' of these wayward women (presumably because they were temporarily deprived of their income whilst their charges were confined and endoctrinated), to have the females taken to hear sermons in the Dominican convent of San Pedro Mártir and to purchase bulls for those who repented.[102]

But the brotherhood's greatest extension of activity was in the fulfilment of pious bequests it received from testators. It has been mentioned that the confraternity was originally forbidden to hold property and rents, but in 1557 the brothers explained that they had changed this policy, 'seeing that it was a greater work of charity to discharge obligations for the souls of the dead than for their bodies'.[103] According to one recent study, the Santa Caridad did not actually own the rents, properties or income it received from testators, but merely served in the capacity of an administrator or trustee.[104]

Table 14. *Income of
the* mayordomo de
memorias *of the
Santa Caridad*[a] *(in
mrs)*

| Year | Income |
| --- | --- |
| 1524 | 63,966 |
| 1531 | 71,870 |
| 1548 | 117,701 |
| 1555 | 105,370 |
| 1566 | 124,912 |
| 1596 | 283,102 |

[a]ADPT, Libros de finados,
Memorias, 1524, 1531,
1548, 1555, 1566 and
Libro de memorias, 1596.

The income the brotherhood received from last testaments and wills, outlined in table 14, increased steadily throughout the sixteenth century. When all the brotherhood's bequests were reviewed in 1660, there were a total of 182, each of which contained some type of spiritual obligation, such as the celebration of masses, vigils or vespers, the covering of a grave, and offerings or prayers given for the souls of the dead.[105] Of the 182 bequests, 47 also included charitable obligations.

Probably the largest bequest received by the Santa Caridad was that of the wealthy *regidor*, Alonso Daza and his wife, García de Renteria.[106] In addition to the money left for spiritual purposes, Alonso Daza also founded many charitable trusts. One was devoted to providing the parish poor of San Justo with bread; another paid for the maintenance of one bed for an incurable pauper in the Hospital del Rey; another paid 100 *reales* to any prostitute who repented of her sins and abandoned her former life; another established dowries for poor orphan girls; and the Santa Caridad directly received 10,000 mrs for the relief of poor or sick parishioners of San Justo and another 10,000 mrs for 'the benefit of the poor'. Far more usual were the smaller bequests, frequently given by a poor brother or sister, such as Marina López (1507) who named the Santa Caridad as her heir and executor and left her houses for the benefit of the poor.

Table 15. *Date and purpose of 47 charitable bequests given to the Santa Caridad*

| | Poor relief | Dowries | Widows | Prostitutes | Hospitals | Prisons | Total |
|---|---|---|---|---|---|---|---|
| 1500–9 | 3 | 1 | | | 1 | | 5 |
| 1510–19 | 3 | | | | | | 3 |
| 1520–9 | 2 | | | | | | 2 |
| 1530–9 | | 1 | 1 | | | | 2 |
| 1540–9 | 0 | | | | | | 0 |
| 1550–9 | 0 | | | | | | 0 |
| 1560–9 | | 1 | | | | 1 | 2 |
| 1570–9 | 1 | | | | | 1 | 2 |
| 1580–9 | 5 | 3 | | 1 | 1 | 2 | 12 |
| 1590–9 | 4 | 2 | 1 | | | 5 | 12 |
| 1600–9 | 4 | 1 | | | | 1 | 6 |
| 1610–19 | 1 | | | | | | 1 |
| Total | 23 | 9 | 2 | 1 | 2 | 10 | 47 |

Frequently the Santa Caridad was named as one of many beneficiaries and was responsible for fulfilling one of many charitable obligations stipulated by the testator. This was the case for the will of another wealthy *regidor*, Juan Gómez de Silva, who left the brotherhood 102,500 mrs (derived from the income of four distinct properties) to care for the poor and sick *envergonzantes* in the months of September and October 'or whenever there is the most need'.

The forty-seven charitable bequests received by the Santa Caridad are outlined in table 15, according to the date the will was notarized and the philanthropic purposes stated by the testator.[107] Throughout the period, poor relief remained the most popular cause. It is difficult to be specific about the exact type of relief given to the poor because in many instances, especially in the early years of the sixteenth century, testators were vague in their specifications. Catalina de Villalobos (1519) left the confraternity 150,000 mrs 'for masses and to spend for the poor according to custom'. García Martínez (1529) ordered the brotherhood to spend all his wealth for his soul and to do good for the poor. By the 1580s and 1590s, when Alonso Daza and Juan Gómez de Silva drew up their wills, testators were much more precise in their instructions as to how money should be spent. Doña Catalina de los Angeles (1594) left bread for the parish poor of San Nicolás, while Diego López de Santa Justa (1570) left money for shirts to be divided among the poor during Holy Week.

Two causes that drew an increasing amount of support in the later years of the century were the prisons and dowries, a trend that is also evident in a recent study of Venetian charitable testaments.[108] Eight of the ten foundations for the prisons were given to help defray the cost of supplying the prison cisterns with water, an expensive proposition in a city chronically short of water. Others were dedicated to paying for the release of poor persons imprisoned for debts, to give the prisoners bread and fruit, or to help pay for the operation of the prison infirmary. For those who could afford it, the most popular charitable foundation of the late sixteenth century were the *suertes de doncellas*, the lotteries whereby young women were selected to receive money to be used as a dowry or, in some instances, to enter a convent. In six of the nine bequests included in the table, the testators stipulated that the recipients should be poor orphans, while the remaining three mentioned only young women. Escolástica Suárez wanted young women to be chosen from her family, but if none could be found, then any needy, honorable female could qualify.

Possibly the increasing number of charitable bequests left to the Santa Caridad in the last two decades of the sixteenth century was a response to the brotherhood's inability to maintain all its increasingly expensive charitable obligations. The assured income derived from testaments may have allowed the brotherhood to dispense charity in a more systematic fashion, but the bequests, usually earmarked for a specific purpose, could not be used to subsidize the open parish relief the brotherhood had practised in the earlier years of the century.

Testamentary bequests also entailed a lot of bookkeeping. Throughout the sixteenth century the obligations stipulated by a testator became more expensive as the income, usually the rent on a property or the interest on a tribute or *juro*, remained stable or diminished. Thus the brothers had periodic meetings with the diocesan officials to reduce the charitable or spiritual obligations of the testament in accordance with the income. On a minor scale this occurred in 1564 and 1614,[109] but it was in 1660 that all the brotherhood's bequests were inspected in what was known as the General Reduction of 1660, carried out under the auspices of Cardinal–Archbishop Baltasar Moscoso y Sandoval. The result of this review, which lasted until 1664, was that all the brotherhood's obligations, whether charitable or spiritual, were reduced, and in some cases the bequest was eliminated completely. Out of its total of 182 bequests, the Santa Caridad retained 132, and those that were eliminated were usually the small endowments that amounted to no more than a few hundred *maravedís* tribute on a house in Toledo. Reading the results of the 1660 reduction one gets the impression that nearly every house in Toledo was in a state of ruin or so overburdened with *censos* or tributes that nothing could be collected. The bequests that fared the best were the largest and most diverse: the *juros*, *censos*, and properties given by Alonso Daza in 1580 still paid 249,274 mrs, more than half the interest paid in 1580, though nearly all the income that had not been lost in *concursos* had been invested in *juros* by 1660.

Obviously no charitable institution, society or giver escaped the effects of the financial reverses that struck seventeenth-century Toledo. While some economy measures were taken earlier, it was in the third decade of the seventeenth century that the Hospital of Tavera began to cut back the number of patients it admitted and was unable to collect many of its rents. The Santa Caridad curtailed its open parish relief in the late sixteenth century, but it was in 1619 that the brotherhood received its last charitable bequest. Dispensation of charitable assistance clearly depended upon the wealth available to maintain these services. Perhaps the charitable societies and institutions of Toledo were particularly hard hit because of the city's dramatic loss of trade and population in the early seventeenth century, but financial chaos and recession struck all seventeenth-century Castile. It is doubtful that many charitable institutions escaped unscathed, or that they were able to provide charitable assistance on the same level they had in the sixteenth century.

# 5

## The recipients of relief

PARISH POOR AND HOSPITAL PATIENTS

No matter how diligently one searches, discussions about poor relief in sixteenth-century Europe are limited by the documentation available. The bulk of the extant records have to do with the finances of charitable institutions or with the individual who was wealthy enough to make a last will and testament, while the recipients of poor relief remain colourless and vaguely defined individuals in among the mass of humanity known as the poor.

The usual recourse for anyone in search of generalizations about the more humble estates of society is a quotation from literary sources, but utilization of contemporary opinions is hazardous. Should one quote from Domingo de Soto:

And who doubts but that in solemn holy days, especially during Holy Week, that the sight and clamour of the poor melt hearts to feel the passion of Christ; (*Deliberación*, p. 122)

or from Juan de Robles:

How much better Holy Week seems now that the services are celebrated in quiet and silence instead of the noise previously made by those persons who neither looked at the service nor considered the mysteries of Holy Week, but only how they could pull money out of the persons from whom they begged; (*De la orden*, p. 268)

or from Saint Teresa of Jesus:

I think I have much more compassion for the poor than I used to have. . . . They cause me no repulsion, even when I mix with them and touch them, and this, I now see, is a gift of God, for, though I used to give alms for the love of Him, I had no natural compassion.[1]

Such quotations offer more illumination about the character and prejudices of the authors than about the poor, and opinions about the poor and poverty were as diverse in the sixteenth century as they are today.

Escape from the neatly documented books of institutional finance, the not so neat but abundant wills of the wealthy, and the observations of poets and theologians, to the illiterate poor of the sixteenth century is not such an easy task. Nor is the escape encouraged by the assortment of humanity sheltered under the ample skirts of poverty. In one recent discussion of the poor, the author has mentioned vagabonds, beggars, gypsies, workers, criminals, *pícaros*, the proletariat, the lower orders, the common people and the dangerous classes.[2] In the welter of candidates jostling for inclusion in the lists, it may be useful to review some of the individuals considered by contemporaries as poor, or in need of relief.

One candidate is a poor woman given a charity burial by the confraternity of the Santa Caridad in 1593.[3] The woman's name is not given, but she lived alone in a room in the city, presumably a rented room. After she was buried her possessions were auctioned off, a normal custom in the case of anyone buried with the assistance of charity in sixteenth-century Toledo. Aside from serving as a poignant example of the limited possessions of the poor, the auction underlines the importance and value of clothes, which seem to have been used until they literally disintegrated. The total number of items found in the woman's room amounted to fourteen (two of which are in-decipherable), and they were sold for a total of 532 mrs or 11 *reales*. In the way of room furnishings she had two waterjars, one of which was broken (84 and 68 mrs), an old chest (68 mrs), a mortar (8 mrs), a small oil lamp (24 mrs), and some old bowls (8 mrs). Her wardrobe consisted of two small headdresses (68 mrs), an old shirt (85 mrs), an old brown mantilla (68 mrs), some pieces of an old blanket (no price given), some old rags (16 mrs) and an old brown mantilla that was given to a poor person.

A larger perspective of the people who received relief can be drawn from the records of Cardinal Tavera, who in 1538 gave 500 *fanegas* of wheat to 238 needy parishioners of Toledo.[4] The cardinal's close associate, Pedro de Campo, and the vicar-general of Toledo, Licenciado de la Gasca, compiled a list of the individuals who received the wheat, and the recipients were selected by the priest of each parish. Among the recipients were doña Jerónima, doña Ísabel de la Pena, the *maestro de muchachos* (possibly the schoolmaster, Alejo Venegas), two weavers, a bonnet maker, a halter maker, a mason, a cloth shearer and a blind man. Unfortunately the occupation of some male recipients is given only in the parishes of San Miguel and San Justo. Since 66 per cent of the recipients were females and 33 per cent of these were widows, perhaps occupations seemed an unnecessary addition to those who compiled the list.

If the most striking fact about the 1538 poor list is the preponderance of females, it is somewhat disconcerting to see that two *doñas* were included and to note that they and the schoolmaster received three *fanegas* of wheat while most of the parishioners were given only two. Yet the inclusion of titled women and their extra *fanegas* of grain was quite understandable to a society which considered that persons of high estate who had fallen upon evil days needed more relief than a poor person who had always had less and was accustomed to eating less.[5] And how shall this list of persons be characterized? It would seem a bit far-fetched to place widows in the category of 'dangerous classes' to whom Cardinal Tavera gave grain 'to stave off social unrest'. Nor will the broad, dispassionate term 'the common people' do, given the presence of two highly-born *doñas*. One is left with the untidy conclusion that poverty, as defined in sixteenth-century Toledo, cut across all social classes.

Partial records for another, much larger alms distribution have also survived.[6] This distribution, made in all the parishes at Christmas time in 1573, was arranged and paid for by Sancho Busto de Villegas, who acted as governor of the Toledo archdiocese after the death of Gómez Tello Girón in 1569 until the appointment of Cardinal Quiroga in 1577. The governor drew up a list of instructions for the parish priests and the *regidor* or *jurado* who actually distributed the alms in each parish, which began by urging that a written list of 'the most principal and honorable poor' be compiled, 'secretly and quickly, so that negotiations and importunities do not occur'. These lists were to be returned to the governor so they could serve as written evidence for anyone who might appear to complain that they had been slighted. The governor urged that young marriageable women or orphan girls 'who are in danger of being lost', virtuous journeymen and small retailers who lacked means, and any person who was sick, be given special consideration in the distribution.

As his last request the governor asked the parish priests to make a list of all the 'idle poor' (*pobres zánganos*) and any children who did not work or learn a trade, 'because, having made this list, they will be removed, half by the ecclesiastical arm and half by the secular arm,

Table 16. *Alms distributed in Toledo parishes, 1573*

| Parish | Amount of money distributed (in *reales*) | Approximate no. of recipients | 1561 population (inhabitants) |
|---|---|---|---|
| S. Juan Baptista | 200 | 39 | 580 |
| S. Salvador | 600 | 41 | 645 |
| S. Cristóbal | 600 | 120 | 1,190 |
| S. Nicolás | 1,000 | 193 | 3,060 |
| S. Miguel | 2,000 | 462 | 3,855 |
| S. Isidoro | 2,000 | 518 | 3,320 |

and more alms will remain for the deserving poor'. When the governor spoke of removing the idle poor, presumably he meant they should be removed from the list of alms recipients. As for the careful balance of responsibility between church and state, though the governor's directive about compiling a list of the idle poor applied only to the parish priests, the actual parish visits, distributions and poor lists were made by the combined efforts of a priest and a city official, who, it appears, were both responsible for deciding which paupers were deserving and which were idle. Clearly the governor was not a believer in indiscriminate almsgiving.

Records survive for the recipients in only six of the city parishes. This is a small number of parishes, but included among the surviving lists are the parishes with the highest and lowest percentage of poverty in 1558 (see table 5). These six parishes are given in table 16, beginning with the wealthy parishes of San Juan Baptista and San Salvador and working down to the poorer parishes of San Cristóbal, San Nicolás, San Miguel and San Isidoro. Also included in the table are the amount of money distributed in the parish, the approximate number of recipients, and the parish population in 1561.

According to the original instructions of the governor, each parish was to receive 600 *reales*, but this fixed quota was obviously modified, probably after consideration of the varying population and poverty levels in the parishes. The small wealthy parish of San Juan Baptista received only 200 *reales*, the medium sized parishes of San Salvador and San Cristóbal received 600 *reales*, the larger parish of San Nicolás received 1,000 *reales*, while the large and very poor parishes of San Miguel and San Isidoro each received 2,000 *reales*. Those who fared best in this distribution were the forty-one needy persons of San

Salvador; the smallest amount of money given out in this parish was 8 *reales*, whereas in San Isidoro the average amount was 2 *reales*. It is difficult to explain why San Salvador, with its 645 parishioners, should receive 400 *reales* more than San Juan Baptista or the same amount as the more populous and poorer parish of San Cristóbal. Those responsible for the distribution in San Cristóbal, the *regidor* Juan Gómez de Silva and the parish priest Andrés Níñez, clearly felt they did not have enough money. In their final summary they apologized for not giving more money to young women and poor journeymen and justified their disregard of the governor's instructions on grounds of the great number of very poor people in the parish.

The figures given in table 16 for the approximate number of people who received relief are based on counting each individual entry on the lists as one. In the case of individuals this is a valid system, but in the case of families it is not. For instance, Juan Sánchez, recorded as having a wife and four children, may have received more money for his family, and the same is true of the many women with children. However, in each parish a slightly different system of recording facts is used. In some cases the reason why a person received extra money is explained, but usually it is not; nor is the number of children in a family always recorded. The only way to achieve consistency among the various methods used in the parish lists is to adopt the system of counting each individual entry as one, but the figures in table 16 are probably an underestimate of the total number of individuals who received relief. In all the parishes except San Cristóbal and San Salvador, a few people received larger sums than the average amount. These were the people who met the governor's criteria of deserving special attention: in San Nicolás, one young woman received 34 *reales* for her marriage; in San Juan Baptista, two women received 18 and 22 *reales* for marriages; in San Miguel some people received as much as 22 *reales* but no explanation as to why is given; and in San Isidoro the priest received 107 *reales* to help with the marriage of young women.

In all six parishes the majority of recipients are females, whether *beatas*, widows, women with children whose husband, if they had one, is not mentioned, *doncellas*, or just women with no distinguishing features given. In San Juan Baptista females account for 64.10 per cent; in San Salvador, 60.97 per cent; in San Cristóbal, 63.33 per cent; in San Nicolás, 73.05 per cent; in San Miguel, 57.14 per cent;

and in San Isidoro, 56.56 per cent. The records for the parish of San Juan Baptista are the most informative, and this parish contained six *beatas*, four of whom worked, numerous widows, some of whom worked (two sold green vegetables and one kept a tavern), or who were described as old, alone, or having children. Instances when the occupation of the women is mentioned are rare in the other parishes.

This lack of information about occupations is also true for the men. In San Isidoro an occasional tailor, bonnet maker, or fisherman is mentioned, but these account for only sixteen of the 518 entries. In San Juan Baptista three tailors who had wives or children received money, because even though they worked they did not earn enough to support their families. Two barbers, one described as old with a sick wife and the other with a wife and three children, also received money, as did two men who 'served', a stocking maker, two tavern keepers and one old man. Those who received assistance in San Juan Baptista were the resident poor who suffered from physical handicaps, sickness, old age, too many children and a small salary, or, in the case of the women, children and no husband.

While some Castilians may have viewed the *moriscos* as carriers of disease, and the Castilian church may have viewed them as heretics, it is consoling to note that the *moriscos* were not excluded from relief. In the parish of San Isidoro *moriscos* accounted for 147 of the 518 people who received relief: 59 women, 10 widows, 23 men who were heads of households, and 55 men. Of the 2,000 *reales* given to this parish, 500 were spent to feed the *moriscos*: meat for those who could eat it, as well as raisins, pomegranates, figs, chickens, apples and bread. The accounts are so incomplete that it is difficult to be precise, but it appears that more money was given for *moriscos* in other parishes. Those in San Cipriano and San Sebastián (one of the *mozárabe* parishes), were also fed and given 4 *reales* apiece, while those in San Isidoro, Santiago and Santo Tomé received mattresses stuffed with straw or esparto and probably some of the shoes, stockings and blankets that were given out.

Possibly one means of distinguishing the varying degrees of poverty that existed in the city parishes is that the poor of San Isidoro, old Christians as well as *moriscos*, received blankets and clothes in addition to money. These were people who lacked every essential of life – clothes, money, housing and an occupation. If much of the governor's Christmas gift was to be directed to the established, resident poor of the community, such as those in San Juan Baptista, the inclusion of the *moriscos* and other people of San Isidoro added the element of destitution to the list.

As for the records of idle poor that the parish priests were to send to the governor, they are mentioned in only two of the six lists. The priest of San Cristóbal reported that there were no such people in his parish, while in San Nicolás, Dr Alonso de Vallos said that he had already compiled such a list which he would forward whenever the governor wanted it.

The lists drawn up for Cardinal Tavera in 1538 and Governor Busto de Villegas in 1573 are similar in that females received the greatest amount of relief. However, the 1573 distribution was a much larger operation, with less relief given to more people. The 2 *fanegas* of wheat (160 pounds) given by Cardinal Tavera in 1538 could have fed a person for six months, while the 2 *reales* of 1573 probably bought a pound of bread. Another discrepancy between the two lists is the absence of *doñas* in 1573. Toledo must have housed as many, if not more, needy *doñas* in 1573 as in 1538, but their absence from the later lists suggests that they received relief by other means. Possibly the governor had a separate list of better-born people who were in need of assistance, or possibly by 1573 the confraternities that offered home relief took care of the *doñas*. Relief of the *envergonzantes* by special confraternities was what Domingo de Soto had recommended in 1545. It is very difficult to find any record of these people since every effort was made to keep their need secret so they would not be exposed to the humiliation of having others see that they accepted charity.

The decrease in the activities of the confraternities that offered home relief has been discussed in chapter 4, but concomitant with their decreasing relief was an increasing selectivity in choosing recipients. By the last two decades of the sixteenth century, the Madre de Dios decided to limit relief to 'widows or honorable poor who cannot go to the hospitals', and, after a consultation with theologians, the brotherhood abandoned its hospice because 'the shamefaced poor should be preferred over all others' and the hospice served another type of needy – the indigent, the beggar and the outsider. By the late seventeenth century the Santa Caridad limited its relief to 'people of the first order',[7] a limitation that excluded silk weavers and other 'honorable' people. Such extreme exclusion was not typical of the late sixteenth century, but it is clear that at this time the brotherhoods were distinguishing between two groups of people who needed relief: those who could go to the hospital and those who could not. In the latter category were the established, honorable city residents, a group that probably included some *doñas*.

Who then went to the hospitals? Presumably the less honorable, less established, but equally impoverished people of Toledo, who could not afford the luxury of viewing a hospital visit as a demeaning' experience. Historians have usually assumed that hospitals housed the vagrants and the transients of sixteenth-century society, the people with no fixed residence who were strangers to a town, the so-called floating population.[8]

Many of the larger Castilian hospitals kept records of the patients they treated and the series of record books preserved in the Hospital of Tavera, which range from 1553 to the eighteenth century, is probably one of the longest in Castile. The exact information contained in these books varies according to the energy and whim of the scribe, yet certain facts, such as the name, marital status, illness and the possessions of each patient when he entered the hospital, were consistently recorded. Attempts were made to note the patient's point of origin, but since the scribes were never certain whether they should record the patient's birthplace (*natural de*), the place where he had established a household (*vecino de*), or the place where he resided (*vive en*), this information is of little value except to say that the patients came from all over Europe though the great majority were born in the Iberian peninsula. As for the patient's possessions, those usually amounted to the clothes each person wore and the Tavera patients seemed to be attired in a monotonous similarity of dress: the men with shirts, tunics, stockings, shoes, a cap and a hat; the women in a skirt, shirt, apron, stockings, shoes and a headdress. The only distinctive feature noted by the scribe was the condition of the clothes, which varied from good, medium, torn or old, the latter condition being the most frequent.

Out of all the facts recorded about the patients, the only useful items consistently listed are the sex and marital status of the patient. A sample of 120 patients, ten for each month of the year, taken every ten years from 1559 to 1649, has been outlined in table 17. According to the percentages of this table, single men consistently comprised the largest group treated in the hospital. Children, distinguished by the scribal notations of *niño* or *muchacho* or the use of the diminutive for the names, have been recorded separately and are not included in the percentages of the patient's marital status. With the exception of 1579, a year of great sickness which apparently drove an unusually

Table 17. *Sex and marital status of 1,200 Tavera Hospital patients*
*(in percentages)*

|  | Men | Women | Children | Single | Married | Widows (Widowers) |
|---|---|---|---|---|---|---|
| 1559 | 74.5 | 20.3 | 5.2 | 57.8 | 42.2 | 0 |
| 1569 | 65.9 | 23.8 | 10.3 | 58.1 | 41.9 | 0 |
| 1579 | 50.7 | 27.3 | 22.1 | 52.8 | 35.4 | 11.8 |
| 1589 | 64.6 | 23.2 | 12.2 | 73.2 | 20.3 | 6.5 |
| 1599 | 65.4 | 29.6 | 5.0 | 66.9 | 22.8 | 10.3 |
| 1609 | 65.8 | 21.8 | 12.4 | 60.6 | 26.5 | 12.9 |
| 1619 | 69.1 | 20.7 | 10.2 | 55.4 | 32.3 | 12.3 |
| 1629 | 70.9 | 17.8 | 11.3 | 63.8 | 24.9 | 11.4 |
| 1639 | 79.0 | 19.3 | 1.7 | 56.7 | 27.0 | 16.3 |
| 1649 | 68.1 | 25.0 | 6.9 | 55.2 | 32.7 | 12.1 |

large number of juveniles to seek the services of a hospital, children accounted for a small percentage of the hospital's clientele. As for the widows and widowers, their absence from the records before 1579 is surprising, given the fact that in 1561 widows alone accounted for 19.3 per cent of the Toledo population. Possibly the change made in the purpose of the hospital in 1569 – from a convalescent to a general hospital – explains the absence of widows in 1559 and 1569.

The predominance of male patients seems to be a characteristic of sixteenth- and early-seventeenth-century hospitals. It is true of two hospitals of Medina del Campo, where from 1578 to 1585 men accounted for 65.80 per cent of the people admitted to the Hospital de la Piedad and from 1620 to 1644 for 63.60 per cent of those admitted to the Hospital de Simón Ruíz.[9] It is also true of the Hôtel-Dieu of Lyons in the sixteenth century, where men accounted for 59 per cent to 70 per cent of the patients.[10] However, by the early seventeenth century the Lyons hospital shows a much higher percentage of women (48.2 per cent) than ever recorded in the Hospital of Tavera.

If table 17 contributes some limited information about the type of person who used the hospital, more details can be provided for certain years. From 1595 to 1608 the hospital employed the same scribe who consistently recorded certain facts about the patients. In the case of the unmarried patients, he noted their age and whether their parents were living or dead, while for those patients who were married or widowed, he recorded the number of their children. For every person admitted to the hospital, the scribe entered the place where they were born in addition to the place where they presently resided. The place of birth, frequently an obscure village in the north of the peninsula, was usually accompanied by the bishopric where the settlement was located, and the place of residence was determined by the town or village where the patient was a parishioner, not where he was a *vecino*.

Since the information available from 1595 to 1608 permits a more detailed study of the hospital patients, another sample has been taken for six years out of the thirteen-year interval. This sample was taken in the same way as the first one, with a certain number of patients recorded in each month, but the total number for each year varies: there are 120 patients for the years 1598, 1599, 1600; 155 patients for 1595; 150 patients for 1596; and 130 patients for 1605, making a total sample of 795 patients, 16.77 per cent of the estimated 4,739 patients who were admitted to the hospital during these six years. Of these 795 patients, 19 fall into the category of unknowns. These are persons who were brought to the hospital in such a feeble condition that they were unable to talk and answer any questions. Obviously they are not too useful for establishing facts about the age, marital status or point of origin of the patients, though they have been included in the percentages of mortality rates.

From this sample, the 516 single persons have been listed in table 18 according to their age group. These age groups have been established with some reference to the contemporary judgment of the maturation of the individual since, in addition to recording the age, the scribe also noted whether the patient was a child (*niño*), a maiden or a young man (*doncella* or *mancebo*), or a spinster or a bachelor (*soltera* or *soltero*). Children from the ages of four to eleven are invariably described as *niños*, though on one or two occasions a patient of twelve or thirteen was noted as a child. Probably the physical appearance of the individual had a great deal to do with the scribe's decision as to whether they were children or adolescents, but since the majority of twelve-year-olds were not included as children, the breaking-off period for childhood had been established at eleven. The same confusion exists as to when maidens became spinsters or unmarried women and young boys became bachelors or unmarried men. Occasionally a twenty-five-year-old woman was listed as a *doncella* and a thirty-year-old man as a *mancebo*. Again, physical appearances and demeanour probably had a great deal to do with the scribe's decision and it would seem safest to say that the turning point occurred sometime in the early twenties for the females and in the late twenties for the males.

Table 18. *Age, sex, and parents of 516 single Tavera Hospital patients*

| Age group | Total patients | Male | | Female | | Both parents | | Father | | Mother | | No parents | |
|---|---|---|---|---|---|---|---|---|---|---|---|---|---|
| | | No. | % | No. | % | No. | % | No. | % | No. | % | No. | % |
| 4–11 | 23 | 13 | 56.52 | 10 | 43.48 | 5 | 21.74 | 4 | 17.39 | 4 | 17.39 | 10 | 43.48 |
| 12–15 | 103 | 75 | 72.82 | 28 | 27.18 | 23 | 22.33 | 10 | 9.71 | 24 | 23.30 | 46 | 44.66 |
| 16–20 | 181 | 127 | 70.17 | 54 | 29.83 | 47 | 25.97 | 22 | 12.15 | 40 | 22.10 | 72 | 39.78 |
| 21–25 | 112 | 99 | 88.39 | 13 | 11.61 | 27 | 24.11 | 9 | 8.04 | 26 | 23.21 | 50 | 44.64 |
| 26–30 | 55 | 46 | 83.64 | 9 | 16.36 | 9 | 16.36 | 0 | | 11 | 20.00 | 35 | 63.64 |
| 31–40 | 26 | 23 | 88.46 | 3 | 11.54 | 1 | 3.85 | 0 | | 1 | 3.85 | 24 | 92.30 |
| 41–50 | 8 | 6 | 75.00 | 2 | 25.00 | 0 | | 0 | | 0 | | 8 | 100.00 |
| 51–60 | 6 | 6 | | 0 | | 0 | | 0 | | 0 | | 6 | 100.00 |
| 61–70 | 1 | 1 | | 0 | | 0 | | 0 | | 0 | | 1 | 100.00 |
| 71–80 | 1 | 1 | | 0 | | 0 | | 0 | | 0 | | 1 | 100.00 |
| Total | 516 | 397 | 76.94 | 119 | 23.06 | 112 | 21.71 | 45 | 8.72 | 106 | 20.54 | 253 | 49.03 |

Table 18 indicates that the majority of hospital patients were males between twelve and twenty-five years of age. Considering that the hospital cared for such ailments as broken bones, wounds, dislocations, bruises, burns and mutilations, it is not surprising that young men, exposed to the hazards of such occupations as building, weaving, transport, forging and the like, and also given to frequenting the local taverns where altercations might occur, should be more prone to injuries. Their female counterparts undoubtedly led a more sheltered, if equally laborious, life at home. In two of the rare occasions where the cause of an injury was recorded, one young man had suffered a nail wound in his foot and another had fallen out of a window in the convent of Santa Fe, presumably while repairing it.[11]

The greatest number of single patients recorded in table 18 are the sixteen- to twenty-year-olds and the numbers decrease progressively for the older age groups. The sharp decrease for the women between twenty-one and twenty-five years old and for the men between twenty-six and thirty years old suggests that the figures reflect the marriage patterns of the poorer city residents. In Valladolid at approximately the same period of time (1590–1605) the average marriage age for women was twenty years and for men it was between twenty-three and twenty-five years, while in mid-seventeenth-century Valencia the average marriage age for women was twenty years, seven months and for men, twenty-four years, seven months.[12]

Although marriage increased the responsibilities of a man, it may also have opened new welfare benefits to him and his family. At least four Toledo confraternities stipulated that no unmarried man was to be admitted to their brotherhood unless he was the son of a deceased brother who filled his father's place.[13] Four confraternities are not adequate evidence to argue that all the confraternities were closed to single men, who may well have organized their own species of brotherhood, but it is probable that membership in a confraternity was a much simpler matter after marriage when a man had permanently settled in the community and established a household.

As for the parents of the single patients, the figures given in table 18 indicate that the great majority were orphans who lacked either a mother, a father, or both parents. That the number of orphans among the Tavera patients is far higher than the norms established in other areas of pre-industrial Europe, which range from one-third to 40 per cent, is not surprising.[14] Hospital records are not, of course, an accurate measure of the norms in a society since many people sought the services of a hospital precisely because they were alone and had no family to help them. Nonetheless the Tavera figures do indicate that a large percentage of young children between the ages of five and eleven were orphans. It is hard to imagine that these young children did not experience some deprivation or neglect upon being left without parents, and possibly this neglect is best indicated by the fact that they sought and were admitted to a hospital. As for the older groups, their prospects of being orphaned would depend upon two unknown factors: the age of the parents when the child was born and the life expectancy of the parents. Assuming that the life expectancy of sixteenth- and seventeenth-century Castile was analogous to other areas of Europe, which means that it varied from the mid-twenties to the late forties with an average in the mid-thirties, then few of the older groups could expect to have parents.[15] In any event, in terms of offering assistance during an illness, the existence of a mother or father probably did little to help these children, most of whom were immigrants whose parents lived too far away to be of much help. Given the plethora of widows throughout Castile, it could be expected that more children would have a mother than a father, but this same pattern is also evident in other parts of pre-industrial Europe.[16]

Little can be said about the married and widowed patients treated in the hospital except that they were a minority of only 260 persons, 33.5 per cent of the sample. The sex and civil status of these individuals, given in table 19, indicate that married male patients were more abundant than women, although the widowers were outnumbered by their female counterparts. Since the scribe recorded the number of children for all those persons who were or had been married, the total number of children for each group has been included in the table. The number of children per patient is less than two, so it cannot be said that the Tavera patients were overburdened with children. This is not a very useful observation without knowing more details about the age of the patient and how long they had been married, but based on the facts available for the hospital patients, it would appear that the high level of population in Toledo owed more to immigration than it did to the abundance of children supported by the poorer residents of the city.

Whether married or single, the majority of the 776 patients were not born in or *vecinos* of Toledo; these people account for only 22.13 per cent of the sample. The largest group, amounting to 49.52 per

Table 19. *Sex and number of children of 260 married and widowed Tavera patients*

|         | Male | Female | Total patients | No. of children |
|---------|------|--------|----------------|-----------------|
| Married | 122  | 70     | 192            | 225             |
| Widowed | 22   | 46     | 68             | 78              |
|         |      |        | 260            | 303             |

cent, are the immigrants, people who were born outside Toledo but gave their residence as one of the Toledo parishes. The second largest group are the people classified as transients who account for 28.35 per cent of the sample. Since these persons were born outside Toledo and gave their parish residence in a city, town or village outside Toledo, it has been assumed that these were in the city on a temporary basis.

Classification of sixteenth-century hospital patients is not easy, even with the consistent and detailed notations given in some of the Tavera hospital books. For instance, the group classified as transients might equally well be called vagabonds, pilgrims, poor travellers or short-term immigrants. The modern reader has no idea what brought them to Toledo or how long they stayed, what they did before coming, while they were there or after they left the city.

Similar problems arise in the classification of immigrants, the people not born in Toledo who had become residents of one of the city parishes. The question of how parish residence was established in sixteenth-century Castile is difficult to answer. Cardinal Quiroga published diocesan legislation prohibiting the *moriscos* from changing their parish without first obtaining the consent of their parish priest,[17] but no restrictions were published for the rest of the population. Did one establish parish residence by first finding a place to live and then attending services at the parish church? And was it incumbent upon the parish priest to inform himself of any new parishioners? These questions cannot be answered, but it does appear that parish residence was a concern of the church rather than the city, a fact that might explain why in 1591 the *corregidor* claimed that the parish priests were the only people who had complete lists of the city's population. The city council was in charge of determining who qualified as *vecinos* of the city, a privilege limited to those persons born in Toledo, to those who married the offspring of a *vecino*, or to those

Table 20. *Residence status of patients from four hospitals (in percentages)*

| City (time span) | Hospital | Natives/ vecinos | Immigrants | Transients | Unknown |
|---|---|---|---|---|---|
| Toledo (1595–1608) | Tavera | 22.13 | 49.52 | 28.35 | — |
| Medina del Campo (1578–85) | Piedad | 20.90 | 70.10 | | — |
| Medina del Campo (1619–47) | Simón Ruíz | 21.03 | 62.66 | | 16.31 |
| Lyons (1575–1625) | Hôtel-Dieu | 45.46 | 54.55 | — | — |

who had resided in the city for ten years and owned property in Toledo.[18] Clearly a newly arrived immigrant could not meet these qualifications, but eventually, with a bit of luck, some of them might.

Table 20 contains the percentages for the various groups of patients admitted to the Hospital of Tavera as well as percentages derived from three other hospitals.[19] The distinction between immigrants and transients is made only in the Tavera figures; for the other three hospitals these two groups are given as one large figure or, in the case of Lyons, it is possible that the transients are excluded completely. Despite these disparities, some valid comparisons can be made. One is the low percentage of natives (native-born and *vecinos*) treated in the Castilian hospitals; the average seems to be 20 per cent to 22 per cent, a far lower percentage than in Lyons where the natives account for 45 per cent, nearly half the patients admitted. The greatest similarity between the Toledo and the Lyons figures is the large number of immigrants assisted in both hospitals, though this comparison is of dubious validity because of the uncertainty about the Lyons transients whose exclusion or inclusion would change the percentage for the immigrants. The combined total of the transients and immigrants admitted to the Hospital of Tavera is 77.87 per cent, a figure that is close to but somewhat larger than the 70.10 per cent and the 62.66 per cent for the Medina del Campo hospitals. These large percentages for the transients and immigrants treated in the Castilian hospitals suggest that the poorer population of Castile was very mobile, possibly more mobile than the poor of southeastern France. If the sixteenth-century Castilian poor laws are to be interpreted as measures designed to prevent the free movement of the poor, it must be concluded that they were not very successful in achieving this goal.[20]

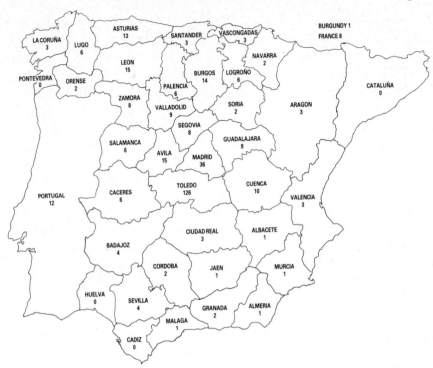

Figure 11. Province of origin of 354 immigrants, patients of the Hospital of Tavera

The immigrants treated in the Hospital of Tavera came from all over the Iberian peninsula and Europe, and the province of origin of 354 of the 384 immigrants is given in figure 11. Since the scribe noted both the village and the bishopric where the patient was born, the task of identifying the tiny settlements where most of the patients originated has been simplified, though in thirty cases the village has not been located and these people are not included on the map. For the most part the patients have been listed in conformance with the modern provinces of Spain, but, in the interests of keeping the map as uncluttered as possible, where the number of patients are few the larger regional jurisdictions are used instead of the provinces (Aragón, Catalonia, Murcia, Valencia, and Vascongadas).

Quite understandably the largest number of immigrants came from the province of Toledo; the practical consideration of distance meant that the villages close to Toledo would lose many of their children to the nearby city. Looking at the overall pattern, however, it is remarkable how many persons came from the northwest of the peninsula, especially from the area defined by the present-day boundaries of Galicia, Asturias and León. The contribution of the province of Burgos is also notable and perhaps bears some relation to the languishing wool trade in that region. The large number of immigrants from the northwest brings to mind the sour observation of Luis Hurtado in 1576 that 'the *moriscos*, Galicians and Asturians have brought so much poverty and sickness to this city' ('Memorial', p. 544). At least the accuracy of the point of origin of the northern immigrants is confirmed by the map. Excluding the *moriscos*, who came to Toledo in 1570–1 under duress, the southerners made little contribution to swell the ranks of Toledo's immigrant population. The movement of people is definitely from the northwest to south, a pattern suggested by several historians and usually explained in terms of the increasing poverty in the north of the peninsula which stimulated migrations to what appeared to be the more prosperous south.[21] A similar pattern of migration is evident in Medina del Campo where from 1578 to 1585 the greatest number of patients came from the regions of Galicia, Asturias and León and the provinces of Valladolid and Ávila.[22]

Such migrations were, after all, what Domingo de Soto had suggested when he argued that the poor must retain their liberty of movement in order to migrate to the richer provinces of the peninsula. If the records for the Hospital of Tavera are accepted as a valid yardstick by which to judge the amount of immigration within one portion of the Iberian peninsula, then it is easy to understand the difficulties in executing a poor law like that of 1540, which decreed that the poor should return to their birthplace to be succoured. Enforcement of such a decree would have caused a displacement of hundreds, perhaps thousands, of persons. Considering the vast and inhospitable country that stretches from Asturias to Toledo and the means of transport available to the poor Iberian in the sixteenth century, it is remarkable how many made the journey; but compared with other peregrinations made in Europe, movements within the Iberian peninsula do not seem extraordinarily long nor unique.[23]

As for persons of other nations, the Tavera records do not indicate a deluge of foreigners. Using the modern distinctions to determine foreigners, the twelve Portuguese, eight Frenchmen and one Burgundian amount to twenty-one people or 5.46 per cent of the 384 immigrants. Nor do the records for the Hospital de la Piedad in Medina del Campo indicate a large number of foreigners. Of the 1,123 people admitted to the hospital from 1578 to 1585, forty (3.56 per cent) were foreigners and half the foreigners came from Portugal.[24] Heavy Portuguese immigration might be explained by the relatively close location of Portugal and the fact that in 1580 Portugal became a dominion of the king of Spain. It might also indicate that if the poor had a difficult time in Castile, things were even worse in Portugal.

The small percentage of foreigners admitted in both Castilian hospitals gives some cause to doubt the accuracy of contemporary estimates as to the number of foreigners treated in Castilian hospitals. Cristóbal Pérez de Herrera stated that 8,000 to 10,000 Frenchmen were treated in the Royal Hospital of Burgos every year, an estimate that has enjoyed great popularity.[25] Possibly a greater number of Frenchmen did pass through Burgos, situated on the pilgrimage route to Santiago de Compostela, than they did through Medina del Campo and Toledo, but even if the Burgos hospital cared for no one other than the 8,000 Frenchmen it must have been the busiest hospital in Castile. In 1606, its busiest year, the Hospital of Tavera cared for no more than 1,624 people, and the average number of yearly admissions between 1569 and 1625 was approximately 900. In the seven-year interval between 1578 and 1585, the Hospital de la Piedad in Medina del Campo admitted 1,123 people, which works out to a yearly average of 160 people. Whether considered as an estimate for the number of foreigners or even for the total number of people admitted each year to the Burgos hospital, the figures of Pérez de Herrera appear to be greatly exaggerated.

Including the Tavera patients who were immigrants to Toledo and the *vecinos* and native-born, some 556 patients resided in Toledo, scattered about in all the parishes of the city. The total number of patients who came from each parish is given in figure 12. With the exception of the tiny parish of San Ginés, which provided only one hospital patient in all the 556, three figures have been recorded in each parish: the first signifies the total number of patients who resided in the parish; the second figure, the number of native-born; and the third one, the number of immigrants.

In any interpretation of figure 12, proximity is an important consideration. In addition to the Hospital of Tavera, Toledo had two other large hospitals – Santa Cruz and the Misericordia – in the interior of the city that treated non-contagious diseases, and a person in need of hospital care probably went to the institution that was closest. Thus it is not surprising that the two northern parishes of San Isidoro and Santiago, closest to the Hospital of Tavera, provided the

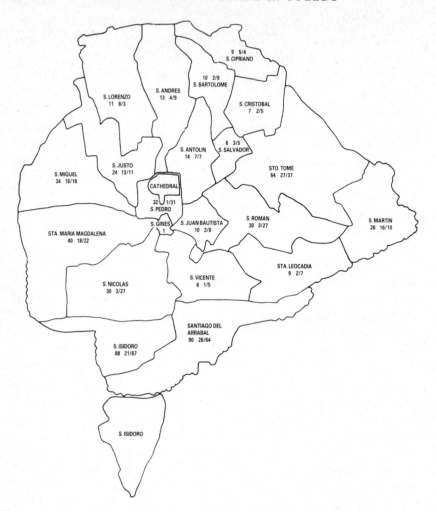

Figure 12. Parish residence of 556 Tavera Hospital patients

greatest number of patients recorded in figure 12. Of the remaining
parishes, the largest number of patients came from Santo Tomé,
probably because it was the most populous parish of the city. It is also
worth noting that the greatest number of patients from these three
parishes were immigrants – 76 per cent for San Isidoro, 71 per cent for
Santiago, and 57 per cent for Santo Tomé – and in all but five of the
twenty-one parishes, immigrants outnumbered the native-born and
the *vecinos*. While the great majority (77.87 per cent) of the Tavera
patients lived in Toledo, the hospital offered the largest percentage of

Table 21. *Percentage of mortality for the Hospital of Tavera patients*

| Year | Percentage | Year | Percentage |
|------|-----------|------|-----------|
| 1559 | 10.2 | 1600 | 28.7 |
| 1569 | 16.5 | 1605 | 12.6 |
| 1571 | 13.4 | 1609 | 11.9 |
| 1579 | 20.8 | 1619 | 17.2 |
| 1584 | 15.1 | 1629 | 13.4 |
| 1589 | 25.4 | 1639 | 14.7 |
| 1595 | 26.7 | 1649 | 12.5 |
| 1596 | 15.3 | | |
| 1598 | 30.2 | | |
| 1599 | 5.5 | | |

Average percentage of mortality: 16.4

its services (49.52 per cent) to poor immigrants, the same people who swelled the ranks of the city's workforce.

Do the mortality rates for the Hospital of Tavera, given in table 21, reflect the periods of subsistence crisis that periodically struck the city? Up to a certain point they do: the years of the highest mortality – 1579, 1589, 1595, 1598 and 1600 – were all years of sickness or grain shortage in Toledo. In so far as the percentage of mortality seems to increase with every crisis, culminating in the 30.2 per cent of 1598, it might be argued that the Tavera figures support the theory of a higher mortality rate among the poor by the end of the sixteenth century, an increase caused by the recurrent subsistence crises and undernourishment of the poor which lowered their resistance and left them an easy prey to disease.

However, certain facts argue against placing too much confidence in hospital mortality rates as an accurate barometer for the health of the community or the poor. For example, how can one explain the high mortality rates of 1598 (30.2 per cent) and 1600 (28.7 per cent) and the mere 5.5 per cent of 1599? Did the scribe forget to record deaths in 1599, or did the hospital send all plague patients to the plague hospital of San Lázaro, conveniently located next door to the Hospital of Tavera? Also, after 1600 the mortality rates show a remarkable stability that seems to ignore sickness and famine. For example, 1649 was a year of war, sickness and grain shortage and the hospital mortality rate is a mere 12.5 per cent. Possibly by the seventeenth century the Hospital of Tavera had become more

selective in its admission policy. Certainly after 1619 the hospital
began to send more patients to the Hospital del Rey, the institution
that treated incurable diseases.[26] Obviously if the Hospital of Tavera
was sending away patients who were seriously ill, its mortality rates
were bound to drop. These questions underline the difficulty of using
hospital mortality rates as a source of information for the health of the
community. The modern reader will never know the exact condition
or ailment of the patients admitted to a hospital and the criteria for
admission may have changed. However, the average mortality rate of
16.4 per cent does suggest that the Tavera patients stood a reasonably
good chance of leaving the hospital alive.

   The hospitals of Toledo have recently been described as disorganized and chaotic, and doubts have been raised as to whether
they served the rich or the poor.[27] It is very questionable that the
Toledo hospitals were more disorganized than the hospitals of any
other sixteenth-century city, and they were certainly organized
enough to respond to the periodic subsistence crises that struck the
city. As for the hospitals serving as 'infirmaries for cathedral canon',
this is not true of the Hospital of Tavera. The one Toledo hospital that
appears to have been more selective in its admission policy was the
Nuncio, where the insane were housed. Admission to this hospital was
determined by the cathedral chapter, and, according to Luis
Hurtado, the hospital admitted only 'poor and honorable insane
people' ('Memorial', p. 557). The actual discussions of the cathedral
chapter are not very informative as to the background of the patients.
In 1575 the hospital housed a *beata* who some canons thought should
be removed on grounds that she was sane, and in 1579 doña Catalina,
a *vecina* of Toledo, was admitted because she was 'insane and very
poor'.[28] Given the small number of people housed in the hospital and
what seemed to be the large number of prospective applicants who
came from all over the Iberian peninsula, the recommendations of a
cathedral canon probably did help in gaining admission to the
hospital.

   However, such a selective admission policy was not typical of the
Hospital of Tavera. In attempting to describe the Tavera patients, it
would be helpful to know their occupation, but unfortunately the
hospital records do not include consistent information about occupations. Occasional notations record a tailor, a weaver, a wool comber,
a carpenter, a seller of old clothes, a slave, a shoemaker, a bonnet
maker, an iron forger, a baker, a silk twister, a carter, and a servant.[29]
Considering the age of the majority of the patients, it is not surprising

that the notations for apprentices and servants are the most frequent. Possibly an occasional vagabond did get into the hospital, but there is no reason to suspect that the institution was crowded with malingerers. If anyone in sixteenth-century Castile was capable of distinguishing a feigned illness it should have been the staff of a hospital. Convinced as he was that idleness is the root of all evil and that work was the best remedy for the poor, it is doubtful that Salazar de Mendoza would look kindly upon such persons as occupants of his hospital beds (*Tavera*, p. 311).

The great majority of the patients were poor, but the hospital did admit persons of 'quality' and had special rooms reserved for them.[30] These persons, like Captain Rodrigo de Ayo y Molino from Alcalá la Real, were very infrequent and they usually gained a lengthy description from the impressionable hospital scribe.[31] As a general rule, the well-to-do were cared for in their own homes and called in physicians to attend them there, so the hospital's special rooms were largely used by wealthy travellers. Other persons occasionally entered the hospital with more possessions than the clothes they wore: Juan de la Peña left a purse containing 79 *reales* in the hospital's deposit chest;[32] women were frequently adorned with silver earrings, beads of jet and necklaces of amber, and several brought along books of alchemy, presumably to assist in their treatment.[33] These are the exceptions, however, who provide contrast in the grey canvas filled with persons whose possessions amounted to little more than the clothes on their back, many of whom were too poor to buy a *bulla de cruzada*,[34] an item every Castilian is thought to have possessed and probably did if he or she could afford it.

There is every reason to believe that the Tavera patients were representative of the type of people admitted in other Castilian hospitals. As Bernardino de Obregón, the founder of a hospital order, explained in the rules and instructions he wrote for his followers:

To help the sick die properly . . . is the primary obligation of our congregation and the most exacting need, because it is of the greatest importance to help a soul and to guide it in that dangerous hour, especially for people so rude and so lost as those who usually come to hospitals. (*Constituciones*, p. 12).

### THE PREOCCUPATION WITH YOUTH

The clientele of the Hospital of Tavera was predominantly young but some special provisions were made for the elderly. In accordance with a stipulation of Cardinal Tavera, the hospital took in six poor, elderly priests who were in some way impeded from celebrating mass, and six unmarried or widowed men over fifty years of age. These twelve persons were permanently housed, fed and clothed by the hospital, and they might be asked to perform some small services for the hospital at the discretion of the administrator. The hospital also maintained any staff member who had served the hospital for many years, thereby providing its employees with the additional benefit of a safe and secure retirement.[35] While these considerations signify that the needs of the aged were not unheeded, they applied to a very limited number of persons in relation to the total number of patients cared for by the hospital.

Out of all the twenty-six Toledo hospitals, only two besides Tavera made provisions for the elderly: the Hospital de Nuncio, which maintained twelve old men in addition to the mentally deranged, and the Hospital de San Pedro, where an elderly person might find sleeping space. No doubt a venerable citizen of Toledo would have been accepted in any of the city hospitals if he sought admission, but the lack of hospitals specifically dedicated to the aged probably implies that there was little demand for such services. It is doubtful that many of the poorer persons of society, those who would normally seek hospital relief, lingered on to an advanced age and those who did were probably cared for by their families or in their own homes by the confraternities. That accommodation for the elderly in the hospitals of Tavera and the Nuncio were limited to men is difficult to explain unless it can be assumed that retirement in a hospital was viewed as unsuitable for a woman.

In contrast to the paucity of provisions for the aged are the numerous institutions, societies and officials devoted to youth. One explanation for the concern for young people is probably related to the age-structure of society: studies in other areas of pre-industrial Europe have found the proportion of children to be 40 per cent.[36] In addition to their abundance, the figures given in table 18 indicate that many children under fifteen years of age were orphans, deprived of the security and guidance usually provided by a father and mother. Aside from the practical considerations, the sixteenth century was an age devoted to inculcating Christian doctrine and morality in all members of society, but, on the theory that good habits are best learned at an early age, children were of special concern. This preoccupation with children and the need to give them a proper moral example as well as occupational training is evident in the Castilian poor laws, which forbade parents to take a child of five years or older out begging and ordered that these children be put with masters to learn some sort of occupation.

One society devoted to youth was the college of the Niños de la Doctrina, which seems to have existed in all Castilian cities and was directed by the municipal authorities.[37] The usual candidates for the college were poor boys less than ten years of age who were fed, clothed and housed, taught to read and write, and instructed in the Christian doctrine. Those with aptitude continued their studies of letters, while others were apprenticed to craftsmen or tradesmen of the city. These children usually accompanied the funeral processions of the wealthy, which served as another means of raising money for the college.

Not all poor boys got into the Niños de la Doctrina. In 1568 the Toledo college housed only thirty boys, though in the 1580s, under the direction of Sancho de Moncada, the college's enrolment was expanded to some one hundred children and women were also admitted. Even with the increased number of the 1580s, some sort of selection process was necessary. In 1576 the Toledo college accepted a boy brought to them by Friar Juan Núñez, who also contributed to the boy's upkeep, while in 1584 a Tavera patient, a widow from Madrid, reported with pride that she had a son in the Madrid college.[38] The recommendation of a respected local citizen, especially one who contributed something to the child's upkeep, probably improved a child's chances for acceptance, and apparently the children did not need to be orphaned of both mother and father to gain admittance. In 1598 Cristóbal Pérez de Herrera implied that the colleges no longer served the children of the poor, but rather served as 'prebends' for children whose parents had somehow gained favour with the city council (*Amparo*, p. 96). On the other hand, in 1626 Pedro Fernández Navarette described the children as 'the sons of the scourge and scum of the republic'. The *arbitrista* argued that the college was overeducating its charges by teaching them to read and write and 'the most ingenious crafts', which contributed to the glut of clerics, friars, doctors, *letrados* and scribes instead of supplying what was lacking in Castile – farmers, journeymen and soldiers (*Conservación*, pp. 301–3).

The Hospital of San Lázaro was another institution devoted to youth, though technically its services were limited to those children suffering from contagious skin diseases such as ringworm and mange. It seems safe to assume that the children who were infected with these ailments and ended up in the Toledo San Lázaro were usually children who lived in great poverty and with very little adult supervision. The rector of the institution, Alonso de Ribera, reported that most of the children were very young boys, many of whom had to be brought to the hospital by force; he also claimed that Licenciado Tejada of the Royal Council had sent him three cartloads of infected boys from Madrid.[39] Apparently these children were without much supervision, or whoever did supervise them was not too concerned to see them packed off to the San Lázaro in Toledo. In addition to being cured of their skin diseases, housed and fed, the children received spiritual indoctrination and were actively employed in work projects. While there is no record of efforts to find permanent employment for these boys, it is probable that the rector attempted to place them with a master before they left the institution.

In 1563 the city of Toledo paid salaries to two officials known as the Padres de los Mozos, or the Fathers of Young Boys. These officials were not unique to Toledo for in 1551 the Castilian Cortes, lamenting the numerous idle young men visible on every side, recommended that all the towns and villages with a population of more than a thousand *vecinos* should have an official to see that these young persons were employed.[40] In Toledo the Fathers each received a salary of 6 *reales* from the city and another *real* for each young man they placed in service, the latter commission paid by the master and his new found employee, each of whom contributed half a *real*.[41] When one reads that the Father was responsible for indemnifying any master who was robbed by his new servant and was also to provide a master with a new servant free of charge if the other one left within three days, it does not appear that the system was always successful for either the employer or the employee, or that the Father and his young charges were the most responsible of persons. However, the Padre de los Mozos, who patrolled the city streets with a staff as an emblem of his authority, probably discouraged any idle youths from conspicuously loitering in public places.

Another preoccupation throughout Castile was the care of foundling children: Seville, Madrid, Valladolid, Salamanca, Córdoba and Santiago de Compostela all boasted an institution dedicated to this purpose, but the Toledo foundation, the Hospital of Santa Cruz, was certainly one of the wealthiest and largest in the peninsula. Actually, foundling children in Toledo had been provided for before Cardinal Mendoza's generous endowment to the Hospital of Santa Cruz in

1495. When the Toledo cathedral canon and apostolic nuncio, Francisco Ortiz, founded the Hospital of the Nuncio in 1483, he made provisions for the hospital to care for thirteen foundling children in addition to the thirty-three mentally disturbed patients. However, when Cardinal Mendoza included the care of foundlings as one of the purposes of his new hospital, Francisco Ortiz decided that his hospital should care for thirteen old men instead of foundlings.[42] Cardinal Mendoza's foundation began to care for foundlings in 1497, but this care was provided in three temporary buildings until the new Hospital of Santa Cruz officially opened in 1514. In addition to the rents left by the cardinal, the foundlings also received a yearly donation of 3,000 *reales* from the cathedral chapter and the prelate (1,000 *reales* were taken from three separate accounts, the *mesa arzobispal*, the *mesa capitular* and *obra y fábrica*). The cathedral chapter appointed a new rector each year as well as two of the hospital's four visitors.[43]

Leaving unwanted infants in or outside the Toledo cathedral was an old custom, but by the sixteenth century the cathedral chapter had made the operation more secure by constructing a wooden shelter inside the cathedral where unwanted infants could be deposited. Despite this modernization, the spot where the infants were left was still known as *la piedra*, the stone, and the foundling children were known as *niños de la piedra*. Infants found in the shelter were carried to the Hospital of Santa Cruz, a ten-minute walk from the cathedral, where they were named, baptized, registered and given to a wet-nurse. Some children arrived with slips of paper relating their name and the fact that they had been baptized, in which case they were merely registered and given to a nurse. The nurses and their charges were expected to participate in the annual procession held on 8 September, the birth of the Virgin, to honour the memory of Cardinal Mendoza.

Of the hundreds of books and papers that must have been kept for the foundling children, very few survive or have been catalogued. A new Libro de Crianza, a book of the foundlings and the women who served as nurses, was compiled each year. Of the 135 books that were compiled from 1515 to 1650, only eleven survive, and one of these, the book for 1609, has been severely mutilated.[44] If the number of books is small, the books themselves are large. Each contains entries for every child the hospital paid for in that particular year, and every child received his or her individual page, except in periods of subsistence crises or epidemics when increased admissions sometimes forced the scribe to put two children on the same page. While each book has a specific date, it contains information about children admitted in earlier years as well as the new infants admitted in the year the book was compiled. The books usually begin with the oldest children supported by the hospital, children who may have been from three to six years of age. These were the children who were placed in service or adopted and each book contains some notes about the placement of the older children. By the late sixteenth century the hospital began keeping another set of books, the Libros de Asientos, which contained information about the placement of each child, but for this early period none of these books has yet come to light. For the younger children, those who were wet-nursing or who had been weaned but were still with a nurse, the notes are usually limited to the payments made to the nurses.

All the surviving books consistently record certain facts: the name of the child, of the nurse and usually of the nurse's husband; the place where the nurse lived; the date when the child was first given to a nurse; any changes made in nurses; and all payments made for each child. Aside from this basic information, other facts were sometimes recorded. By the seventeenth century the occupation of the nurse's husband is always recorded, but this is not true in the sixteenth century. In 1515 the nurses were paid $\frac{1}{2}$ *real* to have the foundling child baptized, an expense that is not mentioned in later books, possibly because the hospital had the children baptized before they were given to the nurses. In two books the approximate age of the infants given to wet-nurses is mentioned: in 1515 they are recorded as being recently born, while in the book for 1632 the age of the infants is even more specific – one month, fifteen days, two or three months and so on. The remaining books contain no notations about the age of the youngest children left with the hospital, but an occasional remark that a child is six months or one year old leads one to believe that these are noted because they were the exception and the general rule was that the children left in the cathedral were young infants.

One of the major problems for the hospital was keeping in touch with the children and their nurses. Until the 1570s the hospital gave the majority of the foundlings to country women who lived a fair distance from Toledo. When a nurse took a child, she received two months salary in advance and at the end of that period she was to come to the hospital again, with the child, to receive her next payment. If the system entailed a lot of travelling for the nurse and the infant, it also afforded the hospital staff an opportunity to inspect the child. In addition to these inspections, the hospital also had a special visitor whose task was to visit the children in their foster homes and see that they were properly treated and to find any children who had not been brought back to the hospital for a long time. The hospital also received some assistance from the village priests, who sent testimonies as to the health or proper burial of a foundling. The most impressive assistance offered by a village priest was during the plague of 1599 when the wet-nurse of a boy named Juan died in the plague. Unable to find another wet-nurse, the priest of Fuensalida gave the boy to a woman who fed him goat's milk until another wet-nurse did appear. After eight months in Fuensalida the boy was returned to the hospital, apparently in good health, and the priest reimbursed for his expenses on the boy's behalf.[45]

The women who served as nurses were poor. The great majority of the village women were the wives of peasants (*labradores*), with an occasional shepherd, labourer (*trabajador*), weaver, wool comber and tailor. For the nurses who lived in Toledo the occupations of husbands are more varied and include cooks, bakers, water carriers, carpenters, gardeners, tailors, bonnet makers and fishermen, but weavers are the most common.[46] The occupations of husbands are humble, and notes from the village priests invariably describe the nurses as very poor. Also, when a child died the nurse was supposed to return any of the salary that remained after the child's death, but the hospital was rarely able to collect this money because of the poverty of the nurses.[47] Presumably it was the salary paid by the hospital that motivated these women to take the foundlings. The hospital paid more for nursing children and less for those who were weaned, but both salaries increased throughout the century. In 1515 and 1548 the price paid was 4 *reales* a month for children still nursing and $2\frac{1}{2}$ *reales* for those who were weaned; in 1568 and 1574 the salary was 6 *reales* a month for sucklings and between 3 and 4 *reales* a month for those who were weaned; in 1599 and 1616 it was 9 *reales* a month and between 3 and 6 *reales*; and in 1632 it was 14 *reales* and between 8 and 12 *reales*. In addition to the salaries the hospital also clothed the infants who, every four to six months, were given diapers, a piece of flannel in which the children were wrapped, a gown, long stockings, shoes, and three pieces of cloth, two of wool and one of linen. For infants who were sick nurses received extra money,[48] and in 1515 they received $\frac{1}{2}$ *real* for their trip home, a custom that seems to have been abandoned in later years.

Given the poverty of the nurses, it is not surprising that abuses occurred. In 1599 a woman took a foundling and her salary and then put the infant back on the *piedra* and left town with the salary.[49] This recorded case is probably one of many. The visitors occasionally found children being mistreated and these children were usually brought back to the hospital and placed with other nurses.[50] In 1518 the visitor found two children nude because the nurse had given the clothes for the foundlings to her own children.[51] However, the fact that these cases are recorded suggests that they are the exception rather than the rule, at least in the early sixteenth century.

As far as the infants born in Toledo are concerned, the hospital seemed to be well-informed about some people who abandoned their children, and also about women who left children on the *piedra* and then appeared at the hospital as nurses for their own infants. The hospital made every effort to locate parents and if the parents could not be found then the closest relatives were made responsible for the child. In 1515 someone abandoned an eighteen-month-old child who was recognized and the child's relatives made responsible for the boy; and in another case the bookkeeper reported that he knew the nurse was the mother of the child and he withheld her salary 'to punish her'.[52] In 1570 a woman recognized the child she was given to nurse and identified the parents, but the child died before the parents could be located; and a priest reported the parents of yet another child.[53] These examples are all taken from people who lived in Toledo, where the local gossip system exercised some surveillance. It is doubtful that the hospital was equally well informed about the villagers who abandoned their infants in Toledo.

The hospital did not usually return infants to parents who came to reclaim them unless it was reimbursed for the money it had invested in the child, and cases of reimbursement are rarely recorded.[54] However, exceptions were made in instances when a woman was extremely poor and her reasons for abandoning a child seemed justifiable. In 1515 and 1616 children were returned to their mothers whose 'great need' had forced them to abandon their children, and the hospital collected only 8 *reales*, a small portion of the money invested in the child.[55] In 1570 Ísabel de Herrera, the wife of an old clothes seller, was allowed to reclaim her infant because she had given birth to twins and was very poor.[56]

Despite the added difficulty of keeping in touch with its charges, the hospital seemed to prefer to give the infants still nursing to village women, though after the children were weaned women in Toledo were used more frequently. At least the hospital preferred village women until 1568, when more and more infants were left with women in Toledo. This shift is evident from the figures given in table 22, which pertain only to the infants admitted in the year the book was compiled, given in column 1, not all the children the hospital paid for in that year. With the exception of 1545, when it is impossible to determine with accuracy the date when the infants were given to wet-nurses, the table includes infants who ranged in age from approximately two weeks to a year.[57] In 1515, 1518 and 1545–6 village women account for the great majority of nurses, but from 1568 until 1599 women in Toledo are nearly equal to or exceed their village counterparts. One possible explanation for this shift is that from 1568 to 1599 Toledo housed more women who were in need of money, a need that drove them to volunteer for a task that earlier generations had rejected. The dominance of Toledo nurses in 1599 might be explained by the restrictions placed on the movement of people during the plague, which may have made it difficult for village women to gain entry into the city. But considering that the hospital managed to place foundlings with some seventy village women, it does not appear that the plague restrictions were observed very conscientiously. It is also possible that the hospital deliberately changed its policy from 1568 to 1599 and sought out nurses in Toledo, though the fact that village women again predominate in 1616 and 1632 suggests that it was the availability of women who were willing and able to nurse infants that determined where the children went, not the hospital staff.

The books contain more information about the nurses than they do the children. The only facts that can be determined about all the children is their approximate age, their sex, and whether they lived or died. An occasional note about the poverty of some mothers who reclaimed their children and the *morisco* infants who began to appear in 1570[58] explains the background of a few infants, but the origins of the vast majority remain a mystery. Since other foundling hospitals in early modern Europe served as a convenient place for country women to drop off unwanted infants, it is probable that many of the children of Santa Cruz were the offspring of peasants, but this idea is difficult to substantiate with facts from the documents.[59] One thing that can be

Table 22. *Foundlings of Santa Cruz: place nursed, male/female ratio, and estimated mortality*

| Year | Infants admitted | Place nursed | | | | Male No. | Female No. | Ratio | Recorded mortality | | Unknowns | | % of recorded mortality and unknowns |
| | | Village | | Toledo | | | | | | | | | |
| | | No. | % | No. | % | | | | No. | % | No. | % | |
| 1515 | 100 | 89 | 89.00 | 11 | 11.00 | 59 | 41 | 1.44 | 11 | 11.00 | 33 | 33.00 | 44.00 |
| 1518 | 73 | 60 | 82.19 | 13 | 17.81 | 30 | 43 | 0.70 | 17 | 23.28 | 21 | 28.77 | 52.05 |
| 1545–6 | 261 | 203 | 77.78 | 58 | 22.22 | 128 | 133 | 0.96 | 58 | 22.22 | 74 | 28.35 | 50.57 |
| 1568 | 100 | 51 | 51.00 | 49 | 49.00 | 51 | 49 | 1.04 | 22 | 22.00 | 26 | 26.00 | 48.00 |
| 1570 | 122 | 66 | 54.10 | 56 | 45.90 | 53 | 69 | 0.77 | 33 | 27.04 | 49 | 40.16 | 67.21 |
| 1574 | 130 | 59 | 45.38 | 71 | 54.62 | 53 | 77 | 0.69 | 43 | 33.07 | 58 | 44.62 | 77.69 |
| 1599 | 142 | 70 | 49.30 | 72 | 50.70 | 78 | 64 | 1.22 | 49 | 34.50 | 61 | 42.96 | 77.46 |
| 1616 | 42 | 35 | 83.33 | 7 | 16.67 | 21 | 21 | 1.00 | 16 | 38.10 | 16 | 38.10 | 76.20 |
| 1632 | 106 | 79 | 74.53 | 27 | 25.47 | 57 | 49 | 1.16 | 37 | 34.90 | 29 | 27.36 | 62.26 |

said with confidence is that the sex of a child does not appear to have been the determining factor for abandonment. The ratios in table 22 indicate that male and female infants were abandoned in almost equal numbers. If the birth of a girl was viewed as a disgrace by sixteenth-century Castilians,[60] it is not evident in the sex of the children who were left to the hospital, probably because the people who left their children were not in a position to keep any infant, regardless of sex. However, demographers have found that births of males outnumber those of females (105 males for every 100 females)[61] so the equal proportions of table 22 may suggest a preference for females, but it is a very small preference.

Eventually the foundlings were adopted or indentured. Adoption of a foundling appears to have been a recourse for a husband and wife who had no children of their own, or at least this was the case of two children in 1515, two in 1570 and another child in 1574.[62] In 1515 another two children were given for adoption to their respective nurses (and their husbands) because 'they loved the child a lot', while in 1599 when the same procedure was followed the explanation given was that it would save the hospital money.[63] In these four cases nothing was said about whether the foster parents had children of their own. Girls were occasionally given for adoption to single women. In 1599 five-year-old Francisca Pérez was adopted by Luisa Baptista, a *beata* who lived in Toledo; and in 1574 señora Catalina de Miranda, the daughter of a deceased architect (no husband is mentioned), adopted four-year-old Agustina de la Cruz and promised either to legally adopt the girl when she reached ten years of age or, if señora Catalina died before the child was ten, she promised to leave her charge 15,000 mrs.[64]

Much more common than contracts of adoption are those of indenture. If village families predominated as nurses, *vecinos* of Toledo predominated in taking the foundlings into service. Whether this was a policy of the hospital or whether the demand for foundling was greater in Toledo than in the countryside is difficult to say, but the foundlings went to people engaged in all sorts of occupations: sculptors, money changers, barbers, weavers, iron-forgers, book printers, masons, tailors, halter makers, quilt makers, the porter of the Santa Caridad, leather dressers, silk merchants, the *mayordomo* of don Francisco de Silva, the 'treasurer of the Bulls', and the cathedral canon, Juan Ruiz, who served as rector of the hospital in 1515, all took foundling children.[65]

In the contract signed by the hospital rector and the prospective master or mistress, the hospital reserved the right to intervene in the interests of the child until the contract of service expired. The duration of the child's apprenticeship apparently depended upon the age of the child when he was indentured: four-year-old Pedro de Sotomayor was given to Pedro de Bargas, barber, for a period of sixteen years, while seven-year-old Lorenzo Niño was to serve his master for only fourteen years.[66] The children remained in service until they were in their early twenties, an age when they would consider marriage and the establishment of their own household. During the apprenticeship the master was to provide the child with food, clothes and medical care, and to teach it the trade he followed. Girls were to be instructed in the labours of the house, or, in the case of a girl given to a nun, she was to be instructed in religion and learn to quilt.[67] The children were considered productive workers at the age of ten, for the contract stated that if the child died at any time after ten years of age until the expiration of the contract the master was to reimburse the hospital for all the services rendered by the child from its tenth year onward. When the apprenticeship expired, the master agreed to provide his charge with a complete suit of clothes, every article of which was carefully itemized, and a certain sum of money, 5,000 to 8,000 mrs in 1515 and 1548, and 10,000 to 15,000 mrs in 1599 and 1616, which would help the newly independent individuals set up their own household or, in the case of girls, to enter religion.[68]

According to Salazar de Mendoza, the foundling children could not be admitted to communities or orders that required 'pure blood', but in the case of religious orders this prohibition could be circumvented by a special dispensation (*Mendoza*, p. 401). One child that appeared to be on his way to escaping this restriction was Cristóbal de Pareja, who at eighteen months was given in service to Diego de Castilla, the dean of the cathedral chapter. In 1579, after the death of the dean, Cristóbal de Pareja was admitted as a choir boy in the Toledo cathedral, an appointment that should have permitted him to consider a professional career, possibly in the church.[69]

The age at which the foundlings were placed in service or adopted varied, but it appears to be earlier in the first half of the sixteenth century. In 1515 and 1518 the great majority of children were placed in their third year and some at two, whereas in 1599 those placed at three are rare; the usual age is between four and six and in one case the hospital was still paying for a ten-year-old child. Possibly the demand for foundlings was greater in the early part of the century than it was in 1599, or possibly the foundlings were less healthy in 1599 than they were in 1515. Remarks about the poor health of some children – ringworm, leprosy, pock marks, weakness, and poor eyesight, probably the effects of syphilis – are scattered throughout the books, but not in such a manner as to allow a systematic study.[70] Nonetheless it is reasonable to assume that the health of the foundlings would be affected by the diseases and epidemics that struck the region, as well as the poor diets and living conditions of many of the parents.

The constitutions of the Hospital of Santa Cruz limited the number of children who could be admitted in any one year to 200, but this limitation was not always observed. In 1580, for instance, the cathedral chapter decided it would ignore the restriction, 'in view of the urgent need of the times and the fact that the constitutions have never been observed with rigour'.[71] Judging by the figures in table 22, the hospital did not often exceed the limit of 200, though apparently in 1580, and probably in 1545, it did. As is true for the Hospital of Tavera, the Hospital of Santa Cruz also responded to meet subsistence crises and epidemics by increasing the number of admissions, another fact that suggests that the foundlings were the offspring of the poor.

It is difficult to conceive how the Hospital of Santa Cruz imposed limitations on the number of children it admitted. If one can envision an adult suffering from a toothache or a vague case of fevers being sent away from a hospital, it is hard to imagine anyone refusing to take in a one-month-old infant who would obviously die if not attended to. Did the hospital put up a sign at the cathedral saying 'no more children', and, if so, what did the poor village woman who had come to Toledo with the avowed purpose of leaving her infant do with her unwanted burden? Possibly she left it anyway, and this might explain why, in June 1515, three children were left on the *piedra* 'for many days' before they were found and all three infants died.[72]

The usually accurate historian, Salazar de Mendoza, claimed that the Hospital of Santa Cruz never lost track of its foundling children, but this is an overoptimistic assessment. In 1518 the hospital rector was concerned about, or had not made regular payments for, twenty-one of the seventy-three infants admitted that year, and in 1570, twenty-three of the older children had not been seen for a year. It seemed to be the older children who were weaned that were most frequently not seen for long periods of time. The fact that they were not seen does not necessarily mean that they were dead, but in most cases the final end of these children is unknown since the visitor's report is not included in the book. One year in which the results of the hospital's investigation to find its lost children is known is 1616. This was a year of depopulation in and around Toledo, and the results of the hospital's investigation reflect this movement of people away from the Imperial City and its environs. In the case of seven older children, the nurses and their families had disappeared, one to Seville, two to Granada, one to Madrid and three just disappeared without a trace; two other families claimed they had never had a foundling child, and two families who had taken a child had never been heard of in the villages where they claimed to live and work.[73] The success of the hospital's system of farming out children rested in large part upon the honesty of those who took the children, as well as the ability of the visitor to retrieve mistreated or forgotten children, but there was little the hospital could do to find infants taken to Granada or to locate people who falsified names, residence, and occupation.

According to the figures in table 22 it was in 1570 that the hospital began to lose track of an increasing number of infants, but before coming to any conclusions taken from this table, the methods used in figuring the estimated mortality must be explained. Each book contains information about mortality, usually consisting of a cross on a page, which is sometimes accompanied by the date of death or a note from a village priest as to when he buried the child. This information, listed in the table as recorded mortality, is an underestimate of the actual mortality, because in many cases the hospital had not seen the infant or the nurse for three months or longer and the condition of the infant was unknown. All the infants for whom payments had not been made for three months or longer have been placed in the category of unknowns. To assume all the unknowns were dead is to err on the side of pessimism: there could have been many reasons other than the death of the infant to explain a nurse's absence. On the other hand, to assume that the recorded mortality is an accurate measure of the actual mortality is to err on the side of optimism, given the large number of infants who had not been seen for a long time. The percentages for the recorded mortality and the unknowns have been combined in the last column, the estimated mortality, which ranges from a low of 44 per cent in 1515 to a high of 77 per cent in 1574 and 1599.

The percentages seem unusually high when compared with figures for normal infant mortality. In Simancas from 1555 to 1600 Bennassar found that 41 per cent of the young infants (*criaturas*) died, while a recent demographic study of one Toledo parish, Santiago del Arrabal, has established infant mortality (0–1 year) from 1621 to 1630 at 30.67 per cent,[74] a figure that is far lower than the seventeenth-century figures for the hospital. Of course one would expect the mortality rates for foundlings to be higher than the norm since they were more likely to suffer from abuse and neglect. Figures for sixteenth-century foundlings are scarce, but according to a study of one Libro de Crianza (1592–6) for the foundlings of Salamanca, the recorded mortality rate is 55.2 per cent, and if the children who disappeared or whose account is incomplete are included, the percentage rises to 93.41 per cent.[75] However, these figures are based on all the children paid for by the hospital in one year (presumably 1596), and some of those recorded as having 'abundant references' or, for the infants, 'initial references', may well have still been alive. For the foundlings of eighteenth-century France the average mortality rate has been estimated at 60 per cent in years of scarcity and 50 per cent in normal years.[76]

The shortage of documents and the various methods of recording and counting foundlings makes comparison difficult, but the figures in table 22 are interesting in their own right. The percentage of recorded mortality increases unremittingly throughout the period, from the amazingly low 11 per cent of 1515 to the high point of 38.10 per cent of 1616. The figure for 1632 is the first reversal of the upward movement, though a 3 per cent decrease cannot be said to be a very dramatic reversal. As mentioned earlier, it was in 1570 that the hospital seemed to have increasing difficulty in keeping track of its charges, a point that is substantiated by the 14 per cent increase in the number of unknowns in 1570. That 1570 should be a year when the hospital lost track of many infants seems strange in one respect, because in this year, as in 1574 and 1599, women who lived in Toledo accounted for half or more than half of the nurses, a fact that should have simplified the hospital's task of checking on the infants. However, since Toledo women account for 49 per cent of the nurses in 1568 and the rate of unknowns is relatively low, and since village women dominate in 1616 and the percentage of unknowns remains at a high 38.10 per cent, it appears that the physical location of the infants made little difference in the hospital's efforts to keep up with its charges. This same reasoning holds true for the recorded mortality rates, which increase throughout the years no matter where the infants are nursed. What the figures of table 22 appear to reflect is the health of the city of Toledo and the nearby villages where the infants were nursed. As discussed in chapter 3, the decade of the 1570s began a forty-year period of poor health in Toledo, followed by the depopulation of the first two decades of the seventeenth century. Depopulation may explain the small percentage of Toledo nurses in 1616 and 1632, but it does not appear to have improved the recorded mortality rate for the foundlings, which remained at a very high level, although by 1632 the number of unknowns had decreased.

Overcrowded and insanitary living conditions, famines and epidemics, minimal and poor diets seem to have been a continual peril to the poor in Toledo, as in most European cities. The constant recurrence of famine and epidemics suggests a cyclical pattern, with periods of misery, starvation and death complemented by the years of good health and abundant grain. However, it does appear that the health and the living conditions of the poor in Toledo deteriorated in the sixteenth and early seventeenth centuries. The ever increasing percentage of mortality for the foundling hospital in the sixteenth and seventeenth centuries and the increasing number of deaths recorded by the Hospital of Tavera, at least until 1600, certainly suggest a deterioration in health. Thus, the cyclical pattern of feast and famine should be drawn on a downward spiral to indicate the deteriorating health and living conditions for the great majority of the city's inhabitants, but especially the poor.

# Notes

## INTRODUCTION

1. Pullan, 'Catholics and the poor', p. 15.
2. Albert Emminghaus, *Poor relief in different parts of Europe* (London, 1873), p. 13; Ernst Troeltsch, *The social teachings of the Christian churches*, trans. O. Wyon (2 vols., London, 1931), vol. I, pp. 133–6, 253; Max Weber, *The Protestant ethic and the spirit of capitalism*, trans. Talcott Parsons (London, 1930), pp. 177–8; R. H. Bremner, 'Modern attitudes towards charity and relief', *Comparative Studies in Society and History*, I (1958–9), 377. For a more detailed discussion and bibliography, see Pullan, *Renaissance Venice*, pp. 11–12, 197–9.
3. Tierney, *Medieval poor law*, pp. 46–50; W. J. Ashley, *An introduction to English economic history and theory*, vol. II (London, 1893), pp. 312–16; Colmeiro, *Historia de la economía*, vol. II, p. 609.
4. Pullan, *Renaissance Venice*, part II.
5. For Lyons, Gutton, *La société et les pauvres: Lyon*, pp. 263–87; N. Z. Davis, 'Poor relief', pp. 231–51. For Geneva, Kingdon, 'Social welfare', pp. 52, 55, 60, 64.
6. For the Italian foundations see Pullan, *Renaissance Venice*, pp. 362–5 and the same author's 'Povere, mendicanti e vagabondi', pp. 1018–19; Gemerek, 'Renfermement des pauvres en Italie', pp. 212–14; Delumeau, *Vie économique et sociale de Rome*, vol. I, pp. 404–5, 411–16. For the French hospitals, Gutton, *La société et les pauvres: Lyon*, pp. 295–349; Chill, 'Religion and mendicity', pp. 400–24; M. Foucault, *Madness and civilization: a history of insanity in the age of reason* (New York, 1965); Hufton, *Poor of eighteenth-century France*, pp. 139–59.
7. Gutton, *La société et les pauvres: Lyon*, pp. 11–13; Gemerek, 'Criminalité, vagabondage, pauperisme', pp. 345–75; Slack, 'Vagrants and vagrancy', pp. 360–79; Beier, 'Vagrants and the social order', pp. 3–29; I. A. A. Thompson, 'A map of crime', pp. 244–67.
8. Pullan, 'Catholics and the poor', p. 34.
9. Bataillon, *Pícaros y picaresca*, pp. 19–27, and 'J. L. Vivès', pp. 141–57; Jiménez Salas, *Historia de la asistencia social*, pp. 79–143; Maravall, 'De la misericordia', pp. 57–88; J. Vilar, 'Le picarisme espagnol', pp. 29–77; Cavillac, 'Introduction' in Pérez de Herrera, *Amparo de pobres*, pp. lx–cciv, and 'La reforma', pp. 7–59.
10. Gutton, *La société et les pauvres en Europe*, pp. 101.
11. Lis and Soly, *Poverty and capitalism*, p. 94.
12. Fortea Pérez, *Córdoba* and García Sanz, *Desarrollo y crisis* both provide much needed information about economic developments in sixteenth-century Castile.
13. García Sanz, *Desarrollo y crisis*, pp. 87–8, 217–18. This is also one explanation given by Fortea Pérez to explain the decline of Córdoba; see *Córdoba*, p. 473.

## I CASTILIAN LEGISLATION, DEBATES AND INNOVATIONS

1. Pinta Llorente and Palacio, *Procesos inquisitoriales.*
2. Noreña, *Juan Luis Vives*, p. 302, gives the following editions: 1526, Bruges; 1530, Paris; 1532, Paris, Lyons; 1533, Strassburg; 1545, Venice; 1583, Lyons.
3. Bataillon, 'J. L. Vivès', p. 143.
4. When Vives wrote his treatise Bruges was in a period of economic decline. See Noreña, *Juan Luis Vives*, p. 51, and Van Houtte, 'The Bruges market', *Economic History Review*, 2nd series, XIX (1966).
5. Pullan, 'Catholics and the poor', p. 29.
6. Bonenfant, 'Les origines', vol. VI, pp. 207–30.
7. For information and bibliography of the early reforms see Pullan, *Renaissance Venice*, pp. 239–40; Lis and Soly, *Poverty and capitalism*, pp. 87–8, 236–7; Gutton, *La société et les pauvres: Lyon*, pp. 251–7; *La société et les pauvres en Europe*, pp. 103–15.
8. Helleiner, 'The population of Europe', pp. 5–40.
9. Pullan, *Renaissance Venice*, pp. 200–1, 216–17; Lis and Soly, *Poverty and capitalism*, pp. 87–8, 236–7; Gemerek, 'Renfermement des pauvres en Italie', pp. 205–17; 'La lutte', pp. 213–36; Favreau, 'Pauvreté au Poitou', pp. 604 *et seq*; Gutton, *La société et les pauvres: Lyon*, pp. 215–18; Misraki, 'Criminalité et pauvreté', pp. 535–46.
10. Burriel, *Informe*, pp. 103–4.
11. Nolf, 'La réforme', pp. ixx–lxvi, lviii, 40–76.
12. Lameere, *Recueil*, p. 268.
13. Nolf, 'La réforme', pp. li, lix.
14. Colmeiro, *Cortes*, vol. IV, 1518, pet. 42, p. 272; 1523, pet. 66, p. 384.
15. Fortea Pérez, *Córdoba*, p. 201.
16. Colmeiro, *Cortes*, vol. IV, 1525, pet. 24, p. 425; 1528, pet. 45, p. 469; 1534, pet. 117, p. 617.
17. *Ibid.*, 1537, pet. 69, p. 658.
18. Pullan, *Renaissance Venice*, p. 286; the ordinance is published in MHSJ, *Monumenta Ignatiana*, vol. IV/1, *Scripta*, pp. 536–43; Pérez-Arregui, *San Ignacio*, pp. 153–7.
19. *MHSJ*, *Monumenta Ignatiana*, vol. 1/1, pp. 161–5.
20. The treatises of Juan de Robles and Domingo de Soto have been reprinted together by the Instituto de Estudios Políticos as: Domingo de Soto, *Deliberación en la causa de los pobres ( Y réplica de Fray Juan de Robles)*, and all citations have been taken from this edition. The quote is on p. 181.
21. Fuente, *Historia eclesiástica*, vol. V, p. 119.
22. March, *Niñez y juventud de Felipe II*, vol. I, p. 219; Gil Calvo, *La Compañía de Jesús*, pp. 32–4.
23. *DHEE*, vol. II, pp. 746–8; Beltrán de Heredia, *Historia de la reforma*.
24. AHN, Clero, 7216/2: Tavera to Toledo cathedral chapter, 12 March 1540; AHT, carp. 102: Escritos en romance de justicia y gobierno del Cardenal Tavera, 1544–5, t. II, 1 July 1545.
25. AMT, LA, No. 2, 16 April 1545: AHT, carp. 102: Escritos, 12 March 1545. Tavera had scheduled a diocesan synod for April 1545, but because he was called to Valladolid by Prince Philip, the synod was postponed until the next year (AGS, Est, leg. 70, fol. 55).
26. AHN, Clero, 7216/2: Tavera to Toledo cathedral chapter, 11 Jan. 1536.
27. AHT, carp. 170: Carta-Quenta del tesorero Rodrigo Quiroga . . . 1 Feb. to 31 Dec. 1539.
28. AGS, PR, leg. 22–75.

29. AGS, Est, leg. 72, fol. 131: Tavera to Charles, 21 April 1545.
30. AGS, Est, leg. 49, fols. 31–2: Tavera to Charles, 2 March 1540.
31. AGS, Est, leg. 49, fol. 42: Tavera to Charles, 8 April 1540; leg. 50, fols 88–90: Tavera to Charles, 26 June 1540. A portion of this latter letter is reprinted in Beltrán de Heredia, *Domingo de Soto*, pp. 86–7.
32. Jiménez Salas, *Historia de la asistencia social*, p. 128.
33. AGS, Est, leg. 50, fol. 271: Charles to Tavera, 6 Sept. 1540.
34. AGS, Est, leg. 49, fol. 179: Tavera to Charles, 13 Dec. 1540.
35. 'Que los pobres piden en sus tierras', *Quadernos de algunas leyes*, 1544. NR, lib. 7, tit. 39, leyes 1–13.
36. Jiménez Salas, *Historia de la asistencia social*, p. 128.
37. In 1547 an English sturdy beggar could be enslaved for two years; in France they were subject to forced labour and galley service; and in Venice they were sent to the galleys. See Leonard, *History of English poor relief*, pp. 56–7; C. S. L. Davis, 'Slavery and Protector Somerset', pp. 533–49; Gutton, *La société et les pauvres: Lyon*, pp. 252–3; Pullan, *Renaissance Venice*, p. 252.
38. Beltrán de Heredia, *Domingo de Soto*, pp. 90, 89, 115.
39. Fuente, *Historia eclesiástica*, vol. v, p. 368.
40. N. Z. Davis, 'Poor relief, humanism and heresy', pp. 259–61.
41. AGS, Est, leg. 70, fol. 28: Soto to Prince Philip, n.d. [1545].
42. For background on the subject of almsgiving see Tierney, *Medieval poor law*.
43. Fortea Pérez, *Córdoba*, p. 201; González y Sugrañes, *Mendicidad y beneficencia*, pp. 3–18.
44. Adam Smith, *An inquiry into the wealth of nations*, ed. R. H. Campbell and A. S. Skinner (2 vols., Oxford, 1976), vol. I, pp. 135–8.
45. Beltrán de Heredia, *Domingo de Soto*, p. 637. In addition to the Spanish and Latin version of the *Deliberación* published in Salamanca in 1545, the author gives (p. 533) the following Latin editions: 1547 in Venice; 1554, 1561, 1566, 1570 and 1575 in Salamanca.
46. *Ibid.*, pp. 775–6; also AGS, PE, leg. 1. Soto was nominated as a candidate for the vacant sees of the Canary Islands and of Granada (AGS, PE, leg. 6) and of Toledo (AGS, PE, leg. 155).
47. Marquez Villanueva, *Espiritualidad*, pp. 115–28.
48. *La pragmática . . . de 1552. NR*, lib. 12, tit. 31, ley 4.
49. Colmeiro, *Cortes*, vol. v, 1555, pet. 122, pp. 695–6.
50. AMT, AS, caj. 3, leg. 3, no. 7: Letter from the Royal Cámara to the city of Toledo, 27 Nov. 1557.
51. Bataillon, 'J. L. Vivès', pp. 151–3; Journez, 'Notice sur Fray Lorenzo de Villavicencio'.
52. Ram, 'Opinion des théologiens'.
53. 'La carta sobre lo de los pobres', *Pragmáticas nuevas*, 1565. *NR*, lib. 7, tit. 39, ley 24; tit. 38, ley 3.
54. *La pragmática . . . sobre los vagamundos*, 1566. *NR*, lib. 12, tit. 31, ley 5.
55. Evennett, *Spirit of the counter reformation*, pp. 37–40; *MHSJ, Monumenta Ignatiana*, vol. I/I, pp. 164–5.
56. Clay, *Mediaeval hospitals of England*; Imbert, *Les hôpitaux en droit canonique* and *Les hôpitaux en France*.
57. Pullan, *Renaissance Venice*, pp. 202–6; Gemerek, 'Renfermement', pp. 208–9.
58. Russell-Wood, *Fidalgos and philanthropists*, pp. 13–17.
59. Baquero, *Bosquejo del hospital real*, pp. 13–26; Sanahuja, *Historia de la beneficencia*, vol. I, pp. 23–34; Teixidor, *Antigüedades*, vol. II, pp. 325–30; Escalona, *Décadas*, vol. I, cols. 1047–9; González y Sugrañes, *Mendicidad y beneficencia*, p. 186.

60. *Copia . . . del testamento . . . don Pedro González de Mendoza*, trans. Andrés Álvarez y Ancil (Toledo, 1915), pp. 20–1.
61. ACT, 0.4 K 5 71, Bull of Alexander VI, 1497.
62. J. M. Fernández Catón, *El archivo del Hospital de los Reyes Católicos de Santiago de Compostela* (Santiago de Compostela, 1972), pp. 31–4.
63. AGS, P E, leg. 142: Foundation of the Royal Hospital of Granada, Alonso (?) de Rojas, n.d.
64. AGS, P E, leg. 195: Copy of 1560 visit in Royal Hospital of Seville.
65. Prescott, *Reign of Ferdinand and Isabella*, vol. I, p. 387.
66. AGS, P E, leg. 39: Report of the Granada hospitals, compiled by the provisor of the diocese (1586–90).
67. Colmeiro, *Cortes*, vol. IV, 1525, pet. 47, p. 425; 1532, pet. 62, p. 556; vol. V, 1548, pet. 131, pp. 428–9; 1555, pet. 55, p. 654; 1559, pet. 52, pp. 833–4.
68. AHT, AF, caj. 11, no. 21: Letter from Charles to Tavera, 5 Feb. 1541.
69. Tarsicio de Azcona, *La elección y reforma*; García Oro, *Cisneros y la reforma*.
70. Sala Balust and Martín Hernandez, eds., *Obras*, vol. I, 41–221; vol. II, 3–20.
71. Aranda, *Vida del siervo de Dios*.
72. Sala Balust and Martín Hernandez, eds., *Obras*, vol. I, p. 61; Aranda, *Vida del Siervo de Dios*, chs. I and II.
73. Sala Balust, 'La espiritualidad', p. 180.
74. Sala Balust and Martín Hernandez, eds., *Obras*, vol. I pp. 84–92, 167–83, 209–21.
75. *Ibid.*, carta 177, p. 852.
76. *Ibid.*, carta 204, pp. 925–6.
77. The traditional version, given by Francisco de Castro and most of John of God's biographers, is that he was born in Montemayor el Nuevo, a village in Portugal, and at eight years of age was transported from Portugal to Oropesa (Toledo) by a cleric. Julio Caro Baroja, *Los Judíos en la España moderna y contemporánea* (3 vols., Madrid, 1961), vol. II, pp. 238–9, concurs with the Portuguese nationality of the saint but argues that he was a *converso*, presumably because of his original name, Ciudad. Gómez-Menor, 'El linaje toledano', pp. 93, 126, n. 24, argues that John of God was born in Casarrubios del Monte, a village near Toledo.
78. Sala Balust and Martín Hernandez, eds., *Obras*, vol. I, carta 45, p. 501.
79. AGS, PE, leg. 39: Report of the Granada hospitals.
80. Sala Balust and Martín Hernandez, eds., *Obras*, vol. I, carta 141, p. 752.
81. *Ibid.*, pp. 751–2.
82. AGS, PE, leg. 140: Visit of the Córdoba San Lázaro, 1592.
83. José Cruset, *San Juan de Dios* (Barcelona, 1958), p. 283.
84. *Ibid.*, p. 289; Serrano, *Archivo*, pp. 266–7.
85. AGS, PE, leg. 39.
86. AGS, PE, leg. 140.

## 2 THE REFORM OF CHARITABLE INSTITUTIONS

1. Pullan, *Renaissance Venice*, pp. 331–5; Imbert, 'L'église et l'état'; *Les hôpitaux en droit canonique*; 'Les prescriptions hospitalières'.
2. Clay, *Mediaeval hospitals of England*, pp. xvii–iii.
3. BL Add. 28.355, fols. 327–48.
4. *NR*, lib. 7, tit. 38, ley 2; lib. 8, tit. 10, ley 1.
5. For background on the *subsidio* see *DHEE*, vol. II, p. 1139; Carande, *Carlos V*, vol. II, pp. 466–86; Ulloa, *La hacienda real*, pp. 597–621. Garzón Pareja, *Diezmos y tributos*, pp. 249–56.

6. AGS, Est. leg. 20, fols. 114–15: Tavera to Charles, 6 June 1530.
7. AGS, CC, leg. 1, *subsidio* of 1543: Las limosnas, which appears to be a duplicate of the list published by Carande, *Carlos V*, vol. II, p. 470, taken from AGS, Contaduría mayor, 1ª época, fol. 13.
8. AGS, CC, leg. 1: Cédula de la merced, 24 March 1537.
9. *Ibid.*, leg. 2; 'Repartimiento del subsidio de 1541' includes details of the papal brief.
10. Colmeiro, *Cortes*, vol. v, 1548, pet. 110, p. 418.
11. *NR*, lib. 12, tit. 12, ley 13. For more details about confraternities see Rumeu de Armas, *Historia de la previsión social en España*.
12. *Constituciones synodales, Toledo*, 1536, fol. 9v.
13. Jedin, *Crisis and closure*, p. 158; *DHEE*, vol. I, p. 419.
14. Imbert, 'Les prescriptions hospitalières', pp. 5–28.
15. Tejada y Ramiro, ed., *Colección de canones*, vol. v, pp. 180–399. AGS, PR, leg. 22–2 for the crown letter to the archbishop of Seville. Martínez Diéz, 'Del decreto tridentino', p. 255, n. 3, explains that no provincial council was held in Seville because the obligations of Fernando Valdés as inquisitor-general forced him to reside elsewhere.
16. Schroeder, *Disciplinary decrees*, pp. 391–2.
17. AGS, PR, leg. 22–1.
18. AGS, PR, leg. 22–36.
19. Tarsicio de Azcona, *La elección y reforma*, deals with the early expansion of the royal patrimony.
20. AGS, PE, legs. 139, 140, 142 contain an abundance of disorganized material relating to the extent and condition of the royal patrimony in the last third of the sixteenth century.
21. Lovett, *Philip II*, pp. 159, 161.
22. AHN, Órdenes Militares, lib. 1064C, fol. 1 (1480); lib. 1067C, fol. 24 (1494); lib. 1236C, fol. 2 (1500); lib. 1075C, fol. 11 (1511); lib. 1079C, fol. 89 (1515); lib. 1080C, fol. 145 (1525); lib. 1081C, fol. 81 (1528); lib. 1083C, fol. 93 (1537); lib. 1086C, fol. 179 (1554); Judicial 51541 (1564–66); Judicial 19786 (1575); Úcles, caj. 382, no. 33 (1582); Judicial 61169 (1593); lib. 5C, fol. 5, lib. 7C, fol. 16; 1088C, fol. 1 (1603); Consejo, leg. 6830, no. 2 (1637).
23. AGS, Cámara, libros de cédulas, no. 44, fols. 152–3.
24. AGS, PE, leg. 27: El obispo de Guadix sobre la visita, 28 July 1590; see also legs. 165 and 31 for more details of the visit.
25. AGS, PE, leg. 39: Report of Granada hospitals.
26. AHN, Cámara, leg. 4413, exp. 30, 6 Feb. 1594; AGS, PE, leg. 40: Report of the president of the Granada chancery, 16 March 1594.
27. AGS, PE, leg. 112: Visit of Royal Hospital of Granada, 20 May 1628.
28. AGS, PE, 174: Pleyto entre Luis Moreno y la cofradía de Nra Señora de la Paz y Corpus Cristi, 1611–15.
29. AMT, LA, no. 5, 7 May and 26 Sept. 1561.
30. AGS, PE, leg. 40: Proceso del ospital de San Lázaro de Toledo, 1592.
31. AGS, PE, leg. 30: Carta de Miguel de Azparren, 5 May 1591.
32. AGS, PE, leg. 40: Proceso, 1592.
33. AGS, PE, leg. 21² (Burgos); legs. 53, 318, 319 (Granada); leg. 140 (Córdoba); leg. 53 (Arévalo); leg. 41 (Seville); legs. 52, 53 (Gijón); leg. 142 (Zamora); leg. 50 (Segovia); leg. 40 (Toledo).
34. AGS, PE, leg. 40: From 1560 to 1580 the Confraternity de las Angustias was unable to find any lepers in Toledo. PE, leg. 41 contains the judgment that leprosy still existed in Seville. The question of whether leprosy existed in Castile

was debated again in 1620; see BL 1322 k 13, *Papeles varios*, vol. i. Stanley Rubin, *Medieval English medicine* (London–New York, 1974), pp. 150–1, gives some ideas as to why leprosy was difficult to diagnose.

35. AGS, PR, leg. 38–51.
36. Goñi Gaztambide, 'La reforma tridentina', pp. 267–76. Nuñez Cepeda, *La beneficencia en Navarra*, pp. 96–101.
37. *Constituciones synodales, Toledo*, 1568, fol. 52v.
38. *Constituciones synodales, Salamanca*, 1584, fols. 97–8.
39. AGS, PE, leg. 139, $5^2$.
40. AGS, PE, leg. 13.
41. BNM, MS 732.
42. AMT, LA, no. 17, 19 Jan. 1583.
43. *Constituciones synodales, Salamanca*, 1584, fols. 190–3.
44. *Constituciones synodales, Toledo*, 1622, fols. 94–106.
45. ADT, iv/1499, Libro de la visita de los partidos de Canales, 1634–6; iv/1240, Libro de la visita a los partidos de Zurita, 1647–8.
46. ADT, iv/1499, fol. 8v for the transfer of money from one pious work to another; fols. 36 and 29 for the refinancing of *pósitos*.
47. *Ibid.*, fol. 27.
48. AGS, PR, leg. 23–190. *NR*, lib. 7, tit. 38, note 2.
49. BL, Add. 28.351, fols. 489–513.
50. *Ibid.*, fols. 487–8.
51. *Ibid.*, fol. 486.
52. BRME, L.I.12–24, fols. 196–9, reprinted in Jacques Soubeyroux, 'Sur un project original d'organisation de la bienfaisance en Espagne au XVIᵉ siècle', *Bulletin Hispanique*, LXXIV (1972), 118–27.
53. BRME, L.I.12–24, fol. 197v.
54. González y Sugrañes, *Mendicidad y beneficencia*, pp. 100, 108, and Cavillac, 'La reforma'.
55. Giginta had described the fate of his 1576 'Representación' in his book, *Tratado de remedio de los pobres*, fols. 2, 2v. A manuscript of the 'Representación' is in BNM, MS/18653 and it has been reprinted in González y Sugrañes, *Mendicidad y beneficencia*, pp. 355–62 and Hernández Iglesias, *La beneficencia*, vol. ii, pp. 1169–76.
56. Boyd, *Cardinal Quiroga*; Salazar de Mendoza, *Crónica de Mendoza*, pp. 287–318; Pisa, *Descripción*, vol. i, pp. 268–71. According to Cavillac, 'La reforma', p. 18, Giginta also dedicated his original edition of *Exhortación* (Madrid, 1581) to Pazos. The more common edition, published in Barcelona in 1583, was dedicated to the city council of Barcelona.
57. Pullan, *Renaissance Venice*, pp. 362–5; 'Povere, mendicanti e vagabondi', pp. 1018–19; Delumeau, *Vie économique et sociale de Rome*, vol. i, pp. 404, 411–16.
58. AGS, PE, leg. $5^1$, $5^2$, 10 and 11 contain the correspondence of President Pazos. Lovett, *Philip II*, pp. 144–6 and Parker, *Philip II*, pp. 28–9, 150 *et seq.* give details of the late sixteenth-century government by junta; for a discussion and bibliography of the early-seventeenth-century reform, see Elliott, 'Self-perception and decline'.
59. Letters from Pazos to Philip, in AGS, PE, legs. 10 (31 March 1579), $5^1$ (12 and 19 Dec. 1578), $5^2$ (6 July 1578), 10 (15 July 1579), and $5^1$ (17 Oct. 1578), respectively.
60. See Cavillac, 'La reforma', p. 43 for Villavicencio's approval. For pressure exerted on the Augustinian to conform to the majority opinion, see AGS, PE, leg. $5^1$.

61. AMZ, leg. 21–30; Broadside proclaiming the opening of the Toledo beggars' hospital, Jan. 1581.
62. *Ibid.*; also AMT, LA, no. 16, 17 Nov. 1581.
63. AMZ, leg. 21–30: Giginta to city council of Zamora, 16 April 1581.
64. AMZ, leg. 21–39, Broadside proclaiming the opening of a General Hospital of Beggars in Madrid, 19 Jan. 1582; there is another copy in BPUG, FC, vol. 7, fol. 118.
65. Giginta, *Cadena de oro*, 'Epístola a don Gaspar Quiroga'.
66. González y Sugrañes, *Mendicidad y beneficencia*, pp. 105–8.
67. *Ibid.*, pp. 71–8, 101–14, 120.
68. *AC*, vol. VIII, pp. 191–2, 240–2, 260–2, 348. BPUG, FC, vol. 67, fols. 128–30 are copies of the material sent out by the Cortes in 1587.
69. *AC*, vol. IX, p. 133; also BPUG, FC, vol. 67, fol. 124.
70. AMT, LA, no. 16, 31 July, 7 Oct. and 5 Nov. 1581.
71. González y Sugrañes, *Mendicidad y beneficencia*, pp. 26, 123–7, 129–30.
72. *Ibid.*, pp. 72–8, 120, 114.
73. BPUG, FC, vol. 67, fol. 122.
74. BPUG, FC, vol. 22, letter to don Juan de Zuñiga, 4 Jan. 1582.
75. BL, Add, 28.361, fol. 160.
76. *Ibid.*, fols. 150–70.
77. AMT, AP, 1589. My thanks to J.-P. Molenat who showed me this document.
78. AMT, LA, no. 19, 23 March 1591. The letter was dated 7 Sept. 1590.
79. *Premática que los naturales destos reynos no anden en ábito de romeros*, 1590.
80. AGS, PE, leg. $5^2$.
81. AGS, PE, leg. 39.
82. *Ibid.*: President of the Granada chancery to Royal Council, 26 Oct. 1593.
83. *Ibid.*: Archbishop of Granada to the Royal Council, 7 Aug. 1593.
84. Saldaña-Sicilia, *Monografia histórico-médica*, mentions an attempt at consolidation in 1570, but does not explain why it was not carried out. Córdoba remained with twenty-two hospitals in 1599; see AGS, PE, leg. 54: Report by Andrés Cerio, 23 Dec. 1599.
85. Information for the consolidations mentioned has been taken from the following sources: Valladolid, Bennassar, *Valladolid*, p. 449; Salamanca, AHN, Cámara, leg. 4410, exp. 208 and leg. 4414, exp. 181; Toro, ADPZ, leg. 166–2; Jaén and Antequera, *DHEE*, vol. II, pp. 1220–1 and 1397 respectively; Medina del Campo, Marcos Martín, *Auge y declive*, pp. 202 *et seq.*; Plasencia, Rodríguez Peña, *Los hospitales*, p. 109; Segovia, Colmenares, *Historia de Segovia*, p. 132.
86. BNM, MS 732.
87. RAH, Papeles de Jesuitas, 89, 75; Órtiz de Zuñiga, *Annales de Sevilla*, pp. 566–73.
88. AGS, PE, leg. 57.
89. F. Morales Padrón, 'La Cuidad del quinientos', *Historia de Sevilla* (5 vols., Seville, 1976–), vol. III, p. 117. For a more flattering portrait of the archbishop, see *DHEE*, vol. I, pp. 382–4.
90. Fuente, *Historia eclesiástica*, vol. V, p. 335.
91. AGS, PE, leg. 10.
92. Trinidad, *Vida y virtudes del siervo de Dios Bernardino de Obregón, compuesto por el R.P.M. Luis Bernardino de Obregón*. This is a dual biography; the notes of Luis Bernardino were compiled after the founder's death in 1600, while Alonso de la Trinidad, writing in the eighteenth century, has added more information.
93. Trinidad, *Bernardino de Obregón*, pp. 316, 364; AVM, 2–420–18.
94. Shergold, *History of the Spanish stage*, pp. 177 *et seq.*; J. E. Varey and N. D.

Shergold, 'Datos históricos sobre los primeros teatros de Madrid', *Bulletin Hispanique*, IX (1958), 74–84.

95. AHN, Cámara, leg. 4412, exp. 176; AVM, 2–420–13.

96. AHN, Cámara, leg. 4409, exp. 38; leg. 4414, exp. 36.

97. *Ibid.*, leg. 4407, exp. 19; leg. 4413, exp. 174.

98. *AC*, vol. XVI, p. 652. In three towns of Champagne, sixteenth-century French charitable givers exhibited a similar antipathy toward the new bureaus of poor relief; see Galpern, *The religions of the people*, pp. 103, 193–6.

99. Rodríguez Peña, *Los hospitales de Plasencia*, p. 109.

100. Fuente, *Historia eclesiástica*, vol. V, p. 418.

101. Callahan, 'An aspect of poor relief', pp. 1–24.

102. Pérez de Herrera has recently been studied in a lengthy biography by M. Cavillac, in the 'Introduction' for a reprint of *Amparo de pobres*, which includes a detailed list of all the doctor's publications (CXCVII–CCII). This edition has been used for all references. For Herrera's *converso* origins, see Cavillac, 'Noblesse et ambiguités', pp. 177–212 and Cavillac and Le Flem, 'La "probanza de limpieza"', pp. 565–76.

103. Pérez de Herrera, *Amparo*, p. 249. This was not an original idea. In the 1580s the beggars' hospital of Toledo had been remodelled by those who lived in it, and apparently the same procedure was followed in Barcelona (see González y Sugrañes, *Mendicidad y beneficencia*, p. 114, n. 4).

104. *AC*, vol. XIII, p. 558; vol. XIV, pp. 455–6, 463–5, 503–7; vol. XV, pp. 724–5, 740–1.

105. According to a scribal notation in AGS, PE, leg. 51, a total of three reports and fifteen certifications were drawn up by Pérez de Herrera to prove his pure blood, his service to the crown and the worth of his albergues.

106. Quintana, *Madrid*, p. 449; Pérez de Herrera, *Epílogo*, pp. 2–4.

107. Pérez de Herrera, *Epílogo*, p. 4; Cadalso, *Instituciones penitenciarias*, pp. 220–31. For more information about La Galera, see Cavillac, 'Introduction', *Amparo*, pp. clvi–clvii.

108. AVM, 2–420–25. *NR*, lib. 12, tit. 26, ley 8.

109. BL, Eg. 441, fols. 101–41. Also see M. Agullo y Cobo, *El hospicio y los asilos de San Bernardino* (Madrid, 1972), pp. 6–12.

110. BL, Eg. 441, fol. 108v.

111. Tormo, 'La de Fuencarral', pp. 226–79.

112. Callahan, *Honor, commerce and industry*, pp. 56–69; J. Soubeyroux, *Paupérisme et rapports sociaux à Madrid au XVIIIeme siècle* (2 vols., Lille, 1978).

### 3 THE CITY OF TOLEDO

1. These figures are taken from BPT, MS 210, Blas Ortiz, *Descripción . . . de la Santa Iglesia de Toledo*, trans. Alfonso de Cedillo, fols. 492–4 (originally published in Latin in 1549); Hurtado, 'Memorial', pp. 534–6; and AGS, DGT, leg. 1301, Inventario 24, fol. 18.

2. Pérez, *La revolución*, pp. 516–17, n. 27.

3. Gómez-Menor, *Cristianos nuevos*, p. 7, n. 7.

4. For a discussion and bibliography of this issue in Castile see Ulloa, *La hacienda real*, pp. 18–19; for households in other parts of Europe see Laslett and Wall, *Household and family*, table 1.6, p. 76; table 4.15, p. 153.

5. For the 1528 census, AGS, CG, leg. 768; for 1561, AGS, EH, 2ª serie, leg. 183. See *DHEE*, vol. II, pp. 682–733 for an excellent discussion of the Castilian censuses. Ruiz Martín, 'Movimientos demográficos', p. 152, gives the 1561 population of Granada.

6. González, *Censo de población*, p. 347. AGS, Cámara, leg. 2158.
7. AGS, Cámara, legs. 2162 and 2163. For a discussion of the resettlement of the *moriscos*, see Domínguez Ortiz and Vincent, *Historia de los moriscos*.
8. AGS, Cámara, leg. 2183. This document places the *morisco* population for the archbishopric of Toledo at 11,957 in 1581, but there is a notation stating that the captives have not been included in this figure and another 3,301 people have been added, making a total of 15,258.
9. AGS, Cámara, leg. 2162.
10. AMT, LA, no. 12, 8 June 1575.
11. AGS, PE, leg. 5.
12. Salazar de Mendoza, *Mendoza*, p. 298; the disease is also mentioned in BNM, MS 13044, fol. 129v, and in Domínguez Ortiz, *La sociedad española*, vol. I, p. 68. For a discussion of the relationship between mortality, food supply and epidemics in England, see Slack, 'Mortality crisis and epidemics 1485–1610', Webster, ed., *Health, medicine and mortality*.
13. The records for baptisms are found in the APSN (parishes of Nicolás, Ginés, Vicente), APSJ (parishes of Justo, Miguel, Andrés), APST (Tomé, Cipriano, Cristóbal, Bartolomé), and APSA (Isidoro).
14. Ulloa, *La hacienda real*, pp. 198, 201–2.
15. AGS, EH, 2ª serie, leg. 182: Francisco de Caravajal to Juan Vázquez de Salazar, 6 May 1586.
16. AGS, DGT, leg. 1301, Inventario 24, fol. 18.
17. Letter from Francisco de Caravajal to Council of State, 27 Aug. 1599, in Bennassar, *Recherches*, pp. 177–9.
18. Trinidad, *Bernardino de Obregón*, p. 389. Escalona, *Décadas*, vol. I, quoted in Casey, *Kingdom of Valencia*, p. 30.
19. Hamilton, *American treasure*, p. 370. The price of a *fanega* of wheat in New Castile was 1204.2 mrs in 1606 and 1123.1 mrs in 1607, the highest prices recorded from 1501 to 1625.
20. 'Memoriales que presentó Juan Belluga de Moncada', in Domínguez Ortiz, *La sociedad española*, vol. I, p. 351.
21. For information about the Toledo School see Vilar, 'Docteurs et marchands', and the same author's introduction to Sancho de Moncada, *Restauración política*, pp. 56–9.
22. For recent studies on the decline of Toledo see D. Ringrose, 'The impact of a new capital city: Madrid, Toledo and New Castile, 1560–1660', *Journal of Economic History*, 33 (1973), 761–91; M. Weisser, 'The decline of Castile revisited: the case of Toledo', *Journal of European Economic History*, II (Winter, 1973), 614–40; and Montemayor, 'Une conjoncture municipal', pp. 183–204, whom I would like to thank for allowing me to read this article before publication.
23. This census has been published in Martz and Porres, *Toledo*, pp. 161–288.
24. *Plano de Toledo*, which is a copy of the original drawing thought to have been executed by El Greco between 1606 and 1610.
25. Porres, *Historia de las calles*, vol. II, pp. 476–95.
26. *Constituciones synodales*, *Toledo*, 1568, fol. 50. *Constituciones synodales . . . por Bernardo de Rojas y Sandoval*, *Toledo*, 1601, fol. 49.
27. Bennassar, *Valladolid*, p. 191.
28. AHT, LRE, 1571, 5, 6, 7 March.
29. BNM, MS 12974: *Constituciones synodales*, *Toledo*, 1601, fol. 75.
30. Tejada y Ramiro, ed., *Colección de canones*, vol. V, p. 409.
31. Domínguez Ortiz, *La sociedad española*, vol. I, p. 349.
32. Casey, *Kingdom of Valencia*, pp. 60–1, 85–7; Hurtado, 'Memorial', p. 525.

33. AGS, CR, leg. 351–27 for the 1560s; Hurtado, 'Memorial', pp. 515–16, 570–3 for the 1570s.
34. AMT, AP, Memorial de los pobres, 1 June 1558.
35. BNM, MS 9175, fols. 149–59: 'Memoria de las fiestas y alegrías'; for a detailed study of the parish of Santiago, see Sánchez Sánchez, *Toledo y la crisis del siglo XVII.*
36. APSA, parish of Santiago del Arrabal baptismal records.
37. AMT, CJ, no. 116, fol. 481.
38. AHT, carp. 205: Bartolomé Bustamante to Ares Pardo, 12 April 1546.
39. For a brief description of the San Isidoro parishioners, J. Gómez-Menor, 'La confradía de Nuestra Señora de los Desamparados', *Anales Toledanos*, V (Toledo, 1971), 170–1. APSA, San Isidoro Libro de Bautismo II, 1566–77; beginning in 1573 the baptism of *morisco* children is noted by the priest.
40. Bennassar, *Recherches*, pp. 177–9.
41. Bennassar, 'Medina del Campo', pp. 481–3; 'Economie et société à Ségovie', pp. 131–7; *Valladolid*, p. 439. González Múñoz, *La población de Talavera*, pp. 137–40, 152–3.
42. Lis and Soly, *Poverty and Capitalism*, pp. 79–80; Clark and Slack, *English towns*, pp. 58, 88, 148.
43. For an explanation of this term and the structural poor, see Gutton, *La société et les pauvres: Lyon*, pp. 52, 53.
44. Bennassar, *Valladolid*, p. 436; Braudel, *The Mediterranean*, vol. I, pp. 453–4; Le Flem, 'Cáceres, Plasencia y Trujillo', pp. 248–98.
45. Casey, *Kingdom of Valencia*, p. 31; Bennassar, *Valladolid*, pp. 176–7.
46. N. Z. Davis, 'Poor relief', pp. 254, 273–5; Gascon, 'Économie et pauvreté', pp. 755–7 and *Grand commerce*, vol. I, pp. 402–5; Pullan, 'Poveri, mendicanti e vagabondi', p. 990; Clark and Slack, *English towns*, p. 121.
47. Antonio, *Biblioteca hispanae*, vol. II, p. 50; San Antonio, *Biblioteca universa franciscana*, vol. II, pp. 304–5. According to Nicolás Antonio, the name of the friar might be Luis Escalera instead of Luis de Scala.
48. Rodríguez, *Asistencia social*, p. 236.
49. Venegas, *Tránsito*, ed. Ochoa, part 3, ch. 17, pp. 101–2. For more information about Venegas see the introduction by Mir, in 'Escritores místicos', pp. xiv–xxvi; R. Ricard, 'En Espagne: jalons pour une histoire de l'acédie et de la paresse', *Revue d'ascétique et de mystique*, 45 (1969), 27–45; Bataillon, *Erasmo y España*, pp. 565–71.
50. Venegas, *Libros*, fols. 165–7. I would like to thank P. Antolín Abad Pérez, OFM, for allowing me to use his copy of the 1540 edition.
51. Bataillon, *Erasmo y España*, pp. 438–70.
52. AHT, AF, caj. 11, no. 21: Bull of Paul III, 21 March 1540; letter of Charles to Tavera, 5 Feb. 1541.
53. AHT, AF: According to a letter from Alonso de Villacorto (6 Aug. 1545), the pope would not give his permission for the hospital consolidation.
54. ACT, LAC, no. 6, fols. 328–30.
55. AHT, AF, caj. 11, no. 21, 28 Feb. 1540.
56. AMT, LA, no. 2, 4 Jan. 1546.
57. AHT, carp. 205, 26 Dec. 1545.
58. AHT, carp. 179: Cuenta de los doce mil ducados, 8 Feb. 1546.
59. AHT, carp. 205, 22 Feb. 1546.
60. ACT, LAC, no. 7, fols. 115v–116 and AMT, Libro de los pobres, 1546.
61. AMT, Libro de los pobres, 1546.
62. For Silíceo's opposition to the Jesuits see Astraín, *Historia de la Compañía de Jesús*,

vol. I; concerning the statute of purity of blood in the Toledo cathedral chapter see Sicroff, *Les controverses*.

63. AHT, carp. 179.
64. For the weights of a *fanega* of wheat, see AHT, 'Gasto de trigo', LB or LD.
65. AHT, Libro de copias, 1 Aug. 1549.
66. The lists of the ten parishes that took in beggars have been published by Redondo, 'Pauperismo', pp. 717–24.
67. AMT, LA, no. 3, 3 Aug. 1547.
68. AMT, AP, 1556–9.
69. AMT, AS, caj. 3, leg. 3, no. 7, 27 Nov. 1557.
70. José Ignacio Tellechea Idigoras, *El arzobispo Carranza y su tiempo* (2 vols., Madrid, 1968).
71. AMT, LA, no. 5, 6 Sept. 1561 includes a copy of the original proposals.
72. AMT, Pósito, no. 61 includes a copy of the original constitutions and a history of the *pósito*.
73. AMT, LA, no. 8, 28 May 1566.
74. BL, Add. 28,357, fols. 226–7.
75. AMT, LA, no. 16, 7 Oct. 1581.
76. Martín Gamero, *Ordenanzas de Toledo*, pp. 27–31; AMT, Pósito, no. 61.
77. AMT, LA, no. 3, 29 March 1547.
78. AMT, LA, no. 10, 3 Oct. 1569; no. 11, 4 April 1572.
79. AMT, AS, caj. 3, leg. 3, no. 26, 26 Oct. 1561.
80. AMT, LA, no. 9, 13 Aug. 1568; AS, caj. 3, leg. 3, no. 11, 12 Sept. 1577.
81. AMT, LA, no. 13, 8 June, 30 Sept., 3, 10, 12 Oct., 7 Dec. 1575 and 9 Jan., 10 Feb. 1576.
82. Salazar y Castro, *Historia geneológica*, vol. I, p. 496.
83. AMT, LA, no. 9, 19 July 1568.
84. AMT, AS, caj. 4, leg. 2, no. 98, 11 Dec. 1557. Libro de los gastos y recibos de los niños de la doctrina, 1576–9.
85. AGS, CR, leg. 619–2: Cargos e descargos de la ciudad de Toledo, 9 Aug. 1586.
86. AMT, AP, 17 May 1581.
87. *Ibid.*; for Quiroga's support of the Jesuits in Toledo see Gil Calvo, *La Compañía de Jesús*, pp. 52–63.
88. Hurtado, 'Memorial', p. 555; AGS, CR, leg. 619–2.
89. AGS, CR, leg. 309–19: La ciudad de Toledo sobre el hospital general; *AC*, vol. X, pp. 184–6.
90. Bataillon, 'Le Docteur Laguna', p. 27; Cavillac, 'La reforma', p. 35.
91. AMT, AP, Petición de Giginta, 17 May 1581; Los provechos, 1581.
92. AGS, CR, leg. 309–19: 15 Nov. 1583.
93. *Ibid.*: San Juan de los Reyes, Oct.–Nov. 1583.
94. AGS, CR, leg. 619–2: Cargos e descargos, 1583–9.
95. AMT, AS, caj. 3, leg. 3, no. 14: Separación de los pósitos, 1655.
96. AMT, AP, 1585.
97. AGS, CR, leg. 619–2: Provisión real, 13 Sept. 1586; Cargos de Francisco de Caravajal, 1585.
98. AGS, CR, leg. 351–27: Diego de Zuñiga, 5 July 1570.
99. AMT, AP: Memorial and letters, 1586.
100. AMT, LA, no. 9, 10, 13 Dec. 1569; CJ, no. 196, fol. 651.
101. AMT, Libro de la hermandad de San Miguel y San Bartolomé, Cabildos, 1559–1623, 1 March 1581 and 20 Sept. 1583.
102. AMT, AP: La orden en el recogimiento, 29 Dec. 1587.
103. AGS, PE, leg. 40: Petición de Juan Pérez de Villareal, 24 May 1593.

104. AMT, AP: Horden de curar, 1589.
105. Bennassar, *Valladolid*, p. 442.
106. Hernández Iglesias, *La beneficencia*, vol. I, p. 15; Jiménez Salas, *Historia de la asistencia social*, p. xi.
107. AGS, PR, leg. 38, fol. 56.
108. AGS, PE, leg. 40: Proceso, 1592.
109. *Ibid.*: Alonso de Ribera to Francisco González de Heredia, 17 Oct. 1592.
110. *Ibid.*: Dr Juan López to Licenciado Tejada, 20 May 1593.
111. AGS, PE, leg. 38: Cristóbal Palomares to Licenciado Tejada, 16 May 1593.
112. AMT, LA, no. 22, 1 Aug. 1594.
113. BPT, MS 210, fols. 210v–212.
114. AMT, AS, leg. 2, no. 85.
115. AMT, LA, no. 22, 23 Aug. 1594.
116. AGS, PE, leg. 41.
117. AGS, PE, leg. 60.
118. AMT, LA, no. 23, 10 March 1598.
119. AMT, LA, no. 21, 11 Aug. 1593; no. 22, 11, 18 April 1594; no. 23, 20 July 1598; no. 24, 2 March 1599.
120. AMT, LA, no. 18, 21 July 1589.
121. AMT, LA, no. 19, 19 March, 19 Aug., 9 Sept. 1591.
122. AMT, LA, no. 22, 11, 18 April 1594.
123. AMT, AP, 4 March 1598.
124. Ariño, *Sucesos de Sevilla*, pp. 45–7; Bennassar, *Valladolid*, p. 437.
125. RAH, Papeles de Jesuitas, 89, 75.
126. Pullan, *Renaissance Venice*, pp. 251, 315–16, and C. M. Cipolla, *Cristofano and the plague* (London, 1973) give examples of the measures taken in Italian cities.
127. Information for the measures taken to combat the plague in Toledo are taken from AGS, CR, leg. 115–4 and AMT, LA, no. 23, 1 June 1598.
128. AMT, LA, no. 24, 18 June, 1 April 1599.
129. AHN, Órdenes Militares, Judicial, 61,716 for Feb. 1599 and 61,654 for Aug. 1599.
130. AHT, LO, 1599, fol. 138.
131. AMT, AS, leg. 4, no. 10; for more information about the increasing popularity of San Roch in Spain, see Christian, *Local religion*, pp. 42–3, 66–7, 209–10.
132. Pullan, *Renaissance Venice*, pp. 270–8, 362.

#### 4 PRIVATE CHARITABLE INSTITUTIONS

1. BL, Eg. 1882, fols. 194–5; Hurtado, 'Memorial', p. 535; ACT, OF, 840, fol. 91. According to Hurtado (p. 559), in 1576 the cathedral cloister grain was given to fifty natives on a daily basis and to any pilgrim or outside pauper for three days.
2. Salazar de Mendoza, *Crónica de la provincia de Castilla*, p. 148.
3. Hurtado, 'Memorial', pp. 554–67. The author says he has listed 27 hospitals and 147 confraternities, but in fact he mentions 28 hospitals and 143 confraternities. See also A. López-Fando, 'Los antiguos hospitales de Toledo', *Toletum*, I, (1955), 96–112.
4. Salazar de Mendoza, *Mendoza*, p. 399. The author does not give the date when Santa Cruz limited its care to foundling children, but explains that the institution lost half its income when the interest rate on *juros* was reduced. I have assumed that this was the reduction of 1608 or 1621.
5. AMT, Libro de los pobres, 1546; AP, Dec. 1556.

6. ACT, LAC, no. 16, 16 Sept. 1580.
7. AMT, AP, Aug. 1589.
8. AMT, Libro de la Hermandad de San Miguel.
9. ADPT, Constitutions of the Hospital of Jesús and San Nicolás.
10. AGS, PE, leg. 203.
11. AHT, carp. 102: Escritos, Oct. 1544.
12. AGS, CR, leg. 115–7; PE, leg. 38.
13. ADT, 669: Libro de quentas del Hospital del Rey, 1632.
14. I have used two copies of the Castilian translation of Blas Ortiz's *Descripción*: one in BPT, MS 210, fols. 589–602, the other in BL, Eg. 1882, fols. 212–16. Both works list 100 confraternities, but Ortiz omitted the parish of San Cristóbal, some confraternities he counted as one are listed separately by Hurtado (for example, San Blas and Santa Susana in the parish of San Salvador), and Ortiz excluded the brotherhoods that operated the Hospital del Rey and the Hospital de la Misericordia from his list.
15. ADT, IV/700, IV/422, IV/1821.
16. Christian, *Local religion*, pp. 185–90.
17. Pullan, *Renaissance Venice*, pp. 34–40, 50–2.
18. AGS, PE, leg. 40.
19. Gil Calvo, *La Compañía de Jesús*, pp. 62–3; Rodríguez, *Asistencia social*, pp. 351–4; Pisa, *Descripción*, vol. II, p. 85. Pisa was a brother of the new confraternity.
20. AMT, Hojas sueltas, 1607–14.
21. Rodríguez, *Asistencia social*, pp. 284–5.
22. ADPT, Libro de finados, 1534; Libro de depósito, 1560–85.
23. ADPT, 1779 review, Juan Gómez de Silva bequest.
24. AGG, Fondos Históricos, Secc. 1ª, negociado 21, leg. 5, 1586. I am grateful to Father Sebastián Insausti for this information.
25. *Constituciones sinodales, Toledo*, 1622, fol. 50.
26. ACT, LAC, no. 12, 17 Feb. 1564.
27. *Constituciones synodales, Toledo*, 1568, fol. 81.
28. *Constituciones synodales, Toledo*, 1601, fol. IIV–12.
29. AMT, LA, no. 2, 16 Apr. 1545.
30. AGS, CR, leg. 115–7.
31. AHT, carp. 102, 1 June 1545; ADT, Libro de registro, no. 96, 20 Sept. 1552.
32. AHT, AF, caj. 7, no. 19, bull of 14 Jan. 1543, 'sobre la unión perpetua de los beneficios de Alia y Garvín al hospital'.
33. AHT, AF, caj. 5, no. 1, bull of 9 Dec. 1560, 'sobre la unión perpetua de los beneficios de Cazorla, El Pardo, Ciempozuelos, Tordelaguna, Canencia y Valdetorres al hospital'.
34. Jago, 'The influence of debt', pp. 218–36.
35. Information about the Tavera family is taken from Salazar de Mendoza, *Tavera*, ch. 15; Salazar y Castro, *Silva*, vol. I, pp. 326–7; and Parro, *Toledo*, vol. II, p. 373.
36. Peers, ed. and trans., *Complete works of Saint Teresa*, vol. I, pp. 232–4, vol. II, p. 45, and *The letters*, vol. I, p. 40.
37. AHT, LD, 1629, Extraordinario, 9 July.
38. For complete details about the architecture and construction of the hospital, see Wilkinson, *The hospital of Cardinal Tavera*; also A. Rodríguez y Rodríguez, *El Hospital de San Juan Bautista* (Toledo, 1921).
39. For the importance of Bustamante's architectural ideas see A. Rodríguez and G. de Ceballos, *Bartolomé de Bustamante y los orígenes de la arquitectura jesuítica en*

*España* (Rome, 1967); Wilkinson, *The hospital of Cardinal Tavera*, p. 32 *et seq.*; Gil Calvo, *La Compañía de Jesús*, pp. 31–9, 94–6. For Bustamante's other activities, see Astraín, *Historia de la Compañía de Jesús*, vol. II, pp. 276, 447–52.

40. BPT, MS 454, Constitutions of 1569, cap. 11, fol. 20.
41. AHT, LD, 128 books, 1553–1700.
42. AHT, LRE, 118 books, 1553–1700.
43. AHT, carp. 127: Eighteenth-century additions to constitutions.
44. Fairchilds, *Poverty and charity*, pp. 96–7, 132, has come to the opposite conclusion in her study of charitable institutions in eighteenth-century Aix-en-Provence.
45. AHT, LD, 5, 12, 15 Jan. 1571; 2–8, 10–12, 15, 18 June 1606. According to Marcos Martín, *Auge y declive*, p. 181, the pattern of admissions is similar for a hospital in Medina del Campo. Concerning the popularity of the months of August, September and October for travelling vagrants, see Beier, 'Vagrants and the social order', pp. 25–6, and Pullan, *Renaissance Venice*, p. 220. The figures of Slack, 'Vagrants', p. 320, show a higher number of vagabonds punished in the spring than the fall.
46. AHT, LRE, 1569, 1571, 1584 are informative years for types of ailments.
47. Recording fevers as the ailment for all patients admitted to a hospital seems to have been a custom throughout Europe and it survived for many years. See Steele, 'Mortality of hospitals', pp. 195–8; Fairchilds, *Poverty and charity*, p. 81; Marcos Martín, *Auge y declive*, p. 191.
48. AHT, LO, penas, 1599.
49. AHT, Libro de copia, 5 May 1618.
50. AHT, LO, 1570, extraordinario, for washerwomen; Libro de copias, 1579 for tailor who mended the patient's clothes.
51. *Constituciones synodales*, *Toledo*, 1536, fols. 60–1.
52. AHT, LR, 1589.
53. ADT, Visitas, no. 142.
54. AHT, LR, 1559.
55. AHT, LR, 1609–11.
56. AHT, carp. 68: Cédula real, 15 Dec. 1605.
57. AHT, LR, 1589 and LR, 1637.
58. For more details about *juros*, see Castillo Pintado, 'Los juros de Castilla' and 'Dette flottante et dette consolidée'; and Ulloa, *La hacienda real*, pp. 118–22.
59. AGS, Contaduría Mayor de Cuentas, 1ª época, leg. 1378. The charitable and ecclesiastical institutions of Valladolid also owned many *juros*; see Bennassar, *Valladolid*, pp. 255–7.
60. AHT, LR, 1589 and LR, 1609–11.
61. AHT, Carta quenta . . . 1579–80.
62. AHT, LR, 1637.
63. For more information about *censos*, see Bennassar, *Valladolid*, pp. 258–65, and Jago, 'The influence of debt', pp. 219–36.
64. AHT, LR, 1609–11.
65. Jago, 'The influence of debt', pp. 229–30, describes the procedure of a *concurso*.
66. AMT, Hojas sueltas, 1607–28.
67. AHT, Carta quenta . . . 1558–9; LR, 1589.
68. AHT, LR, 1609–11.
69. AHT, LR, 1559, 1589, 1609–11.
70. AHT, LR, 1637.
71. ADT, Visitas, no. 142. The hospital owned land in Burujón, Burgelín, Escalonilla, Camarenilla and Alicique.
72. AHT, LR, 1589.

73. ADT, Visitas, no. 142. The diocesan authorities granted permission to Luís Díaz to sell eighteen pieces of silver on 11 Dec. 1626.
74. AHT, LB, 18 Sept. 1619 and LD, 18 Sept. 1649.
75. AHT, LD and LB 1579, 1589, 1600, 1606 and 1619.
76. AHT, LB, LD, LO, LR, 1589; ADT, Visitas, no. 142.
77. AHT, carp. 99, Nóminas de salarios; for food rations see LD for the appropriate year.
78. AMT, Hojas sueltas, 1607–28.
79. ADPT, Interrogatorio de 1557–8, which includes a copy of the 1530 constitutions and a brief history of the confraternity.
80. ADPT, Libro de los cofrades de la Santa Caridad.
81. ADPT, Lista de los cofrades . . . de 1609.
82. ADPT, Constitutions, cap. 3.
83. ADPT, Libro de finados, 1531.
84. Rodríguez, *Asistencia social*, pp. 292–3.
85. ADPT, Testaments.
86. ADPT, Constitutions, caps. 3 and 4.
87. ADPT, Testaments. In 1601 Juana Batista Cordovesa left the Santa Caridad a legacy 'to cure the poor of the confraternity', as did the Jesuit, Pedro Manrique, in 1605.
88. ADPT, Constitutions, cap. 13.
89. ADPT, Constitutions, cap. 10. The Santa Caridad received 3,000 mrs for the funeral of the conde de Cifuentes; see Libro de finados, 18 April 1555.
90. ADPT, Libro de finados, 1524.
91. ADPT, Constitutions, cap. 20; Libro de finados, 1531.
92. ADPT, History of the brotherhood.
93. ADPT, Libros de finados, cargo, 1534, 1586, 1600 and 1622.
94. ADPT, Libros de finados, 1531 and 1566.
95. ADPT, Libros de finados, 1524 and 1600.
96. ADPT, Libro de finados, descargo, 1524, 1576, 1600, 1622.
97. AMT, AP, 20, 21 Aug. 1589.
98. ADPT, Libro de dottadores, 1660, Juana Baptista bequest.
99. ADPT, 1779 review, Juan Gómez de Silva bequest.
100. ADPT, Libro de depósito, 1560–85.
101. AMT, LA, no. 22, 18 Apr. 1594.
102. ADPT, Loose papers, expenses for the prostitutes in 1600.
103. ADPT, history.
104. Rodríguez, *Asistencia social*, pp. 317, 321, 326.
105. ADPT, Libro de dottadores, 1660.
106. *Ibid.*; also review of 1779 and testaments.
107. Information for this table is taken from the testaments, the Libro de dottadores, 1660, and the review of 1779, all in the ADPT.
108. Pullan, *Renaissance Venice*, pp. 164–5, 184.
109. For an example of the earlier reductions, see ADPT, Libro de dottadores, 1660, and the 1779 review for Juan López de Cuenca and Catalina de Villalobos, both reduced in 1564, and Pedro Gallego, Cristóbal Cisneros, Benito García de Griñón, all reduced in 1614.

### 5 THE RECIPIENTS OF RELIEF

1. Peers, ed., *Complete works*, vol. 1, p. 314.
2. Kamen, *The iron century*, pp. 386–412.

3. ADPT, SC, Loose sheet: Los bienes que se hallaron . . . 21 April 1593.

4. AHT, AF: Memoria del repartimiento, 1538.

5. Pullan, *Renaissance Venice*, pp. 229, 373.

6. ADT, iii/Varios.

7. Rodríguez, *Asistencia social*, pp. 175, 190, 335–8, n. 119.

8. Meuvret, 'Demographic crisis in France', p. 519.

9. Marcos Martín, *Auge y declive*, pp. 178–9.

10. Gascon, 'Immigration et croissance au XVIe siècle', p. 994.

11. AHT, LRE, 26 Mar. 1571 and 6 Jan. 1589.

12. Bennassar, *Valladolid*, p. 197; Casey, *Kingdom of Valencia*, pp. 17–18.

13. ADPT, SC, Constitutions, 1530; Constitutions of the brothers of the Hospital of Jesus, 1567; ADT, no. 608 and no. 376.

14. Laslett, *Family life*, pp. 164–5, 170–1, 173.

15. *Ibid.*, pp. 162–3, 182–3.

16. *Ibid.*, pp. 172–3.

17. *Constituciones sinodales*, Toledo, 1583, fol. 65.

18. Martín Gamero, *Ordenanzas de Toledo*, pp. 246–8.

19. For Lyons see Gascon, 'Immigration', p. 992; for Medina del Campo, Marcos Martín, *Auge y declive*, pp. 272, 280.

20. Lis and Soly, *Poverty and capitalism*, pp. 88–96; Weisser, *Crime and punishment in early modern Europe* (Atlantic Highlands, NJ, 1979), p. 104.

21. H. and P. Chaunu, *Séville et l'Atlantic, 1504–1650* (8 vols., Paris, 1955–9), vol. i, p. 247; Castillo Pintado, 'Population', pp. 719–33.

22. Marcos Martín, *Auge y declive*, pp. 272–4.

23. Braudel, *The Mediterranean*, vol. i, pp. 334–8, 415–18; Gascon, 'Immigration', pp. 995–8; Laslett, *Family life*, pp. 50–86, 98–101.

24. Marcos Martín, *Auge y declive*, p. 274.

25. Pérez de Herrera, *Amparo*, p. 40, for the original estimate, which is repeated by Colmeiro, *Economía política en España*, vol. ii, p. 609; C. Viñas y Mey, *El problema de la tierra en la España de los siglos XVI y XVII* (Madrid, 1941), p. 169; Kamen, *The iron century*, p. 393. Not to be outdone by Pérez de Herrera, the Jesuit Pedro de Guzmán in *Bienes de el honesto trabajo*, pp. 123–4, suggested that 70,000 foreigners entered Castile every year.

26. AHT, LD, 1619, 1629, 1637, 1649.

27. Cavillac, 'La reforma', p. 33.

28. ACT, LAC, no. 16, 11 Sept. 1575 and 30 Mar. 1579.

29. AHT, LRE, 1557, 1569, 1571, 1584.

30. BPT, MS 454, fol. 33.

31. AHT, LRE, 11 Dec. 1589.

32. *Ibid.*, 13 Mar. 1595.

33. *Ibid.*, 21 Mar. 1571; 1 Oct. 1559; 3 Sept., 5 Feb., and 11 May 1589.

34. Out of a sample of 120 patients in 1598, 74 had a *bulla de cruzada* and 46 did not.

35. BPT, MS 454, cap. 1, fols. 5–6, cap. 49, fol. 71.

36. Laslett, *Family life*, pp. 63, 88 and 'Mean household size', p. 148.

37. Bennassar, *Valladolid*, pp. 445–6.

38. AMT, Libro de los gastos, 1576–9. AHT, LRE, 16 Sept. 1584.

39. AGS, PE, leg. 40.

40. Colmeiro, *Cortes*, vol. v, 1551, pet. 120, pp. 552–3.

41. AMT, LA, no. 6, 26 Mar. 1563.

42. Francisco de Borja de San Román, 'Autobiografía de Francisco Ortiz y constituciones del Hospital del Nuncio de Toledo', *Brabacht*, 46–9 (1931), 71–98; BPT, MS 210, fols. 479–80.

43. For background of the Hospital of Santa Cruz, see Alcocer, *Historia de Toledo*, fol. cxix; Salazar de Mendoza, *Mendoza*, pp. 384–400. The cathedral chapter

usually appointed a new rector in May: ACT, LAC, no. 7, 4 May 1545; no. 12, 3 May 1563; no. 16, 14 May 1575.

44. The Libros de Crianza in the ADPT are 1515, 1518, 1519, 1545, 1568, 1570, 1574, 1599, 1609, 1616 and 1632. One book survives from the late seventeenth century and there are others from the eighteenth century.

45. ADPT, LC, 1599, fol. 309.

46. The books for 1570, 1599 and 1609 contain fairly consistent notations about the occupations of the nurse's husbands.

47. ADPT, LC, 1515, fols. 70, 167, 277; 1570, fol. 210.

48. ADPT, LC, fols. 8, 243; 1568, fol. 144; 1570, fols. 70, 80; 1599, fol. 6.

49. ADPT, LC, 1599, fol. 377.

50. ADPT, LC, 1515, fols. 228, 264; 1568, fol. 194; 1570, fol. 304; 1599, fols. 19, 260.

51. ADPT, LC, 1518, fols. 10, 37.

52. ADPT, LC, 1515, fols. 184, 216.

53. ADPT, LC, 1570, fols. 180, 304.

54. ADPT, LC, 1515, fol. 35 is one case of a father who reclaimed his child and repaid the hospital for its expenses.

55. ADPT, LC, 1515, fol. 262; 1616, fol. 105.

56. ADPT, LC, 1570, fol. 36.

57. What happened in 1545 was that the scribe recorded an arbitrary date when a child was given to a nurse rather than the correct one. Someone added the correct date for 100 of the 265 children admitted in 1545–6, but 165 dates remain uncorrected.

58. ADPT, LC, 1570, fols. 251, 252, 305, for *morisco* infants.

59. For France see Hufton, *Poor of eighteenth-century France*, pp. 338–9, 345; for England see Pinchbeck and Hewitt, *Children in English society*, vol. I, pp. 131–2, 181.

60. Fernández Álvarez, *La sociedad española*, p. 172.

61. Hajnal, 'European marriage patterns', p. 127.

62. ADPT, LC, 1515, fols. 32, 125; 1570, fols. 31, 44; 1574, loose paper.

63. ADPT, LC, 1515, fols. 16, 19, 124; 1599, fols. 54, 57.

64. ADPT, LC, 1599, fol. 20; 1574, loose paper.

65. ADPT, LC, 1518, fols. 12, 14, 16, 29, 35, 39, 45, 108; 1545, fols. 20, 40; 1574, loose sheet; 1599, fols. 6, 19, 61; 1609, fols. 5, 12; 1616, fols. 20, 132. AHPT, prot. 1620, fols. 942–5, 1005, 1006; prot. 2458, fols. 829, 1073, 1121; prot. 3183, fols. 141, 265, 1445, 1453.

66. AHPT, prot. 1620, fols. 942, 944. For a study of children placed in service in 1503, see Delacour, 'El niño y la sociedad española', pp. 210–21.

67. AHPT, prot. 3183, fol. 141; ADPT, LC, 1515, fol. 4.

68. AHPT, prot. 1620, fols. 943, 944 (for 1548); ADPT, LC, 1599, fol. 50; 1616, fol. 132.

69. ACT, LAC, no. 16, 20 Nov. 1579.

70. ADPT, LC, 1515, fol. 243; 1545, fol. 2; 1568, fol. 144; 1570, fols. 70, 80; 1599, fols. 6, 220; 1616, loose sheet; 1632, fol. 87.

71. ACT, LAC, no. 16, 28 Aug. 1580.

72. ADPT, LC, 1515, fols. 291, 294, 295. Since this was the first year the new Hospital of Santa Cruz was operational, the neglected infants might have been the result of some initial confusion.

73. ADPT, LC, 1616, fols. 1–23, 37, 38, 59.

74. Bennassar, *Valladolid*, pp. 194–5. Sánchez Sánchez, *Toledo y la crisis del siglo XVII*, pp. 142–8.

75. Fernández Álvarez, *La sociedad española*, p. 170.

76. Hufton, *Poor of eighteenth-century France*, p. 342.

# Select bibliography

PRINTED DOCUMENTS AND CONTEMPORARY WORKS

*Actas de las Cortes de Castilla* (54 vols., Madrid, 1861–1936)

Alcocer, P. de. *Historia o descripción de la imperial cibdad de Toledo* (Toledo, 1554)

Antonio, N. *Biblioteca hispanae nova* (2 vols., Madrid, 1783–8)

Aranda, G. de. *Vida del siervo de Dios, ejemplar de sacerdotes, el V.P. Fernando de Contreras* (Seville, 1692)

Ariño, F. de. *Sucesos de Sevilla de 1592 a 1604* (Seville, 1873)

*Cancionero de Sebastián de Horozco, poeta toledano del siglo XVI* (Seville, 1874)

Castro, F. de. *Historia de la vida y santas de Juan de Dios, y de la institución de su orden y principio de su hospital* (Granada, 1588)

Colmeiro, M. *Cortès de los antiguos reinos de León y Castilla* (5 vols., Madrid, 1883–1903)

Colmenares, D. de. *Historia de la insigne ciudad de Segovia y compendio de las historias de Castilla* (Segovia, 1637)

*Constituciones de la hermandad del Hospital de la Misericordia desta ciudad de Toledo, nuevamente añadidas, enmendadas y recopiladas* (Madrid, 1628)

*Constituciones synodales del arzobispado de Toledo hechas por el Cardenal Arzobispo de Toledo, señor don Juan Tavera* (Alcalá, 1536)

*Constituciones synodales del arzobispado de Toledo hechas por autoridad del governador apostólico, administrador general, don Gómez Tello Girón* (Toledo, 1568)

*Constituciones sinodales del arzobispado de Toledo hechas por el Illustríssimo y Reverendíssimo don Gaspar de Quiroga* (Madrid, 1583)

*Constituciones synodales del obispado de Salamanca copiladas, hechas y ordenadas por el Illustríssimo Señor don Gerónymo Manrique, obispo de Salamanca* (Salamanca, 1584)

*Constituciones synodales del arzobispado de Toledo hechas, copiladas, y ordenadas por el Illustríssimo y Reverendíssimo señor don Bernardo de Rojas y Sandoval* (Toledo, 1601)

*Constituciones sinodales del señor don Fernando, Cardenal Infante, Administrador perpetuo del Arzobispado de Toledo* (Madrid, 1622)

*Constituciones y reglas de la mínima congregación de los hermanos enfermos pobres, dispuestos y ordenados por . . . Bernardino de Obregón* (Madrid, 1634)

Covarrubias y Horozco, S. de. *Tesoro de la lengua castellaña o española* (Madrid, 1977, reprint of original edition of 1611)

Escalona, G. *Décadas de la insigne y coronado ciudad y reyno de Valencia*, ed. J. B. Perales (Valencia, 1878–80)

Fernández Navarette, P. *Conservación de monarquía y discursos políticos sobre la gran consulta que el consejo hizo* (Madrid, 1626)

Giginta, M. *Tractado de remedio de pobres* (Coimbra, 1579)

*Exhortación a la compasión y misericordia de los pobres* (Barcelona, 1583)

*Tratado intitulado cadena de oro* (Perpignan, 1584)

254

Guzmán, P. de, *Bienes de el honesto trabajo y daños de la ociosidad* (Madrid, 1614)

Hurtado, L. 'Memorial de algunas cosas notables que tiene la imperial ciudad de Toledo', *Relaciones histórico-geográfico-estadísticas de los pueblos de Espana hechas por iniciativa de Felipe II,* trans. C. Viñas y Mey and R. Paz (vol. III, Madrid, 1963)

Lameere, J. *Recueil des ordonnances des Pays-Bas,* vol. III (Second Series, Brussels, 1902)

March, J. M. *Niñez y juventud de Felipe II: Documentos inéditos sobre su educación civil, literaria y religiosa y su iniciación al gobierno* (2 vols., Madrid, 1942)

*Los manuscritos vaticanos de los teólogos salamantinos del siglo XVI* (Madrid, 1930)

Mariana, J. de. 'Historia de España', *Biblioteca de autores españoles* (vol. 31, Madrid, 1919)

Martín Gamero, A. *Ordenanzas para el buen régimen y gobierno de la muy noble, muy leal e imperial ciudad de Toledo* (Toledo, 1858)

Méndez Silva, R. *Población general de España* (Madrid, 1645)

Mercado, L. de. *El libro de la peste,* ed. Nicasio Mariscal (Madrid, 1921)

Moncada, Sancho de. *Restauración política de España,* ed. J. Vilar (Madrid, 1974, reprint of the original edition of 1619)

*Monumenta historica societatis Jesu: litterae quadimestres* (vols. I–V, Madrid, 1894–1925; vol. VII, Rome, 1932)

*Novísima recopilación* (6 vols., Madrid, 1805–29)

Órtiz de Zúñiga, D. *Annales eclesiásticos y seculares de la muy noble y muy leal ciudad de Sevilla, metrópole de la Andaluzía que contiene sus mas principales memorias* (Madrid, 1677)

*Papeles varios,* BL, 1332 K 13

Peers, E. A., ed. and trans. *The letters of Saint Teresa of Jesus* (3 vols., London, 1951)
    ed. and trans. *The complete works of Saint Teresa of Jesus* (3 vols., London, 1946)

Pérez de Herrera, C. *Amparo de pobres,* ed. M. Cavillac (Madrid, 1975, reprint of the original edition of 1598)
    *Epílogo y suma de los discursos que escrivió del amparo y reducción de los pobres mendigantes* (Madrid, 1608)

Pérez de Lara, A. *Compendio de las tres gracias de la Sancta Cruzada, Subsidio y Escusado, que su Santidad concede a Felipe III* (Madrid, 1610)

Pisa, F. de. *Descripción de la imperial ciudad de Toledo, y historia de sus antigüedades, y grandeza, y cosas memorables que en ella han acontecido, de los reyes que la han señorado y governado en sucessión de tiempo* (2 vols., Toledo, 1974–6; vol. I is a reprint of the original edition of 1605, vol. II is the first publication of an unfinished manuscript of 1612)

*La premática de la pena que han de aver los ladrones* (Alcalá, 1553)

*La pragmática sobre los vagamundos* (Alcalá de Henares, 1566)

*Pragmáticas y provisiones nuevas* (Alcalá, 1565)

*Premática en que se prohibe que los naturales destos reynos no anden en ábito de romeros* (Madrid, 1590)

*Quaderno de algunas leyes que no están en el libro de las premáticas que por mandado de sus magestades se mandan imprimir este año de 1544* (Medina del Campo, 1544)

Quintana, J. de. *A la muy antigua, noble y coronada villa de Madrid: Historia de su antigüedad, nobleza y grandeza* (Madrid, 1629)

Robles, Juan de: see Domingo de Soto

*El sacrosanto y ecuménico concilio de Trento,* trans. I. López de Ayala (3rd edition, Madrid, 1787)

Sala Balust, L. and Martín Hernández, F., eds. *Obras completas del beato Juan de Avila* (6 vols., Madrid, 1952–71)

256 SELECT BIBLIOGRAPHY

Salazar de Mendoza, P. *Chrónico de el cardenal don Juan Tavera* (Toledo, 1603)
  *Crónica de el gran cardenal de España, don Pedro González de Mendoza* (Toledo, 1625)
Salazar de Mendoza, P. *Crónica de la provincia de Castilla, Crónicas franciscanas de España*
  (vol. 6, Madrid, 1977, reprint of the original edition of 1612)
Salazar y Castro, L. de. *Historia genealógica de la casa de Silva* (2 vols., Madrid, 1685)
San Antonio, J. de. *Biblioteca universa franciscana* (3 vols, Madrid, 1732–3)
Schroeder, H. J. *Disciplinary decrees of the general councils* (New York, 1937)
Serrano, L. *Archivo de la embajada de España cerca de la Santa Sede* (Rome, 1915)
  *Correspondencia diplomática entre España y la Santa Sede durante el pontificado de Pio V*
  (Madrid, 1914)
Soto, D. de. *Deliberación en la causa de los pobres ( Y réplica de Fray Juan de Robles)*
  (Madrid, 1965, reprint of the original editions published in 1545)
Teixidor, J. *Antigüedades de Valencia* (2 vols., Valencia, 1895)
Tejada y Ramiro, J., ed. *Colección de canones y de todos los concilios de la iglesia de España y
  de America* (6 vols., Madrid, 1849–82)
Trinidad, A. de la. *Vida y virtudes del siervo de Dios, Bernardino de Obregón, compuesto por el
  R.P.M. Luis Bernardo de Obregón* (Madrid, 1724)
Venegas de Busto, A. *Primera parte de las diferencias de libros que hay en el universo* (Toledo,
  1540)
  *Agonía del tránsito de la muerte*, in *Obras escogidas de varios autores españoles*, ed. E. de
  Ochoa (vol. I, Paris, 1847)
Villavicencio, L. de. *De oeconomia sacra circa pauperum curum a Christo institutam* (Paris,
  1564)
Vives, J. L. 'Del socorro de los pobres, o de las necesidades humanas', in *Biblioteca de
  autores españoles* (vol. LXV, Madrid, 1953)

SECONDARY WORKS

Aldea, Q., Marín, T., Vives, J., eds. *Diccionario de historia eclesiástica de España* (4 vols.,
  Madrid, 1972–5)
Astraín, A. *Historia de la Compañía de Jesús en la asistencia de España* (7 vols., Madrid,
  1902–25)
Baquero, A. *Bosquejo histórico del hospital real y general de Nuestra Señora de Gracia de
  Zaragoza* (Zaragoza, 1952)
Bataillon, M. 'J. L. Vivès, réformateur de la bienfaisance', *Bibliothèque d'Humanisme et
  Renaissance*, XIV (1952), 141–58
  *Le Docteur Laguna auteur du voyage en Turquie* (Paris, 1958)
  *Erasmo y España: estudios sobre la historia espiritual del siglo XVI*, trans. Antonio
  Alatorre (2nd edition, Mexico, 1966)
  *Pícaros y picaresca*, trans. Francisco R. Vadillo (Madrid, 1969)
Beier, A. L. 'Vagrants and the social order in Elizabethan England', *Past and Present*,
  no. 64 (August, 1974), 3–29
Beltrán de Heredia, V. *Domingo de Soto: estudio biográfico documentado* (Salamanca,
  1960)
  *Historia de la reforma de la provincia dominicana de España* (Rome, 1939)
Bennassar, B. 'Medina del Campo: un exemple des structures urbaines de l'Espagne
  au XVIe siècle', *Revue d'Histoire Economique et Sociale*, IV (1961), 474–95
  *Valladolid au siècle d'or: une ville de Castille et sa campagne au XVIe siècle* (Paris, 1967)
  'Économie et société à Ségovie au milieu du XVIe siècle', *Anuario de Historia
  Económica y Social*, I (1968)
  *Recherches sur les grandes épidémies dans le nord de l'Espagne à la fin du XVIe siècle* (Paris,
  1969)

Beraza Guadalupe, M. L. *Diezmos de la sede toledana y rentas de la mesa arzobispal (Siglo XV)* (Salamanca, 1972)

Bonenfant, P. 'Les origines et le caractère de la réforme de la bienfaisance publique aux Pays-Bas sous le règne de Charles-Quint' *Revue Belge de Philologie et d'Histoire*, v–vi (1926–7), 207–30

Bossy, J. 'The Counter Reformation and the people of Catholic Europe', *Past and Present*, no. 47 (May, 1970), 51–70

Boyd, M. *Cardinal Quiroga, Inquisitor General of Spain* (Dubuque, 1954)

Braudel, F. *The Mediterranean and the Mediterranean world in the age of Philip II*, trans. Sîan Reynolds (2 vols., London, 1972–3)

Burriel, A. M. *Informe de la imperial ciudad de Toledo al real y supremo consejo de Castilla sobre igualación de pesos y medidas en todos los reynos y señoríos de Su Magestad* (Madrid, 1758)

Cadalso, F. *Instituciones penitenciarias y similares en España* (Madrid, 1922)

Callahan, W. J. 'The problem of confinement: an aspect of poor relief in eighteenth-century Spain', *Hispanic American Historical Review*, LI (1971), 1–24

*Honor, commerce and industry in eighteenth-century Spain* (Boston, 1972)

Carande, R. *Carlos V y sus banqueros* (3 vols., Madrid, 1944–65)

Casey, J. *The kingdom of Valencia in the seventeenth century* (Cambridge, 1979)

Castillo Pintado, A. 'Dette flottante et dette consolidée en Espagne, 1557 à 1600', *Annales: Économies, Sociétés, Civilisations* (1963), 745–59

'Los juros de Castilla: Apogeo y fin de un instrumento de crédito', *Hispania*, XXIII (1963), 43–70

'Population et "richesse" en Castille durant la seconde moitié du XVIe siècle', *Annales: Économies, Sociétés, Civilisations*, XX (1965), 719–33

Cavillac, M. 'Noblesse et ambiguités au temps de Cervantes: le cas du docteur Pérez de Herrera (1556?–1620)', *Mélanges de la Casa de Velazquez*, XI (1975), 177–212

'Introduction', *Amparo de pobres* (Madrid, 1975)

'L'enfermement des pauvres, en Espagne, à la fin du XVIème siècle', *Picaresque Européenne*, *Études Sociocritiques* (Montpellier, 1976)

'La reforma de la beneficencia en España del siglo XVI: la obra de Miguel Giginta', *Estudios de Historia Social*, nos. 10–11 (1979), 7–59

Cavillac, M. and Le Flem, J.-P. 'La "probanza de limpieza" du docteur Cristóbal Pérez de Herrera', *Mélanges de la Casa de Velazquez*, XI (1975), 565–76

Chill, E. 'Religion and mendicity in seventeenth century France', *International Review of Social History*, VII (1962)

Christian, W. A. *Local religion in sixteenth-century Spain* (Princeton, 1981)

Clark, P. and Slack, P. *English towns in transition 1500–1700* (Oxford, 1976)

Clay, R. M. *The mediaeval hospitals of England* (London, 1909)

Coleman, D. C. 'Labour in the English economy of the seventeenth century', *Economic History Review*, VIII (1956), 280–95

Colmeiro, M. *Historia de la economía política en España* (2 vols., Madrid, 1965)

Cuvelier, J. 'Documents concernant la réforme de la bienfaisance à Louvain au XVIe siècle', *Bulletin de la Committée Royale d'histoire* (Brussels, 1946), 37–115

Davis, C. S. L. 'Slavery and Protector Somerset: the Vagrancy Act of 1547', *Economic History Review*, XIX (1966), 533–49

Davis, N. Z. 'Poor relief, humanism and heresy: the case of Lyon', *Studies in Medieval and Renaissance History*, V (1968), 217–75

Delacour, F. 'El niño y la sociedad española de los siglos XIII a XVI', *Anales Toledanos*, VII (1973), 177–232

Delumeau, J. *Vie économique et sociale de Rome dans la seconde moitié du XVIe siècle* (2 vols., Paris, 1957–9)

Domínguez Ortiz, A. *La sociedad española en el siglo XVII* (2 vols., Madrid, 1963–70) and Vincent, B. *Historia de los moriscos: vida y tragedia de una minoría* (Madrid, 1978)

Elliott, J. H. *Imperial Spain, 1469–1716* (New York, 1963)
'Self-perception and decline in seventeenth-century Spain', *Past and Present*, no. 74 (February, 1977), 41–61

Evennett, H.O. *The spirit of the counter reformation* (Cambridge, 1968)

Fairchilds, C. C. *Poverty and charity in Aix-en-Provence, 1640–1789* (Baltimore, 1976)

Favreau, R. 'Pauvreté au Poitou et en Anjou à la fin du Moyen Âge', *Études sur l'histoire de la pauvreté (Moyen Âge–XVI siècle)*, directed by M. Mollat (2 vols., Paris, 1974)

Fernández Alvarez, M. *La sociedad española del renacimiento* (Salamanca, 1970)

Fortea Pérez, J. I. *Córdoba en el siglo XVII: las bases demográficas y económicas de una expansión urbana* (Córdoba, 1981)

Fosseyeux, M. 'La taxe des pauvres au XVIe siècle', *Revue d'Histoire de l'Église de France*, xx (1934), 407–32

Fuente, V. de la. *Historia eclesiástica de España* (6 vols., Madrid, 1875)

Galpern, A. N. *The religions of the people in sixteenth-century Champagne* (Cambridge, Mass., 1976)

García Oro, J. *Cisneros y la reforma del clero español en tiempo de los Reyes Católicos* (Madrid, 1971)

García Sanz, A. *Desarrollo y crisis del antiguo régimen en Castilla la Vieja. Economía y sociedad en tierras de Segovia de 1500 a 1814* (Madrid, 1977)

Garzón Pareja, M. *Diezmos y tributos del clero de Granada* (Granada, 1974)

Gascon, R. 'Économie et pauvreté aux XVIème et XVIIème siècles: Lyon, ville exemplaire et prophétique', *Études sur l'histoire de la pauvreté*, directed by M. Mollat (2 vols., Paris, 1974)
'Immigration et croissance au xvie siècle: l'exemple de Lyon (1529–1563)', *Annales: Économies, Sociétés, Civilisations*, no. 4 (July–August, 1970), 988–1001
*Grand commerce et vie urbaine au XVI siècle: Lyon et ses marchands (environs de 1520–environs de 1580)* (2 vols., Paris, 1971)

Gemerek, B. 'La lutte contre le vagabondage à Paris aux xive et xve siècles', *Ricerche storiche ed economiche in memoria di Corrado Barbagallo* (2 vols., Naples, 1970)
'Renfermement des pauvres en Italie (xiv...xviiie siècles): remarques préliminaires', *Mélanges en l'honneur de Fernand Braudel* (2 vols., Toulouse, 1973)
'Criminalité, vagabondage, pauperisme: la marginalité à l'aube des temps modernes', *Revue d'histoire moderne et contemporaine*, xxi (1974), 337–75

Gil Calvo, M. *La Compañía de Jesús en la historia de Toledo* (Toledo, 1979)

Gómez-Menor, J. *Cristianos nuevos y mercaderes de Toledo* (Toledo, 1970)
'El linaje toledano de Santa Teresa y de San Juan de la Cruz', *Toletum*, no. 5 (1972), 87–141

Goñi Gaztambide, J. 'La reforma tridentina en la diócesis de Pamplona' *Miscelánea conmemorativa del concilio de Trento* (Barcelona, 1965)

González, T. *Censo de población de las provincias y partidos de la corona de Castilla en el siglo XVI* (Madrid, 1829)

González Múñoz, M. C. *La población de Talavera de la Reina (Siglos XVI–XX)* (Toledo, 1975)

González y Sugrañes, M. *Mendicidad y beneficencia en Barcelona* (Barcelona, 1903)

Gutton, J.-P. *La société et les pauvres: l'exemple de la généralité de Lyon, 1534–1789* (Lyons, 1971)
*La société et les pauvres en Europe (XVIe–XVIIIe siècles)* (Paris, 1974)

Hajnal, J. 'European marriage patterns in perspective', *Population in history*, ed. D. V. Glass and D. E. C. Eversley (London, 1965)

Hamilton, E. J. *American treasure and the price revolution in Spain, 1501–1650* (Cambridge, Mass., 1934)

Helleiner, K. F. 'The population of Europe from the Black Death to the eve of the vital revolution', *Cambridge Economic History of Europe*, vol. IV: *The economy of expanding Europe in the sixteenth and seventeenth centuries*, ed. E. E. Rich and C. H. Wilson (Cambridge, 1967)

Henderson, R. W. 'Sixteenth century community benevolence: an attempt to resacralize the secular', *Church History*, XXXVIII (1969), 421–8

Hernández Iglesias, F. *La beneficencia en España* (2 vols., Madrid, 1876)

Hufton, O. *The poor of eighteenth-century France, 1750–1789* (Oxford, 1974)

Imbert, J. *Les hôpitaux en droit canonique* (Paris, 1947)
  'Les prescriptions hospitalières du Concile de Trent et leur diffusion en France', *Revue d'Histoire de l'Église en France*, XLII (1956), 15–28
  'L'église et l'état face au problème hospitalier au XVIe siècle', *Études Gabriel Le Bras* (Paris, 1965)
  *Les hôpitaux en France* (Paris, 1966)

Jago, C. 'The influence of debt on the relations between crown and aristocracy in seventeenth century Castile', *Economic History Review*, XXVI (1973), 218–36

Jedin, H. *Crisis and closure of the Council of Trent*, trans. N. D. Smith (London, 1967)

Jiménez Salas, M. *Historia de la asistencia social en España en la edad moderna* (Madrid, 1958)

Jordan, W. K. *Philanthropy in England, 1480–1660* (London, 1959)

Journez, A. 'Notice sur fray Lorenzo de Villavicencio agent secret de Philippe II', *Travaux de cours pratique d'histoire national*, ed. P. Fredericq (Ghent–The Hague, 1884)

Jutte, R. 'Poor relief and social discipline in sixteenth-century Europe', *European Studies Review*, XI (January, 1981), 25–53

Kamen, H. *The iron century. Social change in Europe 1550–1660* (New York–Washington, 1971)

Kingdon, R. M. 'Social welfare in Calvin's Geneva', *American Historical Review*, LXXVI (1971), 50–69

Laslett, P. *Family life and illicit love in earlier generations* (Cambridge, 1977)

Laslett, P. and Wall, R. *Household and family in past time* (Cambridge, 1972)

Le Flem, J. P. 'Cáceres, Plasencia y Trujillo en la segunda mitad del siglo XVI (1557–1596)', *Cuadernos de historia de España*, XLV–XLVI (1967), 248–99

Leonard, E. M. *The early history of English poor relief* (London, 1965, first published in 1900)

Lis, C. and Soly, H. *Poverty and capitalism in pre-industrial Europe*, trans. James Coonan (Hassocks, Sussex, 1979)

Lovett, A. W. *Philip II and Mateo Vázquez de Leca: the government of Spain (1572–1592)* (Geneva, 1977)

Lynch, J. *Spain under the Habsburgs* (2nd edition, 2 vols., Oxford, 1981)

Maravall, J. A. 'De la misericordia a la justicia social en la economía del trabajo: la obra de fray Juan de Robles', *Moneda y Crédito*, no. 148 (1979), 57–88

Marcos Martín, A. *Auge y declive de un núcleo mercantil y financiero de Castilla la Vieja: evolución demográfica de Medina del Campo durante los siglos XVI y XVII* (Valladolid, 1978)

Martín, M. A. 'Pensamiento teológico y vivencia religiosa en la reforma española (1400–1600)', *Historia de la Iglesia en España*, vol. III, part 2, *La Iglesia en la España de los siglos XV y XVI*, directed by J. L. González Novalín

Martínez Diéz, G. 'Del decreto tridentino sobre los concilios provinciales', *Miscelánea conmemorativa del concilio de Trento* (Barcelona, 1965)

Marquez Villanueva, F. *Espiritualidad y literatura en el siglo XVI* (Madrid–Barcelona, 1968)

Martz, L. and Porres, J. *Toledo y los toledanos en 1561* (Toledo, 1974)

Melero Fernández, M. I. 'El Hospital de Santiago de Toledo a fines del siglo xv', *Anales Toledanos*, IX (1974), 3–116

Menéndez Pidal, G. *Los caminos en la historia de España* (Madrid, 1951)

Merriman, R. B. *The rise of the Spanish Empire in the old world and the new* (4 vols., New York, 1934)

Meuvret, J. 'Demographic crisis in France from the sixteenth to the eighteenth century', trans. Margaret Hilton, *Population in history*, ed. D. V. Glass and D. E. C. Eversley (London, 1965)

Mir, Miguel. Introduction to 'Escritores místicos', *Nueva biblioteca de autores españoles* (Madrid, 1911)

Misraki, J. 'Criminalité et pauvreté en France à l'époque de la Guerre de Cent Ans', *Études sur l'histoire de la pauvreté*, directed by M. Mollat (2 vols., Paris, 1974)

Montemayor, J. 'Une conjuncture municipale: los propios de Toléde (1540–1660)', *Mélanges de la Casa de Velazquez*, XVII (1981), 183–204

Nolf, J. *La réforme de la bienfaisance publique à Ypres au XVIe siècle* (Ghent, 1915)

Noreña, C. G. *Juan Luis Vives* (The Hague, 1970)

Nuñez de Cepeda y Ortega, M. *La beneficencia en Navarra a través de los siglos* (Pamplona, 1940)

Parker, G. *Philip II* (Boston–Toronto, 1978)

Parro, S. *Toledo en la mano, o descripción histórico-artística de la magnífica catedral y de los demás célebres monumentos y cosas notables que encierra esta famosa ciudad, antigua corte de España*. . . . (2 vols., Toledo, 1857)

Pérez, J. *La revolución de las comunidades de Castilla (1520–1521)*, trans. J. J. Faci Lacasta (Madrid, 1977)

Pérez-Arregui, J. *San Ignazio en Azpeitia* (2nd edition, Zarauz, 1956)

Pinchbeck, I. and Hewitt, M. *Children in English society* (2 vols. London–Toronto, 1969)

Pinta Llorente, M. and Palacio, J. *Procesos inquisitoriales contra la familia judía de Juan Luis Vives* (Madrid, 1964)

Porres, J. *Historia de las calles de Toledo* (2 vols., Toledo, 1971)

Prescott, W. H. *History of the reign of Ferdinand and Isabella* (2 vols., London, 1851)

Pullan, B. *Rich and poor in Renaissance Venice* (Oxford, 1971)

    'Catholics and the poor in early modern Europe', *Transactions of the Royal Historical Society*, 5th series, vol. XXVI (1976), 15–34

    'Poveri, mendicanti e vagabondi (secoli XIV–XVII)', *Storia d'Italia*, Annali I, *Dal fuedalesimo al capitalismo* (Torino, 1978)

Ram, F. X. 'Opinion des théologiens de Louvain sur la répression administrative de la mendacité en 1562 et 1565', *Analectes pour servir à l'Histoire de l'Université de Louvain*, XIV (1856), 87–113

Redondo, A. 'Pauperismo y mendicidad en Toledo en época del "Lazarillo"', *Hommage des hispanistes français à Noel Salomon* (Bordeaux, 1979)

Rodríguez de Gracia, H. *Asistencia social en Toledo, siglos XVI–XVIII* (Toledo, 1980)

Rodríguez Peña, J. L. *Los hospitales de Plasencia* (Plasencia, 1972)

Ruiz Martín, F. 'La población española del comienzo de los tiempos modernos', *Cuadernos de Historia*, 1 (Madrid, 1967), 189–202

    'Movimientos demográficos y económicos en el reino de Granada durante la segunda mitad del siglo XVI', *Anuario de historia económica y social*, 1 (Madrid, 1968), 127–83

Rumeu de Armas, A. *Historia de la previsión social en España* (Madrid, 1944)

Russell-Wood, A.J.R. *Fidalgos and philanthropists: the Santa Casa de Misericordia de Bahia, 1550–1755* (London–Toronto, 1968)

Sala Balust, L. 'La espiritualidad española en la primera mitad del siglo XVI', *Cuadernos de Historia*, 1 (Madrid, 1967), 169–87

Saldaña Sicilia, G. *Monografía histórico-médica de los hospitales de Córdoba* (Córdoba, 1935)

Salter, F. R., ed. *Some early tracts on poor relief* (London, 1929)

Sanahuja, P. *Historia de la beneficencia en Lérida* (Lérida, 1944)

Sánchez Sánchez, J. *Toledo y la crisis del siglo XVII: El caso de la parroquia de Santiago del Arrabal* (Toledo, 1980)

Sellin, J. T. *Pioneering in penology: the Amsterdam houses of correction in the sixteenth and seventeenth centuries* (Philadelphia, 1944)

Shergold, N. D. *A history of the Spanish stage from medieval times until the end of the seventeenth century* (Oxford, 1967)

Sicroff, A. *Les controverses des statuts de "Pureté de Sang" en Espagne du XVe au XVIIe siècle* (Paris, 1960)

Slack, P. 'Vagrants and vagrancy in England, 1598–1664', *Economic History Review*, 2nd series, XXVII (1974), 360–79

Steele, J. C. 'The mortality of hospitals, general and special, in the United Kingdom, in times past and present', *Journal of Statistical Society*, XL (1877), 177–261

Tarsicio de Azcona. *La elección y reforma del episcopado español en tiempo de los Reyes Católicos* (Madrid, 1960)

Thompson, I. A. A. 'A map of crime in sixteenth century Spain', *Economic History Review*, XXI (1968), 244–67

Thompson, J. A. E. 'Piety and charity in late Medieval London', *Journal of Ecclesiastical History*, XVI (1965), 178–95

Tierney, B. *Medieval poor law: a sketch of canonical theory and its application in England* (Berkeley–Los Angeles, 1959)

Tolivar Faes, J. *Hospitales de leprosos en Asturias durante las edades media y moderna* (Oviedo, 1966)

Tormo, E. 'La de Fuencarral: como se puede estudiar la historia de una de las calles de Madrid', *Boletín de la Real Academia de la Historia*, CXVI (1945), 215–314

Ulloa, M. *La hacienda real de Castilla en el reinado de Felipe II* (Madrid, 1977)

Vilar, J. 'Docteurs et marchands: "l'école de Tolède" (1615–1630)', *Fifth International Congress of Economic History* (Leningrad, 1970)

'Introduction' in Sancho de Moncada, *Restauración política de España* (Madrid, 1975)

'Le picarisme espagnol: de l'interférence des marginalités à leur sublimation esthétique', *Les marginaux et les exclus dans l'histoire* (Paris, 1979)

Webster, C., ed. *Health, medicine and mortality in the sixteenth century* (Cambridge, 1979)

Wilkinson, C. *The Hospital of Cardinal Tavera in Toledo. A documentary study of Spanish architecture in the mid-sixteenth century* (New York–London, 1977)

# Index